Empowering Diffe

Empowering

DIFFERENCES

ASHLEY T BRUNDAGE

LEVERAGING YOUR DIFFERENCES TO IMPACT CHANGE

Ordering Information: Quantity sales and special discounts are available on quantity purchases by corporations, associations, and others. For details, contact the author at the address above.

Edited by Alyssa Courtoy
Cover design by BKN Creative

Created in Tampa, Florida of the United States of America.
ISBN: 978-1-7360871-3-8 (print)
ISBN: 978-1-7360871-1-4 (ebook)
ISBN: 978-1-7360871-0-7 (audio)

Library of Congress Control Number: 2020921808

First edition, December 2020.

The information contained within this book is strictly for informational purposes. The material may include information, products, or services by third parties. As such, the Author does not assume responsibility or liability for any third-party material or opinions. The author is not responsible for websites (or their content) that are not owned by the author. Readers are advised to do their own due diligence when it comes to making decisions. The views and opinions expressed in this book are those of the author and do not necessarily reflect the policies or views of her employer. The views, opinions, and life experiences expressed in this book are presented from the author's perspective. The overall intended purpose of this book is to use perceived weaknesses as strengths. How you use this guidance will depend on your individual circumstances. For more information on Empowering Differences, the views of this book, online course, and accompanying workbook please visit our website. www.empoweringdifferences.com

Tributes

Starting off with my power three internal core of support from the mother of my children and wife Whitney, and my two amazing boys Bryce, and Blake. None of what I've accomplished personally, or professionally, could have been possible without your love, compassion, and support. I hope all three of you take the time to know that what you provided me has made all of the difference in allowing me to empower myself and others. I'll never be able to say how appreciative I am, but I do hope that this book helps others in the way in which you all have helped me. This includes understanding the importance of the opportunity that you have provided me to showcase my authenticity. Also, learning and growing to be a more well-rounded person through the years. Love you all so very much.

To my mom Faith, I know it may seem that I didn't always make things easy. I want you to know that many of the things that I've learned as a youth growing up watching you, my single mom work in a male dominated industry, was so inspiring to me. Much of the woman that I am today is built on who I saw as a young child growing up. I want to thank you so much and tell you and Richie how much I love you both.

To my sister Stacey, I love you so much and thank you for your confidentiality, and all the love that you provided me during my self assessment period. The continued confidence that I learned directly from you, alongside the support that you provided me, were instrumental during my mission, regardless of the goal. I hope that you use this book as a tool to help you finish your book because I know that you have the power to help so many people.

To my brother Brian, your guidance through the years has always been extremely calculated. If it wasn't for your guidance, I would not have had my power three mentioned above to guide me through this process. I also want to thank you for always listening to me, even though you may not agree with decisions that I ultimately make. Listening is a major part of being an ally to someone, and for that and many other reasons I love you so much.

For Bill and Mary Lou, thank you so much for modeling appropriate, loving parental relationships. I know you didn't choose me to be your child, but I feel I was able to choose you as my additional parents. Your support and compassion has meant so much throughout the years. Your support has led to the completion of this important project, one that you knew was coming, and for that I thank you again.

To the rest of my family and friends who have supported me throughout this process of my self assessment as well as uncovering these empowering actions, I want to thank you all for being there for me.

A special thank you to all the people who were helpful in my career development and integral to my success, especially these key contributors:

Dustin Becker
Tracy Holt
Aina Ince
Dianne Jacob
Marsha Jones
Joe Meterchick
Melissa Mickle
John Vandermolen

Table of Contents

Step 4   Empowering Actions

Foreword

I remember it vividly. The date was August 12th, 2015.

I'd just walked offstage after delivering a keynote speech to 3,000 audience members of the LGBTQ community. A woman introduced herself, and asked if we could take a photo together.

Her name was Ashley Brundage. She was the first openly transgender person I'd ever met.

Ashley posted our photo on Facebook, and a few days later, when I returned home after the conference, I told my 11-year-old about meeting Ashley. Together, we looked at Ashley's profile, and talked about what it means to transition.

My child paused, looked me in the eyes, and asked... "How would you feel if someone you love transitioned, like Ashley did?" I held my breath, wrapping my head around those words. With a powerful flood of emotion, I said I would always love them, inside and out, no matter what.

Then, exactly one month later, he came out to me. "Mom, I'm your son. My new name is Asher. It means 'lucky change.'" I embraced him and said... "I am the lucky one."

He smiled and said, "Wow, this is going to make a fantastic college application essay!" (Ahhh, that kid.)

A few hours later, I went to Facebook and messaged the only transgender person I knew.

"Hello Ashley! We met briefly at the National Gay and Lesbian Chamber of Commerce conference. I remember your energy and radiant smile. I'm reaching out to ask if I might be able to talk with you privately for a few moments, and get a bit of insight. Is that something you'd be comfortable with?"

Notice how the message sounds so casual? As if I was about to ask for a restaurant recommendation. Yeah, well, I wasn't feeling casual on the inside. I made more than a few typos as I typed those words because my hands were shaking, and the screen blurred through tears in my eyes.

In retrospect, I realize what a painful struggle this had been for him and not just for weeks or months, but for years. It's clear, he was always my son. But it took imaginable courage for him to express that.

I wasn't afraid. In fact, quite the opposite. In that moment, my inner mama bear reared up on her hind legs with a roar from deep in my soul, ready to protect my child from the threat of a judgmental world. I would do anything for him, and yet, I didn't know what to actually do.

When my child came out, I knew who to BE.
But I didn't know what to DO.

That's where Ashley came in. She was my lifeline. Instead of giving me a lecture or vague descriptions, Ashley gave me exactly what I needed: Action steps.

And that, my friends, is where this book comes in.

* * * * *

A quick skim of the internet will give you all kinds of abstract discussions about gender identity and LGBTQ kids. And those articles are important. Crucial, in fact. But there's a missing piece to the puzzle...

What should you DO? What's the action plan? You might be thinking to yourself, "Okay yes, I'm ready! But what are the steps?"

Even the most evolved HR managers and corporate leaders can struggle with empowering differences within their organizations. As the conversation shifts away from well-intentioned labels, there have been many recommendations but never a definitive inclusion playbook.

Even if we all agree on WHY we must empower differences, we're still figuring out the HOW.

At this point in the cultural conversation, everyone pretty much gets the concept of diversity. The problem is that organizations still address it with a capital "D." A proper noun, a word with air quotes. You know, like, "*Diversity*." A department in the company.
A task force. An obligatory training program.

But diversity is not a box to check every few months— it's a priority mindset. Less like scheduling a dentist appointment, and more like flossing.

Just as flossing is a non-negotiable for retaining your teeth, so is diversity essential for retaining your top talent, vendors, customers, stakeholders, and market performance. Without D&I as a centerpiece, you'll embark on the slow, agonizing death-spiral of obsolescence.

(When I put it like that, it sounds like a real drag, huh? Like the expression on your accountant's face when you confess that you neglected to pay taxes this year.)

But hold on. I'm about to let you in on a secret…

Today, diversity is your greatest competitive advantage.

Empowering differences is not a cost, or overhead, or a training manual. It's a gloriously thriving investment. It jumpstarts your people and products. It supports sales and spreadsheets. It's the fertilizer that allows your company to enjoy the fruits of engagement from teams and customers.

Just as with LGBTQ identity, there's no one "right" way to empower differences. But there are patterns. Ashley outlines ten actions we can all take, from educating to influencing.

Empower real change.
Inspire your community.

Educate with new ideas.

Include everyone.

Motivate next steps.

Invest in the future.

Mentor the next generation.

Influence your organization, your community, and yourself.

Access the power of uniqueness.

Enlighten yourself to the possibilities.

* * * * *

In my first *New York Times* bestselling book, *How the World Sees You*, I describe my research inside organizations like Twitter, IBM, and Nike. For a decade, I measured a million professionals to identify what high-performers do differently.

Along the way, I discovered a surprising fact. High-performing people and teams have one thing in common: They not only *embrace* different personality styles, but they seek and actively tap into those differences.

In other words, high-performers tap into their most differentiating qualities. Instead of focusing on *similarities* among team members, they tap into unique, innate characteristics of each person. Great organizations know that different is better than better.

It's good to be better. But it's better to be different.
Different is better than better.

Not only had I spent a decade researching differences, I built my company around it: How to Fascinate. I published a #1 *Wall Street Journal* bestseller describing why differences are not just about personality styles or skills or resumes. *Oprah Magazine* raved about this new perspective on personal branding.

And yet… It wasn't until September of 2015, when my son came out to me, that I deeply and profoundly understood what it means to be different.

And after reading this book, you will too.

Why? Because *different is better than better.*

The world needs more empowerment.

The world needs more differences.

And that means the world needs more Ashley Brundage.

Sally Hogshead
CEO & Founder, How to Fascinate®
New York Times bestselling author
Hall of Fame speaker
LGBT advocate

Introduction

Climbing the Corporate Ladder

How do you get to the top of the corporate ladder? To those high-level management positions that we strive to achieve? Traditional career advice has told us that in order to advance in our careers we need to go to college, get the best internship, and work hard in our respective field of study. The conventional model tells us to start in an entry-level position, with little to no relevant experience. Over time, with hard work and dedication, there will be an opportunity to move through the ranks. First passing through middle management, and then finally arriving at the destination of high level, corporate leadership. Once we reach the top, it is only then that we can begin to dream of one day retiring, although retirement will likely still be twenty plus years away. We are constantly told that if we put in the time and effort, we will eventually be recognized by the organization, and be able to climb the corporate ladder until we've reached a peak. The reality today is that the traditional model is outdated. It no longer fits the way professionals advance in their career, or even get their career started.

Even with a bachelor's degree and some work experience, getting your foot in the door is not an easy task. The job market has become much more competitive as a result of population increases and additional learning options. Thirty years ago, someone with an associate's or bachelor's degree would stand out amongst a group of applicants. Now, those degrees are becoming the bare minimum, even for entry-level positions. What do you do when you are excited about a position, but you know there are twenty other applicants who have similar qualifications? Employers look for something that stands out in a potential employee; something that makes them different from the rest. Getting past the first barriers of digital applications and phone interviews is hard enough, but once you are in that interview room talking face to face with the hiring team, you need to make yourself memorable.

Citing your work experience or the education you have will only restate the qualifications they already know about you. Having a master's degree, or years of experience in a field, are definitely great things to have, but they will only get you so far. You need to be able to highlight what makes you different from all the other candidates that have similar educational or work backgrounds. How you have approached difficult work scenarios, the obstacles you have overcome throughout your life, and what can you bring to the table that someone else cannot, are crucially important. But there is more. The traditional career advice has told us to focus on the experiences that we have had in the workplace in order to prove we are the most qualified person for the job. I would like to present you with a wild new concept; highlighting your differences. In the next section, we are going to dive into highlighting your differences to not only land that awesome new job, but to bring beneficial change to your new organization.

Highlighting Your Differences

Too often, professionals neglect to use their differences as a strategy to advance themselves through the job searching phase, and into their careers. With the way the careers are now, working hard at your job will only get you so far. At some point, you may eventually be recognized for your hard work and rise to a low-level management position where you keep tabs over all of the entry-level positions. It is all too common for low and middle managers to be stuck in these positions for years. It is here that many professionals encounter a glass ceiling, where hard work and producing results won't allow them to punch through. It's time to shatter that ceiling.

This is on top of how volatile the job market is. How often have you heard that someone you know or that a business has decided to lay off a huge number of employees? Getting to a higher level position does not guarantee organization loyalty. There are hundreds of people with similar qualifications that would take your job, given the opportunity. To move up in your career, you need to showcase to your employer and business that you are the best qualified person to be in the position and that you are also irreplaceable.

The people that rise to the top seem like they have it all together. They work hard, have a clear-cut plan, and know how to get to where they want. The truth is, they are able to leverage the connections they have made, and the differences that they have, in order to advance their careers. They do not wait for someone to recognize the work that they have done. They actively seek people out who can vouch for the work they are doing and why they are the best possible person to be doing more.

This is the approach that I took in my career. I was not going to wait around for someone to tell me that I was doing a good job. I actively worked to get to the position I have now, as the Vice President of Diversity and Inclusion of a major financial services institution. Though it took more than just going the extra mile and putting myself in the eyes of my bosses. I used the differences that I have as a way to advance my career. I embraced what makes me unique, brought in business through community engagements, and used my identities as another reason why I should be promoted. I was able to demonstrate enough value over time that my company created my position just for me.

I have gone through my own personal journey of self discovery, and throughout it, I was able to rise from a part-time bank teller to the Vice President of Diversity and Inclusion within a short few years. I had to learn about myself and put my differences on the table. As a Jewish, high school educated, mother of two, 6 foot tall trans woman, I made sure to put my differences on the table instead of hiding them, hoping that nobody would notice. I used them as reasons why I should be advancing further in my career. Highlighting my differences and citing my research, I was able to hold my own in critical conversations with my bosses and able to make a lasting impression that allowed me to rise through my career. The same can be said for you. Your differences are what separate you from the rest. They are what you need to be bringing to the table and what will help you make a case for advancing further up the corporate ladder.

20

What Separates You From the Rest?

I want you to think for a moment about what makes you different. What makes you unique? Things that make you different in a workplace don't necessarily have to be things like bachelor's degrees or high school diplomas. They don't have to be things like how much work experience you have in your field, or what types of internship experiences you have. These are differences that set you apart from other people on a resume, but the differences that are going to be explored throughout this book are differences within yourself. What identities do you have that make you different?

Identities such as your race, gender identity, class, education, sexuality, religion, ethnicity, the languages you speak, and where you are from, to name a few. All of these identities are what makes you, well, you. There are some parts of yourself and your differences that you may not have put much thought into, or have even considered as something that makes you unique. These are things to highlight, not just in a job interview, but throughout your career.

Throughout this book you will be asked to dig deep inside yourself. To discover who you are and what makes you unique. These are the lessons and takeaways from my own lived experiences that have helped me to get to the position that I am in now, and that will help you get to the position you want to be in. These lessons are meant to build upon each other, to get you to understand not only yourself, but the people around you, and to celebrate the differences you have. Your differences are not a hindrance, or something that you need to hide. They are a part

21

of you and should be celebrated as such, in both your career and personal life.

There may be topics and themes in this book that challenge your worldview, and your understanding of yourself and others. All of the lessons and topics in this book are meant to change your perspective; to get you thinking about the way that you interact with the world, your actions and words that you say.

It is my hope you will grow to view your differences as something that will not only advance your career, but also uplift the people around you. Wear your uniqueness as a badge of honor and use it strategically to rise to the position of your dreams. But you will need to decide. Are you ready to take that plunge? Are you willing to dig deep to move your career forward? It is by no means an easy task. Taking time to understand and value yourself is only half the battle. You will need to apply the lessons that are taught throughout this book if you want to move your career forward. If you use the advice and lessons that I give in this book, and take what I've learned to heart, then you will be empowered to achieve the career success you desire.

Step 7

Knowing Yourself

Leading to Empowerment

Empowering Differences is your new go-to reference for adapting change and highlighting your differences in order to help you win in your career development. I plan to help you uncover what it is that makes you unique. I will share my insight on how to capitalize and empower these differences. Throughout these lessons and stories, you may be unfamiliar with some of the concepts and terms that I use throughout this book. I encourage you to flip to the terminology section for a quick reference guide.

In my career, I have twice successfully climbed the corporate ladder. It is this success that prompted me to write this book. In both instances, I was hired in the most entry-level position, and within a few short years moved my way through the ranks of lower and middle management, into senior leadership. I have learned a great deal from my experiences and have managed to overcome and grow from my own personal struggles. From my experience, one of the greatest realizations I have had, is that the best way to advance in your organization is to embrace who you are and to empower those around you.

Career One: Boston Market

I'm going to give context into my work experience to help you understand where I came from and how this started. In 1996, while in

3

high school, I was told by my father I had to get a job. My father made it very clear that if I wanted to have things that I really wanted, I would need to pay for them myself. Things like paying for my own car, gas money, and many other things a high school kid might want. I applied at a handful of different stores near my house, and I got an entry level, serving job, at Boston Market. Having this job at 16, while in high school, was necessary in order for me to have all the things that were important to me at the time. Looking back now, I saw my position as a part-time server at Boston Market as a means to survive. While working to make ends meet, I was also battling with my authenticity each and every day. I was still learning more about myself and what being my authentic self really meant. For a while, all I felt was that I didn't fit in, that who I was presenting as wasn't me. I was only now starting to learn the words and definitions that I needed in order to define myself.

I remember my first day working there pretty well. I was a server making around $4 an hour, non-tipped. I remember watching orientation videos and training material, and thinking that I wouldn't need all this information. As I began working, I realized that I could gain more hours and make more money by doing more things. Seems kind of simple, but as a teenager, a solid work ethic was not that common, at least from what I had seen. I quickly learned all the positions in the restaurant, from server, to cashier to drive-thru. I also learned preparation recipes, cook times, and procedures. Before long, I was navigating proteins and full food preparation. Looking back now, I realize that because I was more adaptable in the restaurant, and wanted to learn more positions, that I was seen as more valuable to the organization. Within about a year of working there, I had, at some point, learned or worked in every role in the restaurant.

The following year was pretty important because that was when I reached a personal exploration moment. Around the time I turned seventeen, I started presenting online as Ashley and as a trans woman. This was the day of chat rooms, before video chat existed. In chat rooms, I could present as whatever gender I wanted. It was a way for me to express and be myself without starting the physical changes that come with transition. Not long after I started presenting online as Ashley, a close family member of mine found out. They advised me to be very careful with what I was doing. They said if I went further down the path I was on, and started presenting as myself and being authentic publicly and in person, that I possibly wouldn't be alive in a few years or have a family like I had always wanted.

I didn't take hearing that very well, as having a partner and children of my own was something I deeply desired. It was this event that led me to move out of my parents house, at seventeen years old, and get my own apartment. This was the first domino to fall in a longline of dominos, that jump started my first career. Now that I was living on my own and working, I quickly realized that I needed to pick up as many hours as possible to be able to afford everything and keep a roof over my head. I started doing more strategic moves at the restaurant to gain additional shifts and make more money. This is when I started to improve my skills in all of the positions that I was working. On my scheduled days off, I would actually show up and see if any of my co-workers wanted to take the day off. This was especially bold as the extra shifts would often cause me to go into overtime. Before long, I was working on average about fifty hours a week. Being a teenager, I certainly showed a whole lot of audacity to be able to convince others to give me their hours.

As my eighteenth birthday approached, I figured I could easily execute being a manager in the restaurant. I began taking my role much more seriously at this point, and had discussions with the general manager about being an hourly manager. It was necessary to at least be eighteen to have that role, so shortly after my eighteenth birthday I shifted into an hourly manager role within the organization. As a manager, I really had no clue what I was doing and had to learn on the fly how best to manage other people. While I was struggling to learn how to perform in my new role, I was still grappling with what my close family member had told me. The desire to transition and the worry about what that meant was constant and it weighed on me whenever I had a moment to myself. I kept pushing through it though, concentrating on work and trying to perform well as a manager.

I learned more about the certified training process, and helped shift curriculum within the organization on this program. This helped get me on the map with corporate leadership. In addition, I started going to other stores and offered to pick up shifts. My willingness to go where needed and solve potential problems that existed really helped me grow quickly in my career. My goal in working in the restaurant was not to have a career, it was literally just a means to an end.

I was still in high school pulling fifty hours (plus) per week, and living on my own. Naturally, my grades had suffered during my last year and a half. My priority was not school, it was survival. I was laser focused on how I was going to make it to the end of month, wondering if I would even have enough for groceries. I had grand plans to go to college, but those never materialized. Once I graduated from high school, I focused all my efforts on my work. My focus on survival is what helped me get through each day, at least for a time.

After working for two years as an hourly manager, right around the time I turned twenty, I was promoted to a corporate manager. This promotion included a salary position in the organization. I was one of the youngest, if not the youngest, corporate manager in the entire company. After this promotion, it became clear to me personally, that this was my career, and I needed to focus hard to continue to move forward and take myself to a higher level. Through the next year, I focused intently on sharpening my management skills, and enrolled in multiple training programs. This is where I learned profit and loss (P&L) management, as well as human resources policies and programs. Working in the restaurant industry is a constant recruitment of people, which I used as a way to study and learn habits of others. The more I learned, the more I progressed. Shortly after my twenty-first birthday, I was promoted to general manager. Managing my own store was a big accomplishment for a twenty-one-year-old. I had a very sound understanding of the business, but was still lacking in management experience, especially when it came to managing an entire store.

Looking back at this time frame, this is the point where knowing what I know now, and all the things that I've been through, leads me to believe that my privilege had a lot to do with getting the job that I got. I was always invited to everything because it just seemed that people generally were comfortable around me. I was presenting as a white, cisgender, straight man, and I fit in with the rest of the corporate environment and my co-workers. This was one of the reasons why I very closely hid my status as a transgender person. I felt that if I were ever to be outed, that I would not have been able to survive working in the restaurant industry at that time. Especially given that, at the time, trans women were only seen as sex workers or a quick punchline in a TV show. I knew that it would sink my career and I'd be without a job. So over the next seven years as a general manager, my only focus was on surviving.

While working as a general manager, I was able to learn more about the corporate environment and developed my ability to overhaul areas that needed improvement. Looking into different locations, I would examine everything from top to bottom. This action of process improvement was something I noticed I was pretty good at. I was able to analyze a situation and make changes necessary in order to move the business forward. I started to get noticed for the work that I was doing, and in my third year, I was awarded the "General Manager of the Year award". The ironic part was, even though I wasn't able to move forward in my gender transition, I was focused on change management and transitioning different locations to be able to better perform. I knew the irony of the situation and I started to question myself more and more.

During this time of working in a corporate environment, I made the choice to have kids. This was the best decision I have ever made. Having my kids to care for literally and physically saved my life. My firstborn came in 2005, and then my second child in 2007. As much as I tried to bury myself in my work and put off the thoughts of being transgender, it would eventually build up and constantly affect me mentally. I was struggling to keep going, to get up every day and keep living a lie. Every time that I thought that living this life was not worth it, that I wanted to end everything so that I didn't have to suffer anymore, I thought about my kids. What would it be like to leave them behind, to leave them without a parent? Every time I had those dark thoughts, I thought about my kids and what they meant to me, and I kept going. I kept pushing myself to get up every day because I would never want to leave them. I love them with all my heart, and they need me to be there for them.

My last year working at Boston Market was in 2008. This year was met with numerous tumultuous situations. Having two very young kids, struggling with my gender identity, and an impending financial crisis. All of these things were eventually going to bubble over into each other, and it felt like there was nothing I could do to hold it all together. This all led to a perfect storm. The first domino was my focus at work. I was really slacking because of my personal battles. I could no longer balance it all while taking care of myself and my family. This is what ended up leading to the end of my employment at Boston Market. I needed time away from my career to focus on myself and the family. At the same time, we still had bills to pay, and more than ever needed a stable income. As a family, we made the decision that my wife Whitney would gain employment and I would be the primary caregiver for our children.

2008 -2010

Being a stay-at-home parent became my job overnight. The time that I got to spend with my kids, and the investment I got to make in their lives was priceless. Spending time with my kids helped me survive the gender identity struggles that I was trying to manage on a daily basis. I wasn't able to be authentic and real on a daily basis, but taking care of my kids and being around other stay-at-home moms, it felt right. I was comfortable being around the other moms who were taking care of their kids because I felt like I fit right in with them. We were all caregivers and for me, this allowed me to explore, navigate, and experiment with my true identity. Unfortunately, my time was cut short because we found ourselves greatly impacted by the 2008 housing bubble burst and recession.

My family and I felt the severe effects of the housing market crash. In 2006, we made the decision to sell our townhouse and purchase a larger home for our growing family. We thought it would be best to first purchase the new house, and then sell the townhouse, to create a more seamless move. Mortgage loan requirements were much more lenient prior to the market crash. When we applied for our new house, we were automatically approved for an additional mortgage, without having to show how we would pay for it. The townhouse eventually sold, but the house that I now owned, for which I should have never been approved, was now severely undervalued. My house was basically worth about 30% of what I paid for it. The undervalued house and over budget mortgage, culminating with both Whitney and I both being out of work, led to the bank taking our house back.

With my oldest starting kindergarten, and the looming possibility of being homeless, I decided that I needed to find a new career. I was able to start working from home, but the pay was not enough to support a family of four. I desperately needed to find a new career where I could be comfortable. I quickly realized that because of the financial crisis, most companies weren't hiring someone with middle manager experience like myself. I was constantly told that I needed to start at the bottom and prove my worth, that I had to work myself up the ladder again.

When I finally realized that I would need to start a career from the ground up, I decided that I would only do it if I was able to be my true authentic self. Having to combat my true identity in my prior career was just too taxing on me personally, and negatively affected my productivity. With my newfound courage, I started to go on interviews presenting as my authentic self, Ashley. This led to an immediate change of how I was viewed by potential employers in person. This was the first time in my life I had ever faced real discrimination.

Some of the responses that I would get from employers were downright shocking. I was told everything imaginable: "you have the wrong address", "you don't have an interview here today", "please leave", "we would never hire anyone like you", "I'm going to call the cops", and having a door slammed in my face, literally. When I actually got to sit down and have a job interview, the average time for these interviews was about 15 minutes, I could tell I was being asked the bare minimum number of questions.

Nothing was working and I needed to change my strategy. That's when I began empowering my differences. What I came up with was to utilize the empowering word of educating to make a difference in the interview process. I would work in education about the transgender community, and the LGBTQ community in order to bring a sense of normalcy to me as a candidate for the job. I started to see real results as my average interview length moved from 15 minutes to about 45 minutes. Many of the employers that interviewed me had never even heard of the word transgender, let alone met someone who was trans. This clearly presented a huge problem. Having dialogue with the interviewers in order to educate them about my gender identity, I was able to hold my own and empower my difference. In a way, I also became an educator and an expert in my identity. This is the moment that I look back on now and claim when I saw the power of being a subject-matter expert (SME). Someone who is a SME is going to craft a better job than someone who is not one.

At this point in my job hunt I had probably interviewed with close to 30 companies. The interviews were going much better, but I still had not been offered a position. I decided to think a little deeper and fall back on my experience as a hiring manager. What was it that I was missing in the interview process? Then it finally hit me, I not only needed to educate, I needed to empower the hiring manager to know what the business case was for hiring a transgender person. I poured time and energy into researching my differences, so that not only was I going to educate, I was going to provide the empowering data behind why I was the best candidate for the job.

Now my job interviews were about me, my authenticity, educating others, and then linking all of my differences to the data that I was providing, and why all of this made me the best candidate. I would talk about why it's crucial to have someone like me on the team and backed it up with statistical business case data. I would bring a research study, with information about the buying power for my community and other various research statistics. This included studies and statistics from the Williams Institute at UCLA, National Center for Transgender Equality, and Nielsen. All ranging from sheer numbers of trans and LGBTQ+ people, to data on having diverse talent in organizations. I cited and quoted these statistics during the next several interviews, obtaining 2nd and 3rd round interviews with some companies. After interviewing with more than 40 companies, I was finally offered a position that had future growth potential. That is when I started working as a part-time bank teller for a major financial services organization.

New Gender, New Home, New Job, New Career

I remember my first day in training like it was yesterday. Walking into the training room and seeing the most diverse group of people in one hiring class that I could have ever imagined. It was pretty crazy. From what I could tell, it was very intentional that the organization wanted to increase the diversity of the workforce. For starters, I was not the only trans person of the twelve people in my class, which was virtually unheard of at the time. The group was extremely diverse with every person coming from their own unique background, each diverse in different ways. From race, gender, class, ethnicity, education, to sexuality, each of us came from different backgrounds, and we all immediately bonded with each other. Even our training instructor was from an extremely diverse community. Being openly gay, he really went out of his way to welcome me, like I was part of the family.

Instantly I felt so comfortable, and I felt that I made the right decision to take this job. Of course in my mind it was more than just a job, it was going to be the launching pad for a new career.

Working at an organization that values diversity and inclusion, I felt like I was at home. The next important milestone for me in this process was my first day working in a retail branch. It was the last day that the bank was operating under their prior name, and it was my first day. Basically, the bank and I were both transitioning at the same time. I reached into my repertoire of important things that I had learned along the way during my transition. The empowering word "educate", was one of my most important tools to use during this time frame. I would educate others on what was happening so that they could feel knowledgeable and comfortable during the bank's transition. After a couple of weeks, I really started feeling a part of the team at my local branch. Having team members who showcased compassion and general interest in me, as well as supporting me, made a world of a difference. This helped to boost my confidence and helped to define where I wanted to take my career. I started to rely on all of the knowledge that I had learned throughout my prior career about running a business, from my sales background to P&L management. All of these tools were important foundational resources that helped me become a banker pretty rapidly.

During the first few months of working at the bank, my family and I were able to finally move into an apartment after our house was taken from us by the bank. While in the first few months of working in my new career, while transitioning my gender, we also had to finish moving. When I look back on this moment, I have to wonder if we could have picked anything more stressful to do at one time? Granted, a majority of those things were out of necessity, but it doesn't dilute how hard it was to navigate them. I cannot stress how important it is to have a person or group of people by your side who are there supporting you in a positive way. Whitney and I were able to move through this extremely difficult time, and all of the obstacles that came with it because we did it together as a team.

When I was promoted to banker, I took on the role at another branch. Once again, I was greeted by such a supportive, diverse team. It was no accident. This was now my third team. I could not believe I had the pleasure of working with so many people who were all intersectionally diverse. This led to cohesiveness and a feeling of family. We had each other's backs, and that was unmistakable.

Early on in my career with the bank, I made the decision that I didn't want to go into branch management. For me, I felt being a branch manager would not highlight my strengths. At this point in my career, I felt I needed to be an individual performer in order to build myself up while investing in my clients. This was a strategic decision. It was clear to me that the fastest way to grow in my career would be to skip branch manager. After being a banker for a year and a half, I was able to really start my work externally. I started going to networking events at least three nights a week, at various groups. Of course, I started in my comfort zone, which was the LGBTQ+ community.

I remember showing up to my first LGBT Chamber of Commerce event in Tampa. Honestly, I was expecting to see other people from the trans community. And to my surprise, there weren't any actively

15

involved in the organization. The chamber of commerce desired to have more transgender representation, which landed me a seat on the board after going to my second meeting. Now granted, at that point I had already been on the board of Transaction Florida, a statewide organization that was working to bring inclusion for the trans community. They were actually the organization that changed the department of motor vehicles' policy surrounding gender marker changes. I was proud to serve on that board and help them raise money, but serving on the chamber of commerce board was better aligned with my day job. Everything was business focused from member businesses to corporate members. Being involved in the chamber of commerce created a domino effect for my business pipeline, and eventually my career.

I highly recommend if you are a salesperson to be involved with a local chamber of commerce. One of the difference makers for me as a member, besides being actively involved in the organization, was building relationships in a way that brought others value. In some cases, that was never going to be them banking with me, but it could have been me assisting them, or making a strategic introduction that could help them grow their business. Too many times while networking I saw people who were only in it for themselves. This is a dangerous way of networking, and does not lead to everlasting relationships.

Eventually, all of the networking was beginning to pay. I was a top performer each of the three years I worked in the retail bank. My performance led to many accolades, including me being invited to the annual sales awards ceremony, invited on various trips, and receiving public recognition. At the same time, I was also expanding all of my community volunteerism. At one point in those three years, I was serving on four boards, and close to 20 committees. Then in 2015 I had a very interesting turn of events. Because of the position I held in several organizations locally, I became a media contact for the LGBTQ+ community in Tampa. I started speaking on news outlets, talking about various issues, and giving the local response to national celebrities announcing that they were going through gender transition. I was also speaking out against anti-transgender legislation being presented. It was my action of being visible in news outlets, not my volunteerism that led to more exposure.

Continuing as a banker was something that I thoroughly enjoyed. I had the ability to help business owners create a business plan, help individuals create a budget, and help repair or build credit. These were all things that I had extensive experience in and it really played to my strengths. My extensive knowledge of business management came from my prior career. I naturally thought that was going to be the best way for me going forward. I had my eyes set on becoming a business banker. I was already essentially doing the job of business banker, just from the retail bank. I applied to be a business banker and was interviewed, but did not earn the job. I learned that the only reason I was interviewed was because of my stature in the organization, and that the hiring manager never wanted me on the team. I took this as a learning opportunity. I learned that I needed to grow more and learn more about the organization and other roles that could be available for me.

This led me to have stronger conversations with senior leaders in the organization, which was one of the changing points in my career. Upon speaking with one of the senior leaders, she wondered if I would ever consider getting my investment securities licenses. This encounter led me to start asking questions about myself and my career path. I understood the process of investments, but being a book learner was not really one of my strong suits. She suggested that obtaining these licenses could open the door for other potential lines of business that might have openings, including wealth management. I took her advice, and her sponsorship, and began the process of studying for my security exams. I had to take a small step back from some of the community volunteerism I was doing, but the end result was me passing those security exams at the end of 2015.

Upon passing, I had my eyes set on a new role in wealth management. With my licenses now in hand, I applied for one of the open positions. I came with more determination, energy, and enthusiasm than ever before. When the interview came, I was thrown a curveball. Honestly, I was so determined to find a new role and move up, I had missed something critical. The role I was applying for really wasn't the best fit for my skill set. Even after getting my certification, the role did not fit in line with my experiences and what I wanted to do. I needed a better strategy, so I turned to my mentors and sponsors.

Here I am at the beginning of 2016. I'm navigating my sales results, my volunteerism in the community, being a local media contact, and volunteering with the regional diversity council at my job. My next role needed to involve all the things that were important to me. It was going to be the key for me to take an important leap in deciding my career trajectory.

After strategically building a network of advocates, mentors, and sponsors within the organization to match what I had done outside the organization, I felt I was finally ready for my next move. I cannot stress how important each key person in my network was for my overall career growth. In fact, one of my major sponsors within the organization, who had coached me several times, decided to have a meeting with me to discuss my career path. She is the one who reminded me that I know so many influential people in the organization and that I should begin to circulate what I really want to do with those key leaders across the organization.

I had been stressing to her that I loved the work that I did through the diversity council, and how I wished that I could do that on a larger scale for the organization. It was in that meeting that I decided I needed to create a business plan. I had been tracking metric results for years relating to all of my community efforts. It seemed pretty logical to create a business plan showcasing those results, and then connect it to the organization. My business plan included an executive summary, highlighted the community organizations, and the results that were tracked from those organizations. Some of those results were branding and marketing, online impressions, new businesses that were brought on, and even strategic introductions to centers of influence (COIs). Then, I included how this could be duplicated across all of the markets for the organization.

A couple of weeks later, I managed to schedule a sit-down conversation with one of the c-suite leaders of the organization. During the meeting, I highlighted my background, everything that I had been through already in my journey, why I created this business plan, and why I should be a strategic part of the organization's diversity and inclusion efforts. In short, this executive really appreciated my presentation, but was not certain where funding for this role would come from. Together we worked with my other strategic sponsors to find the funding.

With funding in hand, we were able to create a pilot program to highlight the efforts I was doing. For the next year and a half, I worked alongside the diversity and inclusion team, continuing to track my results, and assisting the team in various tasks. This included the execution of our annual diversity and inclusion conference, and other various events. The following year, a permanent position opened up on the diversity and inclusion team: running the regional diversity and inclusion council program. Immediately I was shifted into that role as a program manager. Now today, I serve as a key part of the organization's diversity and inclusion efforts. I love the work that I do and I love that I am able to strengthen community partnerships through diversity and inclusion.

The path was certainly a long road, and of course there may have been times I made it harder than it had to be. The main takeaway is that I wanted to be true to myself and my values. I did not want to settle for something that was not going to be the best for me. There were times when I was offered positions with other organizations that paid more. Honestly, I was looking at my time at the organization as an investment and I chose to invest in my career in every way that I could.

Ground Rules for
Empowering Differences

What Does Empowering Differences Mean?

Now that you have my background and my backstory, I will lay out the ground rules I have learned to set for myself. These rules have allowed me to advance further in my career and get to the position I'm in now. These rules are like an outline for this book. The lessons that are taught, and the experiences that are shared throughout, if you follow them, will help you on the path of your own career success.

You first need to understand the basis of this book. What does empowering differences mean? Empower means to give power or authority to. Difference means a point or way in which people or things are not the same. When you put it all together Empowering Differences equates to "Using power and authority for yourself or others while positioning ways in which you are not the same as the people around you." Using your differences, what makes you unique, to empower yourself and others to move your career forward.

Think for a few minutes about who you are and where you have been. Think about what knowledge you have gained along the way. Each experience moves you or changes you during your life. Throughout this book, we will work to get you to celebrate and activate these differences to help you move your career development forward rapidly. **So, what are the ground rules?**

1 - Knowing Who You Are

The first rule is that you need to understand yourself and who you are before you are able to do anything. In order to activate your differences and use them strategically, you have to know what they are and who you are as a person. This means more than simply, listing the different identities that you have. It's not enough to say, for example in my case, that I am a white, Jewish, U.S. born, mother of two, 6 ft tall, transgender woman who has found success with only a high school degree. Listing out those identities was only the first step in understanding who I am.

I had to learn and understand what it means to walk throughout the world with the identities that I have. How do they affect me on a daily basis? What privileges or disprivileges do I have because I have certain identities? How could they affect different social and business situations that I'm in? How do they impact and affect me in normal everyday things like shopping or picking up my kids from school?

For some of you reading, the way that your differences affect you and those around you may be clear as day. You may have been able to identify and understand the social position that you are in because you have had to learn from an early age how your differences affect you. For example, if you grew up poor, you probably noticed how little you had compared to some of the other kids who grew up middle or upper

22

class. Getting hand me down clothes from an older sibling, as opposed to new clothes at the start of the school year. Having your food options limited because you were not able to afford more expensive grocery stores like Whole Foods.

For some of you, you may not have realized how the world treats you differently from others because you've never had to question your identity or think deeply about who you are. It's easier to identify how the world treats some people differently because of their race, their gender, or their religion, and think that it's terrible how they are treated without considering how the world treats you differently from them. Oftentimes we try to imagine what it's like being in someone else's shoes. We try to think about things from their perspective but are oblivious to the privileges that we have. Take for instance, if you are a Christian and you see a Synagogue while driving down the street. That might be a rare sight. You may think about how few Synagogues are in the area and then wonder why there aren't more. What you might not realize is how many Christian-based churches are in the area, how the area primarily caters to Christian people, and how that may affect the Jewish community.

It's easier to recognize the disprivileges that other people have because of the contrast to our own lives. People who have the right to vote typically don't think about that right until they hear a story from another country that has limited the ability to vote. Men in the workplace typically don't think about how women are treated until they hear a news story covering a sexual assault allegation. Middle and upper-class people typically don't think about how many kids survive off of school lunches until they hear a story about how a school is

23

ending its meal program from kids living in poverty. It's typically not until we see through the eyes or hear the stories of people who are disprivileged that we realize the privileges that we have. This isn't to say that privilege is an inherently bad thing, or that people who have privilege are at fault for the problems in our society, but that it is important to recognize the privileges and disprivileges we have, and how they affect our lives on a daily basis.

For some of you, you may be in the middle of the spectrum of understanding your differences. You might be able to recognize how some of your identities affect you on a daily basis, while not thinking about other facets of your identity. There may be some parts of yourself that you have not even taken into consideration as a difference, and part of what either hinders or helps you to move throughout the world. Regardless of where you fall on this spectrum, the important takeaway is that you are able to understand yourself and how the identities you have affect the way that you walk throughout the world. Whether you know it or not, the way you present yourself, the way you speak, the color of your skin, the clothing you wear, the way you walk, and the way that you carry yourself on a day-to-day basis when you step out your front door has an impact. It's typically not on a grand scale, but it does affect the way that people think about you, talk about you, and talk to you. Which is why understanding yourself is crucial. If you don't know what impact you are having on others, you will not be able to make the impact you want to make when you need and want to.

For me, I was painfully aware of how people would perceive me in a corporate setting and speaking in conferences. I'm a 6ft tall, trans woman. I knew that if I didn't have my stuff together, then my ideas would be overlooked or judged, and hard. I had to make it a point to stick out in the minds of my bosses. I did this by bringing statistics and data to meetings and interviews. Making sure that I stuck out in their minds, but that I also wasn't seen as the black sheep of the team. I had to be confident, not only in what I was presenting, but also in myself and who I am as a person. I had to be sure my differences are what set me apart from the rest of the team, and could have a huge positive impact on the organization and team I was working with. Once you are able to understand yourself, you are able to start making a change in your life.

2 - Knowing Those Around You

In learning about myself and the way that I am treated walking through the world, I realized that I also had to learn about other people's differences and their experiences if I wanted to connect with not only my bosses, but also my co-workers. This is the second ground rule, once you understand yourself, you have to understand other people's lived experiences and identities.

Knowing how you are able to navigate throughout the world, you'll start to notice the ways that people treat you in different situations. If you are a man, people might listen to your points and take into deeper consideration the suggestions you make at team meetings, as opposed to the women in the same room. Typically, in a corporate or meeting setting, a man's ideas will be heard more than a woman's, even if they present the same ideas. The ways that your co-workers and bosses interact with you are not the same ways that they would talk to another co-worker with differing identities. Knowing the issues and struggles that your co-workers are facing because of their identities, you will be able to step in when needed and create a more inclusive workplace. Understanding other people's identities and what their needs are, puts you in a leadership role where you are solving workplace issues that many may not have known existed.

Companies and businesses aren't run by a single person, they are run by a team of people. Understanding and building connections with that team is what will help you move forward in your career. What is one of the number one things that an employer looks for in a potential hire? If they are capable of doing the job? Sure. But equally important, is the potential new hire a team player? Here are some things to ask yourself. How well are you able to resolve conflicts in the office space? How well do you get along in a team environment? What would you do in certain challenging office situations? Employers and managers want to know that you are able to connect with the rest of your team and able to work cohesively in order to get the job done.

With that in mind, you also need to keep in mind the ways that you interact with other people. Whether you know it or not, words have a huge impact on people's lives. Small compliments about a person's appearance or work can make their day. Conversely, small demeaning comments about a person can tear them down. A lot of the time we do not think of the immediate impact that our words can have on others. Our words matter, and they can have huge consequences and repercussions on the mental health and well-being of others. We may not be able to see this impact in real time, or at all unless the person feels safe enough to share their experience with you.

Even comments that are not explicitly aimed at a person, but a group of people, may have repercussions that you may never be aware of. Thoughtless or negative comments can perpetuate stereotypes and negative ideas about certain groups of people. For example, if the only thing you've heard about gay people is that they are openly flamboyant and feminine, then you might assume that everyone who fits that archetype is gay, and put that person down because of your presumptions. We often do not see the repercussions of certain things we say or do because they are not visibly apparent, or because we block them out entirely from our conscious. Regardless, the words we say matter. You may not see the impact on someone else's life, but imagine the impact that certain words or phrases would have on yours. Part of getting to know others means understanding the ways that you are interacting with them.

Moreover, in understanding the people around you and the identities that they have, you are able to forge connections with them and are able to relate to one another. This can be seeking out a potential mentor or someone who has a higher position than you. Getting to know their background and knowing the needs that they have keeps you in their mind and can come back to aid you when you are applying for a promotion or trying to pitch a new idea. Having a sponsor, or someone who can vouch for you, is immensely helpful for when you are trying to prove yourself. Having a mentor to back you and share that you are not only up to the task, but also why you need to move up in the business.

For me, in order to connect with other people and fit into different social circles, I had to learn what other people's experiences were, and learn about their differences. Being in a room full of men talking about Monday night football, I'm the one who stands out, unless I prove to them that I know what I'm talking about. Because I am not a man, I am not a part of the inside group. I have to find a way to connect with the group in some way if I want to be included in the social circle. In doing so, I am able to gain their respect and connect with them on a more personal level. When I need it most, I will have their support.

Apply this to talking with a group of your superiors. If your bosses are all talking about ways to attract new customers, for example, and you want to make an impression on them in order to introduce yourself, you need to speak their language and know what they are talking about. Doing your research is a part of that. You need to be sure that when you are included in a conversation with your bosses say, at a cocktail party, you need to know how they talk and interact with one another to fit in. You gain their respect, and they will listen to you and the ideas that you want to put forth.

3 - Developing Your Strategy

The third ground rule is to take the knowledge that you have learned and put it into action. Having all of this knowledge about yourself and others is great, but you need to know how to apply it in the right situations in order to showcase your differences. Putting knowledge into action doesn't necessarily mean highlighting your differences every time you are talking with your co-workers or manager. What it means is utilizing your differences in a strategic way to either help you or someone else.

Understanding the backgrounds of your superiors, and ways to connect with them, are key ways for you to stick out in their minds. Connecting with them on a personal level about something they are passionate about is a good way for them to take notice of you and the work that you are doing. Say your boss comes from a poor background and you know that they try to give back when they can. For example, if you know about a local giveaway drive for children in poverty coming up, and your organization has the ability to sponsor that drive, bringing up that idea to your boss is a great way to connect with them. It will show them that you care about the community and also share a similar interest with your boss. Now your boss has your name in mind when it comes to performance review, or even connecting on a more personal level. Being able to connect with your boss because you recognize their differences will help you in the long run.

That's a specific example, but the groundwork is the same in any situation. If your boss has an interest in local sports, or is trying to be supportive of a local community, recognizing and making a connection with them will help your career. Even if your boss has no idea about differences and inclusion, or why it's important. Highlighting the positive impact of having a diverse management staff can make on an organization through statistics, data, and even personal experience, and why you are the best person to lead can create new opportunities that would never have existed. You have to understand your identities and the identities that your bosses have in order to create the opportunities you want.

In terms of co-workers, nobody advances through their career alone. Hard work and putting in extra hours will get you noticed, but getting recommendations and acknowledgments from your co-workers will allow you to move up much quicker, and to higher positions. This isn't to say, learn about your co-workers just to get their recommendation letters, but that you should actively learn and understand other people's backgrounds and identities to be able to use your differences more effectively. As mentioned before with your bosses, connecting with your co-workers means understanding their backgrounds, their interests, and actively understanding where they have come from.

Understanding the needs of your team, you can show your bosses that you know how to identify the needs of others. As a result, you know how to make a better work environment, not just for yourself, but also for others as well. This demonstrates leadership and a driven commitment to teamwork, which will create a more conducive work environment.

Getting to know your co-workers allows for you to share your story and your experiences. A personal example is when I started at the financial services organization. I made intentional connections with several of my co-workers, and months down the road, I was nominated by those co-workers for an organization award because of the connections. Because of the nomination, I was able to meet with the C-suite of executives at the financial services institution. It was at that meeting I was able to present my ideas about creating the position that I have now. Where I am today would have never been possible if I didn't purposefully put myself out there, get to know my co-workers, and actively understand their stories. I listened to them, and in turn they listened to me. We were able to connect with one another, and months down the road it paid off in a big way.

In crucial conversations with my bosses and potential mentors, having two kids would be the best thing I would highlight. Quality of life and work-life balance is a valued trait at many companies, so if you don't have kids, think about highlighting your family or maybe a child or teenager that you mentor. Talking about my kids and the things I do for them is a huge dimension of me. I love to highlight things our family does because for me it is a way of normalizing a conversation. Many people are floored when I share about my kids because they have unconscious bias towards people like me.

Another thing I highlight is that I didn't go to college, not because I did not want to, but because at seventeen life happened. I moved away, working long hours to provide for myself. Some may see my lack of higher education as a disadvantage on paper, I see it as an advantage because it shows tremendous work ethic. College or continued education is not for everyone and it is a privilege to have access to it. If an organization only hires college graduates, they will be excluding a large demographic of people and are losing valuable people that can bring new ideas to the table and have a great work ethic. Recognizing that my educational background is something that I can bring up as a positive difference gives me a unique perspective of the world, that not everyone has. There is always value in a different perspective and a different way of thinking.

4 - Empowering Others Through Action

Once you have reached the point where you are using your differences and your identities to your advantage, you are able to empower others differences. That is the fourth ground rule for this book, once you are able to understand yourself, others, and how to use your differences strategically, you need to empower others to do the same. Lead by example, let your authenticity shine, and inspire others to follow in the same footsteps that you have taken.

There are three reasons for this. The first, is that only using what you've learned to benefit yourself is not the way to go, you move through the corporate ladder as a 'group'. This doesn't necessarily mean literally moving up with a group of people all rising from part-time positions to vice presidents, but that you can't use people for your own benefit. Vain attempts to get to know people, and shallow understanding of others will only be met with rejection and disdain,

You have to be the person that leads and empowers other people. You can do that by giving support, showing compassion for what they are going through, and willingness to help them when they need it. Be an ally for your colleagues when they need it the most. If a co-worker's opinions aren't being heard or addressed, bring that up and stand up for them. If someone is being verbally harassed, that's where you need to step up and say something. Peer support means doing the little things that make a difference in people's lives. You may never know the impact you have had on someone by simply asking how their day has been going, and then actively listen.

The second reason is, you can't be seen as a lone wolf in a business setting. Being seen as someone who acts on their own, disregards the thoughts, opinions, and suggestions that other people make, is the way to isolate yourself from the rest of the office. As mentioned before, employers and bosses look for people who value the team and work cohesively with others. Being seen as the person who runs off and does their own thing without caring about anyone else, is the exact thing that drives people and opportunities away.

Following that, you need to be seen as the person who puts others first, which is the third reason. You have to be recognized by your peers as someone who genuinely wants to help other people in the office, whether that's through mentoring, helping out on a project, providing advice, etc. Being seen as the person who is trying to not only improve the workflow, but also help out other people when needed, will get you recognized.

That's how I was able to move up so quickly at Boston Market. I was actively learning and helping those in other positions, while at the same time learning their roles. Getting further into that career, traveling to different locations, and helping out in their stores showed my bosses that I was a 'go getter' who was willing to help out wherever needed, regardless of what it was.

The last ground rule is that you repeat this process. You constantly get to know more about yourself, more about others, use what you've learned to your advantage, and empower others. Take this as a cycle. We are all constantly learning about anything and everything, whether it's about the world, another person's life, or our own lives. We never stop learning; we never reach this pinnacle where we have all of the knowledge we can know. Throughout your career, you will continue to learn. The important thing is how and when you use what you learn. Follow the ground rules listed and you will continue to find career success as you develop yourself and your peers.

Chapter 3

How to Empower Differences

Ways of Empowering Differences

Throughout the ground rules, I mentioned several times the importance of empowering not only yourself, but also others. But what does that look like? What does it mean to empower yourself and other people? And what differences are you empowering? This guide will give a starting point of ways to empower people and how best to empower specific differences that you or other people have. This is by no means a "be all, end all" list. These are simply how I think best to empower each difference. You may be able to think of better ways that work best for you, or have your own personal experiences, and that's perfectly fine. These are the 10 most empowering words that were used by me in my career journey that allowed me to take a huge leap and propel to the top of the corporate ladder in only a handful years.

I will make a note about how to use this. This is first meant to be used to empower your own differences. The differences that you have are the ones that you want to focus on first, as they are the ones that you will connect to the most, and as such, will have the most impact on you. For example, if your ethnicity and age are what make you different from a majority of your co-workers, then focus on those two first. You don't need to look and remember every single difference.

34

This is meant to be a reference that you can come back to when you need or want to. With all that being said, here is the list of empowering words and the list of differences:

The Ten Empowering Actions

Empower - As mentioned before, this means to give authority to someone to help them achieve their goals. It is to create the space for someone who typically doesn't have it. Working in a male centric space, empowering a female co-worker to speak out and present her ideas at a team meeting. You are able to use your position to create a more inclusive space, it doesn't have to be grand gestures, and can be simple everyday things that you can do for others.

Inspire - This means sharing your story and providing a space for others to share theirs. Showcasing where you've come from, what it's taken for you to get to where you are now, the hardships that you've gone through, and how you've overcome them. Working to inspire others to share their stories and strive for more. Speaking up about your story inspires people to share theirs. It gets a conversation moving and has people talking and thinking about their own lives in ways that they probably would have never thought about before.

Educate - This means to educate others about differences that they may not be aware of, as well as educating yourself about a difference that you don't know about. This can be as simple as educating someone on why they shouldn't use certain words or phases. It can be teaching a single person, or a group of people, about the struggles a community of people face in a training session. It can also mean doing your own research to learn more from others about their experiences in having a certain identity. It also means listening and trying to understand a person's experiences, or doing your own research online.

Inclusion - Being sure that you are mindful that you are not excluding certain people or identities in all that you or your business is doing. Also, being sure that you are including everyone and that no one feels excluded in any way because of a certain identity that they may have. This can be through small things like trying to make sure that a LGBTQ+ co-worker feels included and comfortable mingling and talking with the rest of your team. On a larger scale, this can be making sure that there are LGBTQ+ protections in place and that LGBTQ+ employees aren't excluded in any way. An example would be, making sure they have the same benefits as other workers, and worker protections, so that they can't be fired for being LGBTQ+.

Motivate - Being there as a supportive ally to a person. This can be through simple actions, checking in with a person after an important meeting, being there for them when they need, and encouraging them when they need it the most. This doesn't have to mean literally being there for a person 24/7 cheering them on in an important meeting or in the back of the office like a cheerleader. Being an ally to someone is something that everyone needs, small actions that build a person up can literally save a person's life. You never know what a person is going through and even the smallest actions can have a huge impact on them.

Mentor - This is a person who helps educate and guide another person. The guidance could be related to work experiences, advice that you have to give to another person, lessons that you've learned along the way, or how to understand and use a person's differences to build them up as a confident person. If you share a common identity with someone, for instance only having a high school degree, you're able to share the lessons that you've learned about how you've made it to the position you're in.

Invest - This means investing in others by getting to know them, where they come from, and helping them where you can. Investing in another person financially, if you have the ability to. Financial investments don't have to be huge investments in a person, and don't only have to refer to money. Investments can also mean helping them with a ride to work, or helping them get a certification. Also, investing in development programs, professional mentorship programs, or even sending a group of people to a leadership development conference. The people you are investing in may be the ones to help you in the long run, and by extending that olive branch, you can see lasting returns down the road, sometimes when you need it the most. For me, it wasn't until I was much older that I actually truly understood the importance of personal investment. I remember managers of mine who spent additional time coaching me. Knowing what I know now, I wish that I would have been more appreciative towards them for investing in me.

This also means investing in yourself. Taking the time to understand how you are able to move throughout the world compared to others because of the identities that you have. As mentioned before, once you have a solid understanding of yourself, you are able to understand and help others.

Influence - You have the power to change the way a person or a group of people think. Whether you are trying to be supportive of a person, change the way someone thinks, sticking up for a co-worker, or trying to get policy changes in your organization, you have the ability to influence people and create change. You are able to be there when people need it the most which will help create a more inclusive environment. Take for example, if you overheard a group of your co-workers talking negatively about another colleague because of their background. You're able to stand up for that person and influence the way that group talks about your co-worker.

Access - By this I mean both figuratively and physically. Access is physical access like access to a building; not everyone has the ability to walk up the stairs for instance. Access is also being able to access the same opportunities that other people have. Language is an example of this. Not being able to speak or understand the common language that is spoken presents an accessibility barrier for people who don't speak the common language. Another example of access can mean access to key C level leaders in an organization. Having access to the people who are able to create real change is a huge benefit that not everyone has. Gaining access to these people can mean working in the home office, or being invited to an event where the executives are gathered.

Enlighten - Empowering people through emotion. Emotionally connecting with other people to understand where they come from. This means sharing your story and your experiences, as well as listening to another person's story and background. What has brought you to this moment in time, and the position that you are in currently, and vice versa? Sharing purposeful stories that have an important point, will lead people to have that 'aha moment' in which they realize something about themselves or the world. The more open and real we are with other people, the more we are able to understand each other and support one another.

Common Differences

Note: Keep in mind these don't represent every single difference and identity a person has. There are thousands of differences that you can highlight and empower strategically. This is a short list of common differences that are by no way more or less valuable than any other difference. There is also no ranking for any of the differences that are chosen for this list. They are only put in alphabetical order. Through my experiences and listening to the experiences of others, this is what I've seen as the best way of empowering each of them. As mentioned, you don't need to memorize every difference in this list. This is meant to be a reference guide that you can come back to when you need to, especially as you learn more ways to empower others..

Ability is how we are able to physically and mentally travel through the world day to day. Being able to walk anywhere with both legs is a privilege that not everyone has. Physical movement is something that many people take for granted. Many people may not think twice about the fact that the world is built around being able to physically move and do different things. Ability is also being able to move through the world mentally. It's something that more people are recognizing, but a person's mental ability can drastically affect the way they are able to go about their daily lives. A person with PTSD may not do well in close spaces, or a person with severe anxiety may not be able to present a project update on their own.

The crucial thing is access. Making sure that the people who need it have access to the places they need to go. Listening to the concerns that people have, if they are able to traverse and do the things that people without a disability are able to do. Making sure that their needs are being accommodated and that their concerns are being heard and addressed.

Accessibility is the key thing here and making sure that the people have access to the things that they need. Some companies and businesses have been purposeful in making sure that accessibility is not a problem for their employees. Creating different accessibility programs that are designed to teach their employees about people with disabilities, making sure that policies are in place so that every employee has access to what they need, and working to create a more inclusive environment. Since the passing of the Americans with Disabilities Act (ADA), companies and businesses can no longer discriminate against a person with a disability.

41

Though this doesn't mean that every person is granted the same treatment on a social and employment level. A person with a disability, especially one that is not visible, may not want to self identify that they have a disability because of the backlash that they can receive. The way that co-workers interact with a person with a disability may be demeaning and harmful, and the way that they are treated by their bosses can vary depending on the person. There are numerous reasons and scenarios that a person with a disability may not want to self identity. Just because the ADA is in place and has been expanded, doesn't mean that it's being implemented where needed and that everything is suddenly fixed because of it.

This leads into investing. Investing in the person and taking the time to learn about the struggles that a person with a disability is going through is crucially important. You may not be in a position to create policy change, or change how easily a person is able to access your office building, but you can be there as an advocate and ally. Be in someone's corner, whether that is through listening to their concerns and struggles, or advocating on their behalf for changes that should be implemented.

Also investing in different programs. You could make sure that websites are user-friendly for someone with a disability, that there is training to educate employees, and that people are able to access the offices. Making sure that accommodations are being met and that recommendations by people with disabilities are being heard. You may not be in a position to create the policy changes that are needed, but you are able to advocate with and/or on behalf of people with disabilities. Adding your voice and concern adds to the pressing need for change in your organization, to your bosses, and shows support for your co-workers that have a disability.

This leads to education and enlightening. Many able-bodied people don't consider the systematic struggles that people with a disability go through because they've never had to consider what it's like to go through the world with a disability. Take note that not everyone in your workspace may be able-bodied, whether physically or mentally, and educate yourself on what they might need. Listen to their concerns and let them take the lead on addressing what's best for them and what they need. Listen to their stories, what they've gone through and what has led them to this point in time. Having that space to open up is immensely helpful, you may not be able to relate to a person's life experiences, but you can have that empathy and compassion that we all need.

Having a solid understanding of the needs and concerns of people with a disability, work to create a more inclusive environment that they feel comfortable being in. By this I mean providing the space that they need in order to perform their best. Making sure that they are included in different organization functions, events, and even conversations about the organization itself. Providing the space or materials that a person with a disability needs in order to be their best self. Also being there and motivating them to continue to push towards the goals that they have. Be there as an ally, not just in the sense of listening to a person's concerns, but also encouraging them to keep going. Nobody will ever truly know everything someone is going through on a daily basis, but being there for them consistently, and building them up to be the best person that they can be, will help them in the short and long run.

Throughout all of this, you are working to empower people with disabilities to speak out, to be more confident in themselves, and in the workplace. Empowering one person can create a chain reaction. One person empowered in their identity and their differences can open the way for more people to speak out. To inspire other people to share their story through sharing their own. Not all disabilities are physical and readily identifiable. Not everyone wants their disability to be known by their co-workers for a number of reasons. Some may never want others to know, but there are many people with disabilities that fear retaliation if they speak out.[1] Inspiring one person can inspire and empower a number of co-workers to also speak out. A more inclusive and understanding environment means that more people will feel comfortable expressing their own opinions and concerns with their colleagues.

If you are a person with a disability, by sharing your personal story you are able to influence others to create positive change in your work environment. Reach out, find an advocate or ally that will have your back. Understanding who in your space is someone who will support you and back you up when you voice your concerns about changes that need to be implemented, will give you more ground to stand on. The more people that recognize and support your needs, the more urgent they become, and the more quickly change can occur. Similarly, being an advocate and ally for a person with a disability, you are able to influence the way that people think, act, and talk about people with disabilities. If a conversation came up about a disability or certain co-worker, you have the power to speak up and change the perspective of your colleagues. Put what you've learned into educating and changing the perspectives of those around you.

44

Mentoring would be used if you are a person with a disability teaching another person who has a similar disability to your own. It could mean guiding them on how to move up the corporate ladder, what the office environment is like, and who the allies are in the office. Helping to teach someone who was, or is, in a similar position to you and how you have been able to navigate the organization. This can also mean mentoring an ally, teaching them what they need to know, and how to be a better advocate for people with disabilities. Educating an ally about the needs that you have and what needs aren't being met. Build an ally system. Have a go to a group of people who you know you can trust and who will be there for you when you need it.

Mentoring can also be teaching a person with a disability how to empower their difference by using what you've learned throughout this book, and imparting the lessons learned onto them. You don't need to have similar identities to help teach others about the lessons you've learned. The ways that they will be able to use their differences to make change will be different from yours, but this is also why it's important to educate yourself on other people's differences. Not everyone will be able to use the lessons taught here in the same way that you will be able to. Understand the unique positions that people with different identities have and you will be able to help teach others how to go about empowering their differences.

A great example of putting this into action is through a program or organization like Best Buddies.[2] Best Buddies is a national organization that aims to provide support, and a friend, for people with Intellectual or Developmental Disabilities (IDD). Being an advocate for someone through the organization, you can help someone with IDD develop leadership skills, find employment, and overall being there for someone with IDD as a friend. This is but one specific example of an organization that you can be a part of to help mentor someone and pass down what you've learned.

Speaking on his experiences and the importance of including people with disabilities into the conversation is Greg Pollock. Greg has been advocating for people with disabilities, and he shares the close connection that innovation has with accessibility.

Greg Pollock, Accessibility Officer

One of my goals is to shift the narrative surrounding people with disabilities. People with disabilities like myself are consistently navigating a world that was not designed for us. As a result, we are inherently conditioned to recognize and solve for the flaws of modern-day design. The flaw in these designs are generally easy to spot, they lack accessibility.

Accessibility is rapidly gaining interest across the nation for its role in catalyzing innovation. It continues to transform products that we use and enjoy: smartphones, ridesharing, online shopping. You name it, all of the new product ideas and innovations are all rooted in accessibility. More often than not, these products were created to make an experience easier for consumers.

Their eye for accessibility makes people with disabilities a natural source of innovation and disruption. Since learning the value of accessibility, companies are now competing to create products that are more accessible and convenient. This makes people with disabilities extremely valuable in the marketplace.

For instance, deaf and hard of hearing people like myself, have been text messaging for decades before text messaging was implemented on phones (via TTY/TDD). Back then everybody was using phones but text messaging was not formally introduced as a feature until about 2004 with the emergence of modern cell phones. Now, text messaging is largely preferred to speaking over the telephone. For decades before 2004, this was the only means of communicating over long distances for deaf and hard of hearing constituents. There are countless more barriers that people with disabilities are addressing in our society that will likely become the hottest thing 15-20 years down the line.

Much of the pushback to innovation and accessibility stems from cost-conscious middle managers, people who have been working the job for years and years and don't want to institute change. These individuals subscribe to the mentality of "if it isn't broken don't fix it" or that if we change one thing then there will be a myriad of downstream implications that need to be changed. These changes are often made to seem like this impossible task that could never be done or is not worth it. The flaw in the logic of "if it isn't broken, don't fix it" is that it doesn't factor in the notion that it's only not broken because the user is able to access it. In other words, accessibility.

This logic continues to dominate the marketplace, even with laws like the Americans Disability Act (ADA) which provides what is commonly viewed as a very basic standard for access. For instance, at minimum, a facility must provide wheelchair access. Once this condition is met, it is met regardless of experience. That ramp could be in a back alley surrounded by garbage cans. These minimum standards are harmful to people with disabilities if not coupled with a desire to create a positive, accessible experience for all people. A community that believes in the inherent and economic value of people with disabilities can be a powerful catalyst in shifting the narrative for people with disabilities. When accessibility is factored into all design, we can ultimately create a more inclusive, accessible experience for everyone.

Empowering
DIFFERENCES

Age

For age, there are five different generations of people in the workforce. Each of these generations all come together to work towards a common goal with each having their own input, their own lessons to teach to the other generations, and lessons to be learned from the other generations. Every generation has grown up in their own time, carrying with them the experiences and knowledge of their time that can help to teach others the lessons they've learned.

The first two ways of empowering someone's age difference is through mentoring and education. Regardless of what age you are, and what experience you have, each age group has their own expertise that they bring to the table. For the younger crowd, they are able to mentor the older generations being more technology savvy, teaching the language, and culture of the younger generation. They are also able to teach how to appeal and interact with the younger generations. They can help them understand popular cultural references that are being spread a lot more quickly because of social media and the internet. Younger generations are also speaking out more about discriminatory language and actions that have been acceptable for decades, but haven't been widely discussed or publicized. Whether that's hateful language, or misogynistic behavior, younger people are leading the way in calling these behaviors out. It is important to not only listen, but educate yourself on the concerns that they have.

For the older generations, it might be teaching the younger people in the office what they've learned throughout the years, and how to navigate through the corporate chain. Older generations have years of experience working in a field, learning the ins and outs of their industry, and the organization that they are working for. The lessons that they've learned can be imparted onto the younger generations, teaching them the tips and tricks of how to get to where they are. It goes both ways; each generation has something to teach and learn from the other. Each generation also has a lot to learn about the struggles that each one has gone through. There are many intergenerational issues that generations face, such as student loans and climate change, but there are many issues that have become more prevalent during their time. In recent years, more attention has been drawn towards wages and how many jobs a person working at minimum wage needs just to survive. Educating yourself on the issues that different generations face gives you the knowledge you need to understand where a person comes from and the struggles they deal with. Educating yourself and others about different generational issues leads to more cohesion in your office space, and opens the way for new opportunities for yourself and others.

Something that has been happening more within companies is the hiring of young people to run their social media accounts. More corporate chains are posting memes that appeal to the younger generations because they are written by the younger generations who understand the cultural references that are being shared across social media. This is the influence that the younger people have in a marketing sense. They are able to bring new ideas to the table that may not have been thought of by someone from a different generation, and are able to capitalize on it effectively. Each generation carries their own influence and skill set. Older generations have the years of experience in the field, and know what has worked, and what hasn't. Take for example, if your office space is predominantly older generations and there are only a few younger people on the team, your older co-workers might be set in their ways, not wanting to hear from the younger crowd about what changes they think could be beneficial or how to reach out to newer audiences for your organization. If you're a part of the older generations, you have the ability to influence their thinking and stick up for the ideas that the younger generations have.

Bringing different mindsets and age demographics creates a more inclusive work environment where everyone's ideas are being heard at the very least. A united front that works together will always be better off than one which constantly ignores both the ideas and concerns that a group of people have. If you are in the majority of age demographics, work to bring your co-workers together and stick up for the minority group in your office when you are able to. If you are in the minority of age demographics, be strategic in seeking out a sponsor or an ally. Someone who can help amplify your voice and back you up when you need it the most.

In bringing people together, and creating a more inclusive work space, you are able to enlighten other co-workers about your experiences and the way the world sees you. Each generation has their own conventional wisdom about the world. Through different generational struggles, world changes, and how each generation is perceived by the others; each person has their own lessons that they are able to teach another. Enlightening a person, sharing where you've come from, and what you've experienced, you'd be surprised how many people of different ages share either the same experiences, or have endured the same hardships as you. Connecting with one another brings people together, building a support network that will be there for you and others.

This also means investing in people, getting to know where a person comes from, and helping them to learn the skills they need in order to move up in their career. Having a vast number of years in a field, you have the ability to teach younger co-workers who are starting out about the tricks that you have learned: how to interact in your office space, communicating with the executives, who in the office are potential sponsors and people to connect, etc. On the other hand, coming into a career field, invest in teaching the people that have more experience what it is you know. As mentioned before, the younger generations are able to mentor and teach the older generations, and it will be the older generations that give you the recommendations you need to move up. Investing also means investing in education programs, and teaching each age group how to navigate and understand the world as it is today. The world is constantly changing and moving faster than ever, thanks to social media and the internet. Keeping up with the world means investing in educating people about understanding new technology, new systems, and ways of thinking.

Empower and motivate people with different ages to speak out and speak up. If they are the minority in the room, motivate them to speak louder and share their ideas. Being the minority in the room is difficult. Younger people are often told that they need more experience in the field, or that they need more years of experience in management to secure an Executive level position. It's the paradox of needing experience to get the job, but needing the job to get the experience. If you notice someone struggling with this, motivate them to strive for more, and encourage them in their ability to achieve the higher level positions, even if they do not think they can. Having the experience is definitely a positive, but what gets the foot in the door is being in the right place and talking with the right people.

This leads into ensuring that everyone has the same level of access in your organization to move up throughout the organization and make it through the hiring process. Working in an organization that has a large demographic of young people, don't discount someone who is older who is trying to be hired as a social media manager because you have an unconscious bias. There are preconceptions of what we expect different people to look like in different positions. How old they are, the level of experience they should have in their field, and the typical age demographic. Take for example, the typical age for executives. We tend to imagine them as older, typically in their 40s+. Seeing a young person in a higher level position is an outlier. Being the outlier in these situations may lead to an unconscious bias, but they can also be a reason why you should be the one to have certain positions you are applying for. Having an outlier can help to increase the diversity in the organization, and bring in a new voice that can jump start new ideas.

The last way of empowering someone's age difference is by inspiring another person. That's what I hope to accomplish with sharing my story about working for Boston Market. I was a young kid at the time and what I did was for survival. Figuring out how I can survive starting out as a part-time worker, and how I rose to corporate management from that. Inspiring people helps them push beyond what they think they can do and what they think they can achieve. Share your roots, the struggles that you've had to endure, and you will be surprised when other people say that they have either had similar experiences as you, or open up about times of personal strife that they have gone through. You're able to build each other up and have someone who understands your personal story, and vice versa. Someone that inspires me and has shared some of her story is Debra Quade. She has made sure that she works to pass down what she's learned throughout her career to the next generation and empower people of all generations to share their knowledge and wisdom as well as speaking out against injustices.

Dedra Quade, Director of Supplier Diversity for Kellogg

When I started my professional career, there weren't a lot of women mentors, formalized mentorship programs or recognition and appreciation for diversity of thought. Mentorship from the preceding generations were casual things like, "hey have you read this book?", or once a leader told me I should always sit at the head of the table because he perceived that as being the power position. I'm not sure if that's even true anymore but for him and his generation those were words of wisdom.

Throughout the years, my generation (Baby Boomers) has become more proactive in mentoring and passing on what we know to those that are coming up behind us. We are the transitional generation between a workplace of predominantly white men and the current workplace which is a much more inclusive environment. Millennials and Generation Z are largely driving the change, stating what previous generations might have thought, but were unable to say because they didn't feel empowered to speak out. For example, calling out the lack of inclusion in organizations and advocating for more representation of diverse people to drive change. We're by no means where we need to be, but it's easier to have the discussion today and more organizations and people are taking steps in the right direction.

I've been working in corporate procurement for 20 years and I've seen it become more diverse each day in terms of who is working in the field and also the suppliers that companies are utilizing. That has happened in large part because of the inclusion of young people and diversity of thought. Corporate procurement has become a profession filled with people from different generations, backgrounds and experiences.

We all can learn a lot from each other, and each generation from one another. Don't discount what someone might have to say because of their age. We limit the number of experiences and knowledge that we can gain by stereotyping people or discounting what they say because of this. We stand on the shoulders of giants, and I am not a giant by any means, but I want to be those strong, stable shoulders that give others a boost up in the world.

The class that you fell into (poverty, lower, middle, and upper class) when you were growing up, and where you fall today, shape a lot of the opportunities that you have had in your personal life. It also usually shapes our ability to maintain certain jobs. For people who have access to more capital, the more you have, the easier it is to traverse the business landscape. You're able to afford a car, able to afford a place to live, you have access to a computer if need be to work from home, or apply for a job online, afford work appropriate clothes, able to go on business trips or to conferences, you're able to go to college, and have access to more opportunities. For people who are in the lower class and who have grown up poor, the things I have just listed are issues in accessibility.

People with lower incomes may not have a car, having to resort to a bus or some other means of public transportation. Affording a place to live is a struggle on a tight budget and limited income. Many people don't have internet access, having to resort to borrowing from a friend or using the computers at a public library. This means that it can be harder to apply for jobs, or even be aware that there are more job opportunities, as more and more applications are pushed online to websites. Affording multiple pairs of appropriate work attire can be difficult if a person is spending everything they have to maintain their living, food, and transportation to their job. Being able to go on organization trips, or to training conferences is not an option unless all parts of the trip are prepaid for, and it is considered time "on the clock". College isn't cheap and not everyone can afford to go, especially while trying to provide for themselves and/or their families. Access is the key thing that changes how freely we are able to move throughout the world, especially in an organization.

This leads to education. If you are a person who has never struggled financially, or has only had short periods of financial struggle, educate yourself about what extra hurdles people with lower incomes have to face. For example, think about a person working two minimum wage jobs at 60 hours a week. They might be a single parent and have to take care of their child without any help from family or friends. For me, I had to work harder than anybody when I was working part-time at Boston Market, and also when I started as a part-time bank teller. The former, I had to figure out how I was going to survive. I was on my own and nobody was going to swoop in and save me if I lost my job. I had to make sure that my efforts were noticed and pick up every shift that I could because that's what I had to do to survive. For the latter, I had to provide for my family. I had to make sure that I was doing everything in my power to get more hours and to make sure that I had the financial resources to provide for my kids as they were getting older.

Throughout both times, I was struggling to survive and make ends meet. Everything that I made was going into the roof over my head, or providing for what my family needed. As I rose through the ladder in Boston Market and became a manager, things got a little easier. When I was able to buy my house it was almost like a foray back into the middle class. Then 2008 happened and all of that was ripped away from me. I was brought back to work, paycheck to paycheck, barely making it through each week, and having to squat in my family's old house as it was taken by the bank. I had to work my way up the ladder again to get to the position I'm in now, and I did everything in my power to get to where I am and its given me perspective.

I had grown up in a middle-class family, but I've also lived much of my life working paycheck to paycheck. I know what it's like to wonder how I'm going to put food on the table, and even a roof over my head. I didn't openly choose to live in poverty, barely scrounging to survive. I didn't openly invite myself to be discriminated against, I was not asking for it, and if I had another option, I would've taken it. Anytime my class level lowered, it was for the greater good of my existence and being. For as rough as my experiences have been, they've made me realize that no one ever openly invites to be poor. There are specific circumstances that lead people to either be pushed into one class bracket or another, and it's not as easy as, "just work harder" to get a stable financial footing.

Educate yourself first on what people with lower incomes are struggling with, and your own privileges that you have depending on the amount of income that you have. The more income that you have, the more privileges that are granted to you, and the less you have to worry about. You'll start to notice how intersectionality comes into play heavily with both race and class. Disproportionately people of color, and marginalized people, are the ones who are in the lower-class brackets. Marginalized communities are repeatedly denied opportunities to advance in their careers and aren't able to afford the same opportunities that other people have. The gender pay gap is real. White women make about 81 cents per a white man's dollar, but the gap widens when taking into account race. Black women make about 65 cents for every dollar a white man makes, and Hispanic women make about 61 cents for every dollar a white man makes.[4] Understanding class differences, you will start to understand systematic oppressions that are put in place to keep lower-class people in the lower classes.

Accessibility issues will become easier to identify as you learn more. Once you have a solid understanding, reach out and ask what a person with a lower income might need. You may be able to help them overcome some of the accessibility hurdles that they face. Offering to carpool to work together, or informing the person about new openings in your workplace, small actions can make a huge difference in someone's life. Invest in a person who is struggling. Get to know their personal struggles. Find out what they have to deal with on a day-to-day basis, and what you can do to make things easier for them. Assisting them in different programs that they wouldn't have access to, or different programs that help provide them with funding. Listening to their concerns is important, but it's crucial that you listen and act when they need you to.

Empower a person who is struggling to speak out. Help show them that their struggles don't have to be something to keep to themselves, but are something that can be used strategically to advance their career. To showcase to their bosses that they are able to relate to other people that are in a similar position to where they once were, or still are. A community member that understands the struggles, who can reach out to a larger audience base. Communities of any kind listen and trust someone who shares a common identity. For me, I made sure that when I was engaging community members, whether in a LGBTQ+ or women centered space, that there was a financial tie in. I used those connections as data and results to present to my bosses.

If you are a person who is middle to upper class, you are able to influence the way that others perceive lower income people, and employees who are on the ground level. Take for example, if you are working in the headquarters of an organization, you are likely around the executive heads of the organization, who are in their own ivory towers, and have no idea what it's like working an entry-level position. Being in a similar position or close to them, you are able to influence and speak on behalf of the entry-level employees, and influence the way that the executives perceive them. The best case, improving the benefits that they receive, and highlighting the importance of giving back to lower income communities.

Mentor a person with a lower income. Show them how to navigate the corporate environment in order to move forward in their career. Teach them what you have learned, and show them the channels they should go through in order to achieve their career goals. If you come from a similar background, or have similar experiences as the person you are mentoring, you are able to better teach them and give them the tools that they need to succeed. This also means seeking out a mentor. Every person has something new that they can teach you, whether it's in regard to the specific organization that you are working at, or the field that you are working in. Finding someone who knows the industry tips and tricks is someone that you want to be learning from.

Being a person with a lower income, be intentional about finding an advocate. Find somebody in your job that will be there for you when you need it. Find someone who recognizes the concerns and struggles that you have, and who is able to alleviate some of those concerns and influence others to help amplify your voice. You won't be able to move up on your own. Having a supportive group of co-workers will help you in the long run to alleviate some of the accessibility struggles that you have to deal with on a constant basis.

The climb up the corporate ladder is not easy. Advancing in your field from the very bottom is an arduous task, which is why motivating a person to keep pushing forward is important. To move forward and keep pursuing the opportunities that they may not see are available to them. For many lower-class people, it can feel like there is a glass ceiling. Given the accessibility issues that a person may be struggling with on a daily basis, working paycheck to paycheck for years or decades, it weighs on a person especially when all they get is a pay raise of about 50 cents per hour every year if they perform well. Keep motivating and being there for them. Help them to create their own opportunities and keep pushing forward.

Throughout all of this, work to create a more inclusive work environment where everyone has the same opportunities. Do what you can to level the playing field so that everyone has the same access. Making sure that conferences and trainings are accessible for those that are on a limited budget, and that information about opportunities aren't gate kept by selectively placing information in areas that not everyone can have access to. Creating a more inclusive environment based on class, means working to make sure that no one is denied opportunities, and that everyone has access to the same opportunities. Do what you can to lower the hurdles and accessibility issues that people with lower incomes face.

Part of my hopes in sharing my story is to inspire you using my own personal triumph. I hope to impart success to you by sharing what I've had to do in order to move forward in my positions, and the lessons that I've learned. These are the last two ways of empowering someone's class difference; enlightening and inspiring them. Share your own personal story with someone, what hurdles you've had to overcome, either through growing up, later in life, or what you are struggling with now because of a lack of capital. Sharing your story and your background, you can impart the lessons that you've learned and help teach another person in a similar position how you were able to overcome your struggles. Then you inspire others. Encourage them on their journey of reaching a point where they are no longer financially struggling to get by, and are able to live their truth.

Empowering
DIFFERENCES

Education

Conventional wisdom has told us that having a bachelor's degree or higher is what we need in order to enter the workforce. With an increasingly competitive market, for many jobs having a bachelor's degree seems to be the bare minimum requirements for any lower level or starting position in a field. Unfortunately, not everyone is able to either afford to go to college, or have the time to learn. I certainly wasn't able to go to college, and not for a lack of trying, but because life happened and I never found an opportunity to be able to go. To this day, I still only have a high school education. What I had lacked in college experience and internships, I had to make up for in learning how to manage and work in a corporate environment.

Going to a 4-year accredited university and getting a bachelor's degree are privileges, but they also do teach a lot about corporate management and how to navigate the business world. That, and having an internship through college, shows you the ropes about what you will be doing in your career field and gives you that baseline level of experience. Not having that background experience coming into a field, you have to educate yourself as you are working the job. There is no instruction manual when you move up the corporate chain on how to effectively perform your job or how to lead a team of people. These are skills that are learned through doing the job or are taught to you by other people, whether that is through someone who is training you on how to do the job, or a mentor who is giving you insight and tips on how to perform your job effectively.

Seeking out mentors, and listening to the advice and lessons that they have taught me is part of the reason that I'm in the position I have today. They were the ones who pushed me to go into different fields, to try different things, and encourage me when I didn't know what direction to move forward in. They didn't have the exact same background as me, but they were willing to listen and be there for me when I needed it the most. Regardless of what educational background you come from, everyone could use a mentor to help them learn more about the field they're in, and the path they want to go down. If you are able to, be a mentor to someone who is newer to the field, or who didn't go to college. You work to teach someone the tips and tricks that you've learned, and you also showcase to your bosses that you are a team leader, someone who actively works with your team to teach them the things they need to know.

Through this you are also investing in the person, making sure that they have the resources and the knowledge that they need in order to perform their job effectively. Investing in them as a person, getting to know what they need in order to succeed, what struggles they are facing and what you can do to help overcome them. Investing can also be on an organization wide level. Many companies actively invest in their employees through different types of training. Whether they offer developmental training, leadership, speaking, mentoring, there's a wide variety of different training that companies hold and invest in for the betterment of your team. Talk to your HR managers about the importance of having leadership training, and the impact that these can have on your team. You are not just uplifting the one person that you are investing in, but an entire team that is able to learn business management skills that they may have never had the ability or access to learn.

Access is a crucial thing when it comes to education, especially in making sure that people aren't barred from receiving better opportunities because they don't have a college degree. Working your way up through an organization is one thing, but starting from scratch and applying to multiple jobs online, there are many employers who won't even consider an application unless they have some form of a college degree. If a person has about five years of experience in their field, they might be overshadowed by someone who has two years of experience, but a master's degree in business management. Getting that first foot in the door is the hard part, especially when applying online. Being on the inside of an organization, if you are able to, you can look at the level of access that people without a college education have and recommend policy changes to be implemented.

Get to know the people in your office space that don't have a college education and listen to their stories. Listen to the concerns that they have and work to amplify their voices. As I've said before, excluding an entire demographic of people only works to hinder the perspectives that can be brought in and the positive impact a diverse team can have. People that don't have a higher education and rise to management positions show a great work ethic and a commitment to the job. These are points that you are able to advocate to your bosses as reasons why policy changes should be enacted at your job, and you can also work to create an inclusive work environment. Making sure that everyone has an equal standing and that no one is treated differently because of their educational background.

In working to create a more inclusive work space, share your story or encourage someone to speak out and share theirs. Enlightening someone through storytelling and overcoming personal challenges can change a person's preconception about people who don't have a higher education. Having a higher education and even going to some form of college has become the new normal, to a point that if you don't, then you're the outlier. Part of sharing my own personal background working at Boston Market was to knock down the preconception that you need a degree in order to rise to a high-level management position. To change the notion that in order to be a leader in your community or office space, you need to spend 4 years in a classroom learning how to be one.

At first glance, my education resume on paper might not look so great. Having only graduated from high school, many would see this as a disadvantage. Education is a wide range of factors, it's more than just how many degrees someone has on their wall. Education is how versed you are in a particular subject, if you have any certifications in a specific field, and street smarts. It can be how well you pick up other people's habits and patterns of interacting with one another, how well you are able to code switch, and interact with different groups of co-workers and executives.

Something that I did to help me move up in my career with only a high school degree, was studying people. You can learn so much just from watching how your co-workers and boss handle situations, even how you yourself handle certain situations. I watched, observed, and absorbed all of my surroundings and I caught on quickly to how I should be interacting with people. I learned what I needed to be saying to get my foot in the door with the higher ups. I watched my co-workers and how they did business, mimicking what they were doing and learning from them what I could be doing better. I made sure that I wasn't set in my own ways and acted like a sponge around my co-workers and bosses, taking in how they do business and molding that into my own.

Upon seeing this and learning from them, I decided that gaining certifications to become a registered investment advisor was going to be my plan. In order to become one, I had to get two licenses from the Financial Industry Regulatory Authority (FINRA), Series 7 and Series 66 licenses.[3] The tests to get the licenses are hard, and there is a time window from obtaining one license that you have to get the other. I had to study for months while still producing results at the level at which my supervisors were accustomed to me producing. It was a grueling couple of months, but at the end I had both licenses in hand.

After obtaining those licenses, I had to think very strategically what my next move would be. Upon getting these licenses, I suddenly had offers from several other financial advisory firms wanting me to become a part of their team, and potentially take my client base with me. They offered me signing bonuses if I took their offer, and other benefits to signing on with their firm. As a registered investment advisor, I could start my own investment practice focusing on the LGBTQ+ community.

Ironically though, I never ended up using those licenses. For me, it was the threat of those licenses, the possibility that I could start my own practice, or the idea that I could leave, that made me a more valuable candidate all around for any line of business in the banking world. They were both a recognition that I was versed in multiple areas of banking, but were also a powerful negotiating tool that I was able to use to help move my career forward. The licenses may not have been used in the way that I had originally intended them to, but they were instrumental in my career. The degrees and certifications that you can put down on a resume may not be immediately helpful or relevant in your field, but they do showcase your knowledge and your own unique skill set.

There are lessons in everything that we experience, it's a matter of what we take away from those experiences and how we put them to use. Through sharing your story and getting people to relate, you are able to influence their perceptions about the importance of investing in others. The importance of making sure that there is educational training available to those that want to be a part of them. You get to open people's eyes and change the way they thought about people who never got the chance to go to college or finish it.

If you are a person who has a college degree or higher education, be an advocate for someone who doesn't. It can be extremely hard for people without a higher degree to be recognized and respected by other co-workers who do have a higher education. Be the person who motivates and supports them. Amplify their voice when they present their ideas at a team meeting. Especially if you share a similar background as the person. Motivate and encourage each other to speak up, share your ideas, and support one another whether in team meetings or throughout the workday.

Through motivating and mentoring a person, if they are able to, drive them to inspire others. Encourage them to speak out and share their story about the trials and tribulations that they have gone through, and how they've come to where they are today. Powerful, meaningful stories have more of an impact than you know. Inspiring others through sharing your story, you are able to increase their drive to push for more and achieve more than they thought possible. You also empower other people in similar positions to speak their truth and share their stories of adversity. Empower and encourage these people to see their identity and educational background, not as something shameful, but something to highlight in key moments. Organizations need people who are not college educated to provide a different perspective. A team with all college educated level members is not a truly diverse team.

Ethnicity refers to the shared cultural and social background of a person. This can be nationality, language, religion, and other aspects about a person's culture. What clothes they wear, the way that certain people speak and communicate with another, behaviors that certain people have, etc. A Caucasian person from the U.S. and one from Germany share a similar race, but their ethnicities can vary widely. Ethnicity also refers to a lineage or group of people that a person belongs to or has descended from.

For many office environments, there is a standard and typical way that we are supposed to dress, act, talk, and behave. An office etiquette that we are supposed to follow in order to be seen as a professional in our respective fields. While it is important to have that professionalism, the social rules that are put in place in an office environment can restrict how authentic a person can be in their ethnicity. Take for example, if there are a few Middle Eastern women who are working on your team, some may choose to wear a hijab to the office because they have grown up feeling more comfortable with it, but you overhear a few co-workers tossing around slurs and harassing one of the women. They soon decide that it's better for them and their safety to not wear their hijab in the office.

This is where you empower someone to live their truth, to not put down their ethnicity in how they dress and interact in the office. It should not be on the one person to assimilate into the trends and norms of how other people are, but be able to celebrate what makes them unique. Stand up for them in that moment and show them that they have an ally in their office space who not only listens to their concerns, but works to do what they can. Talk with your co-workers about why the language and words that they are using are harmful, and if it becomes a larger problem, ask the person who you are supporting if you want to take this to Human Resources. An important note about empowering someone is to not go over their head about reporting issues or speaking out for them. Let them dictate what they need from you, not the other way around. For some people, taking the issue to your bosses may only bring more problems down on the person and more harassment to their door.

Part of empowering someone is educating yourself on their culture and what barriers they face on a daily basis, be it socially, politically, in the workplace or otherwise. Have cultural dexterity to get to know a person's culture. The way they talk, interact, and the ways that people perceive others with a differing ethnic backgrounds. There is a history to the stereotypes that we put on a person's ethnicity, and a reason why we don't say certain words or phrases. The way that different groups of people are discriminated against has a history and a legacy of discrimination. Educate yourself on that history and what discriminations a person with a different ethnicity faces.

Part of educating yourself comes with understanding the way that you walk throughout the world because of your ethnic background; how the world perceives you and how you act accordingly. Educate yourself on your own ethnicity. Learn your cultural background, what makes you unique and examine what you are doing when you are talking to other people who don't come from the same background. Oftentimes, we code switch when talking to certain people without even realizing it. We typically don't talk to our parents the way we talk to our best friend, and we don't talk to our co-workers like they are our parents.

Subconsciously, we change the way we act, dress, and what we talk about depending on who we are interacting with and who we are around. Once you have an understanding of your own ethnic background, you're better able to understand others ethnicities and the influences that it has on them.

By educating yourself about your ethnicity, and other people's ethnicities, you have the ability to create a more inclusive environment. Being part of a clique who has a similar background to other co-workers, you are able to influence the ways that people perceive others who come from different ethnic backgrounds. Harmful stereotypes are consistently perpetuated in the office space, whether you are aware of them or not. Phrases like, "Oh where are you really from?", "I didn't know you were one of those people", "Did you hear about x person? I heard they were from x country". Microaggressions that may not be immediately harmful to a person but perpetuate harmful language in an office space that is meant to put a person down. Put what you've learned to use and educate them about the words and language that they are using. You don't need to make a grand show or have them sit down for a lecture. Simply speak up, say what was wrong, and let the person know what they said was wrong. If the situation calls for it, educate the people about the impact that their language can have.

Also investing in another person, getting to know their background, where they have come from, and how you can help to make a more inclusive environment. Whether that is simply listening to them and their concerns, or speaking out for them about issues they don't feel comfortable addressing on their own. Being the only one in a group of people who stands out in any way, we often put our voice down. Not wanting to disrupt the status quo, or be seen as more of an outlier in the group. Having someone who is also speaking out and showcasing support makes that easier.

Do what you can to create a more inclusive environment for everybody. Whether that's being an ally, stepping up when needed, or trying to make sure that there are policies put in place that prevent the discrimination of employees based on a person's ethnicity. Encouraging an ethnic minority in your office space to speak out and enlighten other people about what struggles that people with different ethnicities have to endure and go through. There is a very real emotional struggle of going day in and day out, having to constantly disprove who they are, and prove to others that they are capable and are up to the task of different positions. One story can inspire another person to speak their truth, and if you are an ethnic minority in your office space, enlightening others can work to change the office environment. Inspire other people in your office to live their truth through living your own, and sharing your story.

The unfortunate truth is that, institutionally and in many corporate environments, being inclusive isn't a priority, or even a concern at all. As much as we like to assume that the world at large is starting to celebrate differences and accept people from vastly different backgrounds, there are still vast levels of discrimination, whether its through a single person, a group of people, a community, a business, and even institutions at large. Because of this, it can be hard for a person who is an ethnic minority to even get a job, but also, once they do have a job, they are the ones who have to work harder in order to get the position that they want. They have to work harder to prove in their bosses eyes that they deserve to move up and be in a higher position. If you look at the C-suite of executives at most major companies, the people who are higher up are typically white men. That's become the norm, and it's who many people think of in their heads when they hear the word executive.

Being an ethnic minority in an office environment, they have to prove that they have the ability to lead and move up in their field, but also overcome stereotypes and preconceptions about them that create an unconscious bias in their boss's mind. If you are a person who is an ethnic minority, and who has overcome your own struggles in advancing, share what you know about the organization or the field. How you were able to get to the position that you were in, and be there as an ally and mentor for someone who really needs it. Use your position and educate people who can create change in your organization. Being a person who is struggling to advance in your career, find a mentor or someone that understands your struggle and can help you reach your career goals.

This is why it's also important to keep a marginalized person motivated. To be there for them and cheer them on so that they can achieve the things they want to achieve. Having a supportive person in your corner means more than you think, especially if a person doesn't have anyone else that they can turn to or ask for help. Someone who can speak to how important it is to have an inclusive environment, and people around you that support you, is Ambar Basu. His experiences have shaped how he works to ensure that no one is excluded.

Ambar Basu, USF Associate Professor & Graduate Program Director

As an academic of color by profession, I have, over the years – first as a doctoral student at Purdue University and then a faculty at the University of South Florida – experienced varied levels of inclusion/exclusion. I have been subject to exclusionary practices in determinations of achievement and awards; I have also witnessed my colleagues and friends work actively to create avenues for including my and other similar voices in institutional policy-making. My goal as a practitioner in the knowledge industry, has, however, been to consistently invest in creating platforms of inclusion and access. An investment in inclusion does not mean working towards including difference into the melting pot of this multicultural U.S. culture.

I come from India and in my initial years in the U.S., I tried hard to acculturate to what I thought was a U.S. culture, which, by the way, I thought while in India, was all about the glitz and comforts of New York City and Los Angeles. I learnt soon that the U.S. was no uniform culture and hence, acculturation would not be possible. I have spent my years since trying to acknowledge the fact that the U.S. is truly multicultural, and that the best way to become multiculturally-adept was to learn to respect the multiplicity of cultures in this country. I have come to live by this cultural motto: Difference is normal!

Looking ahead to the future, I'd like to invest my resources and my position in academics to include difference as difference, not with the goal of transforming that difference into deference to a larger mainstream culture. This can, in my head, only happen by way of creating avenues of access for those that continue to be marginalized by our society. This includes access to material resources – food, housing, water, clothing, and employment, access to medicine and health, access to education and finances, and above all, access to those platforms, such as media and policy, that enables the stories of disenfranchisement and underprivileged to be listened to in a manner that leads to positive transformations in socio-cultural-economic-political structures.

Empowering
DIFFERENCES

Gender

By gender, I mean more than just the traditional male, female binary. Gender encompasses more than the typical male/female dichotomy. It includes the lived experiences of transgender men, women, and non-binary people. I will refer to people of all genders as gender diverse, or people with differing genders. Each gender carries with them their own privileges and disprivileges, both in life and in the work environment.

The most important way of empowering people through gender differences is to make sure that your office space is inclusive of all genders and all people. That means making sure that all people feel comfortable and respected in the office; that everyone has a voice and that their concerns are being heard and addressed. Making sure that people's pronouns are respected and that people have access to basic necessities, like being able to, and being comfortable using the bathroom. Be sure there are policies in place that protect people of all genders from being discriminated against, that no one is denied opportunities from speaking out, or denied opportunities from moving forward in their career because of their gender identity. Work to create policy changes that protect people on the basis of gender identity, be there for people of differing genders in your office environment, and help educate others when needed.

Educate yourself about your own gender, what privileges you have, and what you can do to help be an ally for your co-workers with different genders than your own. Know if your gender identity grants you certain privileges in your office space, and how you can help other people who have the same gender identity as you, or some who are in a more disprivileged position because of their gender identity. Being a woman in the workplace, you understand what it's like for other women, and the struggles that you all face collectively in the office environment. Work together to create the policy changes that you want to see in your workplace and change the environment. If you are a man in the workplace, understand the struggles of people with different gender identities and what you can do to work towards being an ally to create a more inclusive work environment. Speak out and educate others when the time calls for it, work with gender diverse people to create inclusive policies, and listen and understand their concerns.

When working to create an inclusive work environment, you also need to understand the lived reality that people of a different gender than your own have to endure. You've seen a little about what I have had to endure, and the hurdles that I have had to overcome, especially with trying just trying to get a foothold and start a career from the ground up again. You don't need to know everything that me, or another trans person, or even another woman has endured, but having a foundational understanding of the basics that we need, and what accessibility problems that we face that prevent us from doing our jobs.

There are varying accessibility issues that face people with differing genders. From even finding a job, to trying to advance in their career. There was a study where two people of the same qualifications applied for a job, the difference was that one was a man and the other was a woman. They both went to the same job interview and were asked the same questions by the same interviewer. The interviewer had no idea that this experiment was being done at all. This was tested at multiple job sites. Majority of the time, the man was hired over the woman, who had the same qualifications. This is an example of the unconscious biases that we hold towards people of differing genders.

Picture what a CEO or an executive would look like. Then, picture a secretary or an assistant. More than likely, a man is pictured when thinking of an executive, and a woman is pictured when thinking of an assistant. We tend to gender certain jobs, or think that a certain gender is more suited towards a certain job because that's who is predominately in those roles. Men are predominantly in the roles of higher level executive jobs, while women are predominantly in lower positions, or secretaries for the executives. In the case of looking for a leader on a team, we typically ask and look towards the men in the room to "man" the booth. To take the lead because they are the most trustworthy to lead. Unconscious biases like this lead to not investing as much into the employees that have a different gender than a man, and lead to non-men employees having to work twice as hard to get recognized and move up in their careers.

Accessibility also means having access to the basic necessities that everyone should have access to. Feeling comfortable in an office environment is a huge factor in how a person is able to do their job and perform in their role. For many women, we have to deal with workplace harassment constantly. Whether that's deeming comments about what a woman is wearing, comments about their physical appearance, touching a woman inappropriately or non consensually, being overtly and sexually aggressive towards a woman, etc. More than 3 out of 4 women have been verbally harassed in the office space, and more than half of women have experienced unwelcome sexual touching in the workspace.[5] All of these lead to women feeling unsafe in the workplace, avoiding certain people or areas of the office, and generally not speaking out against it because of the social and career repercussions that can follow.

For trans and non-binary people, on top of making sure that our gender identities and pronouns are respected by people in the office, one of the larger accessibility issues comes with restrooms. Not every trans person feels comfortable using a particular restroom, and trans and non-binary people are already terrified of being harassed in a restroom. There are multiple cases of trans people being thrown out of a public restroom, or being harassed in the restroom by other people. About 60 percent of trans people have avoided using public restrooms because they fear being harassed or assaulted.[6] Being a cisgender person, the only thing you should be concerned about is if trans people wash their hands before they leave.

Which leads into investing in people with differing genders than your own, understanding their concerns, and what you can do to help alleviate some of those concerns. Whether that is talking with certain people about their behaviors, implementing new policy changes, or even something as simple as walking with the person to make sure that they feel safe and that they have someone that they can turn to. Be an advocate for someone and let them take the lead on what they need in order to feel safe in their space. It's a lot harder to think about what you need to do to advance your career, and even do your job, when you are looking over your shoulder worried about how certain people in the office are treating you or if your office is a safe environment.

Investing also means different training and programs that actively educate your office community about the struggles that certain people go through. Whether that is training on how to be more inclusive towards trans and non-binary people, or training on appropriate behaviors and language in the office space. Also, investing in mentoring and management programs, and trying to push for gender diverse people to apply and be in those programs. Too often people do not push themselves to go for higher roles, or go to different training because they don't see the worth or the benefit of what would be learned in a training. Try and push these people to attend, and possibly offer to go through the training with them. The training can have a huge impact on a person's career. Training can help fast track a person's career through what is taught, and help build leadership skills that employers and bosses want to see in prospective employees.

The type of investing that I received after beginning my transition was even more empowering. I was selected to participate in a media training workshop through Equality Florida[7] and the Gill Foundation[8]. This weekend long workshop really highlighted a huge investment in transgender leaders in the state of Florida. They brought in professional speaker and political correspondent, Sally Kohn, to help facilitate the training. This training also included videotaping our mock interviews with news sources. This practice and the video recordings that I received afterwards, made a huge difference in my public speaking engagements. It was the type of investment that the transgender community in Florida really needed. It couldn't have come at a better time, as this was when we were facing annual bathroom bill attacks from state legislators. This training prepared many in our community to speak out against discriminatory bills. We were equipped and able to speak out, voice our concerns, and articulate the positive aspects of our community while influencing others around us.

Being a part of a clique, whether that's through gender or through your position in an organization, you are able to be a positive influence on your co-workers and create a more inclusive environment through a multitude of different actions. People tend to listen to others who share commonalities as them. Being a man in the workplace, you are better able to influence the other men you are working with to change their behavior or language. Being in a group of other men, you can pull someone aside and work to change the behaviors and actions that they are doing. If someone is constantly making sexual or demeaning remarks to a woman, you can step in and influence them to change their behavior and stop them from harassing someone. Influence the people around you, be an educator to work towards creating a more inclusive work environment for all people.

You can also influence a person to view their gender difference, not as something to 'hide', but as something to highlight. Take the lessons that you learn from this book and use them to teach another person to embrace their differences. Empower other people to be their authentic selves and help them highlight their differences in critical conversations, either with their bosses, or even casually to advance their careers.

Recounting my story and struggles in applying to multiple positions and careers, I hope to shed light on the fact that it is extremely hard for people of differing genders to gain access into the workplace. I also hope to show that I was able to experience forward momentum through owning my identity, and taking on the role of an educator. Becoming an educator and educating people on my gender identity was part of why I was able to get a job and also rise to a higher position than I had ever thought possible at the time. I've had to learn how to frame my story and my experiences in a way that enlightens others on the benefits that I bring to the table. That my identity and the communities that I'm a part of are assets that separate me from the rest and the amount of positive change I was able to bring to the organization.

Through enlightening other people about your story, you can also inspire others to speak out, to be their authentic selves, and live their truths. Showing a path of career success for other people and the steps that you had to take in order to get to the position that you are in. Enlightening people in your office space can also work to inspire change to take place for people to become advocates and allies. We often don't think about what the office environment is like, or what changes should be implemented because we are largely unaware of them if they don't directly impact us. Inspire people to help create change, to be an ally that will help bring a positive impact in the office environment.

If you are a marginalized person who has a higher position in an organization, be a mentor for a gender diverse person. Teach them what you've learned to rise through the corporate ladder, and what tools they need in order to succeed. For example, being a woman in the workplace who has a higher position, be an advocate and mentor another woman in the workplace. Be there for each other, don't tear each other down to meet someone else's expectation. Help other women rise up in the workplace, and they will be there for you. Be there as a support system and someone who motivates others to keep pushing towards their career goals. Not seeing any change and being denied opportunities are demoralizing, and can stop a person in their tracks. Be there to motivate others and keep them going. Help them back on their feet, start from scratch, and keep going. There is always a path forward, you just have to keep working towards it.

There is a growing need for more bilingual people in the workforce[9], specifically in service jobs where there is a lot of day to day customer interaction. Companies and businesses are recognizing that there is a growing need to reach out and connect with different communities and that there is a language barrier that prevents them from doing so. Being bilingual is a valuable asset to put on a resume and something to definitely highlight. Though not everyone who is bilingual speaks perfectly and understands perfectly in both languages. There are many people who are in the workforce that are struggling to speak and learn English.

The best way to empower someone who speaks another language and is struggling to learn English, is to mentor them. You don't have to be a translator for them walking them through day-to-day life 24/7, but being there as a mentor who helps them get through daily office life. Especially if you are someone who speaks the same language as the person who is struggling. For instance, if you speak Spanish as a second language and you know a native Spanish speaker who is trying to read and speak English, you have the ability to help teach them what they need to know. Whether that's through helping them understand certain documents, talking them through certain conversations with other people, or explaining to them how a second language is a valuable asset in an organization.

Access and accessibility are key concerns when it comes to language. Take into consideration the accessibility issues that can come up when you only know so much of a language. It can be difficult to understand contracts and other important documents. Navigating a world that is designed for people who speak English, especially getting into a job interview, can begin to feel impossible. Reading through a resume is one thing, but once a person is in a job interview, everything about a potential hire comes into question, even a person's accent. Depending on your background and your accent, people will receive and treat you differently.

Society at large looks towards people who have a European accent as someone who is elegant and cultured, as opposed to someone who has a Spanish accent, who might be judged as lesser and uneducated. This can lead to stereotyping a person and denying them opportunities because of the way they speak. That means these people have to work twice as hard to be recognized for the work that they are doing, or for the work that they have done. Be an advocate for these people and a resource. If they are applying for a higher position, be the person that writes them a recommendation letter, or be a sponsor on their behalf and advocate for them why they should be in the position in which they are applying.

Many Americans have their own prejudices against other languages and accents. This can lead to many bilingual, and non-English-speaking people, to refrain from speaking their native language if it isn't necessary or safe to do so. Empower people who speak another language to speak out, be an advocate for them, and stand with them when they do speak out. Be the supportive person in the room that will be there and stand up to people when, and if needed. Having just one supportive person in your corner, who is working to empower a bilingual or non-English-speaking person, can mean the difference of being afraid to speak at all, and feeling safe to speak their truth.

Going throughout the world, day by day, receiving degrading looks and comments based on the way that you speak, is demoralizing. People who struggle to speak English, or have a non-English accent, can be overlooked or denied opportunities in favor of someone who is able to speak fluently. As an English-speaking person, be there as a mentor, but also as an ally. Motivate them when they are down, and push them up higher when they are striving to meet their goals. Support them when needed, and listen to the concerns that they have. A simple, "how are you doing today", can make all the difference in a person's day.

Educate yourself on what it means to walk through the world only being able to understand some of what is being told and presented to you. Not being able to communicate at the level you can now, and having people look at you with odd or disgusted faces the moment that you open your mouth to respond to someone. If you've been to another country that doesn't speak English as a first language, you understand some of the struggles that people who speak a second language face. The struggle of trying to ask for the basics, of wondering who speaks your language and worrying about making a fool of yourself in front of the locals. That feeling is what it's like to be an 'outsider' who doesn't speak the language. That feeling is real for so many people in the U.S. who are struggling to learn English as a second language, and who are struggling to adapt and fit into U.S. society.

Part of educating yourself can also be learning a second language. Being able to speak a second language can be a valuable asset in any setting, especially being a person who is interacting with clients on a regular basis. Anyone has the ability to learn a new language, all it takes is the time and dedication to see it through. In learning a second language, you'll also come to understand the struggle that non-English-speaking people have to face on a daily basis. Struggling to communicate and to get another person to understand what you're saying is a frustrating thing, and the people who understand that are better able to relate and help others in a similar position.

Take notice of every label, every sign, document, and website and notice if there is a translation option. See if it's accessible by people who don't speak English as their first language. In your daily life and in your office life. You'll start to notice that not everyone is able to read and interpret all the signs and documents that people who speak English as a first language take for granted. This leads into investing. Investing into translations and making sure that anything that is written and printed is able to be understood by anybody who is reading it. This could be organization websites or contract documents, making sure that they are accessible to those who need it.

Investing also means in terms of your co-workers. Making sure that they have the tools that they need in order to perform in their roles. Say you're working in a predominantly Spanish-speaking part of town, and most of your team only speaks English with only one person who speaks Spanish. Push for a program that teaches the team the basics of the language and what they need to know in order to communicate with the Spanish population.

In doing this, you will work to create a more inclusive environment through educating others and being an advocate for bilingual and non-English-speaking people. You are working to create change in your office environment, whether that is through policies, changing minds, or educating your co-workers and bosses about the accessibility issues that your organization has. In doing this work, you will ensure that there is not a language barrier that prevents someone from having the same opportunities as another because of a difference in language abilities.

If you know someone who is struggling with language ability, share your own story with them and listen to theirs. Learn about their experiences and let their story enlighten you on what it's like to be a person who is bilingual or non-English speaking. Pay attention to the struggles that are endured and how they have managed to overcome them. Their story and experiences may also showcase areas in the workplace that can be improved upon. Inspire them to speak out, to enlighten other people through their story, and work collectively to create change in your office space.

Be in the position of an advocate to influence others in your work environment to be more inclusive. Challenge the preconceptions and educate your colleagues when needed. When you take time to learn about the needs and concerns of bilingual and non-English-speaking people, you are able to influence your co-workers and your bosses about the importance of having an inclusive work environment. You will have the ability to share why inclusion is needed and how it will help the employees of the organization, and also an entire population of people that your organization serves. I've asked Zora Carrier, Executive Director of Florida Museum of Photographic Arts, to speak to her experience being an immigrant in the US, and having to adapt and create a new home for herself.

Zora Carrier, Executive Director, Florida Museum of Photographic Arts

Language represents big words and small words. Language carries weight and those words can be light as a feather. Personally, as a relatively recent immigrant to the United States, what I found fascinating is the different meanings of language, hence the different applications of similar words in different cultural, political or historical contexts. The basic meaning is the same, but the 'final product', so to say, may come out surprising at it's best, or unrecognizable at it's very worst. So then, how is the language we contemplate here, heard, perceived and consequently used?

Most of the population, those on the bottom of the power structure, bottom meaning 80% of the population, are not empowered by originality or creativity in their language. Underneath all the social structure therein lies the language that is used by the majority of the population. This language contains and carries the vocabulary of empowerment and the words that are operative here, are all words that belong to that vocabulary.

It is the monopoly of higher echelons of the privileged, to empower, inspire, educate, include or exclude and lastly and comically, to enlighten. The word Inclusion, when used in accord with the top 20%, is perceived with disgust. They are the ones who dictate the proper form of speech and how language should be shaped and used in accordance with everyday life and especially in a business environment.

When used outside that framework, the way that language is used by those in power, these same words are seen as threatening. Each one of these words from their naked core can be dressed as an ideological tool, part of the language of oppression. In such a climate, sensible people create their own language, perhaps using slang in friendly circles, in order to circumvent words and their meaning as practiced by the close community. When it comes to living outside the corrosive socio-economic environment, in my own personal life and struggle, a life, in which words and their meaning is pure, of course I know each of these words and their effects!

America is the quintessential country of immigrants. One leaves the former homeland, as it lost the desired and nourishing attributes of a home. The loss can be, and often is both material, emotional, and spiritual. The word "inclusion" plays a central role here. An individual feels a loss of connection, either by being pushed away and reminded of their otherness or by gradually developing a sense of alienation. The shared collective story, the narrative, that binds people together, has lost its truth to them. Emigration, if at all possible, becomes the choice and the new reality.

I arrived in the US in 2004, leaving my past life behind. To be accepted, liked, and consequently included, that was the prime hope of mine those days. I was well-educated, I spoke the language, I was experienced, and well-traveled. I prided myself on my adaptability, which I have proven to possess many times in the past. I was introduced to what was supposed to become my new community. The ethnic, cultural, and religious identity of the local population in Grand

Rapids, Michigan was that of Dutch extraction. The community was tight-knit and friendly.

So I thought. On the surface, on Day One, I was viewed as "one of them". Blond curls, blue eyes, European. I love cheese, tulips and find windmills lovely and picturesque.
None of that helped. Once my accent was detected, and it was actually rather mild, smiles faded, a curtain fell, and I was perhaps gently, but firmly reminded: "If you are not Dutch; you are not much!". I am not and never will be one of them. A foreigner without a possibility of parole.

This was not the only experience that I faced, it was the first one. Hence, more memorable. It led to my own improvement. I came to the US with a set of ideas and hopes. I was not willing to let go of them. Any negativity or inhospitality agitates my sense of empathy and it came down to this: if I was seen as poorly compatible, just because of mild inflection in the sound of some words I utter, what about those individuals, citizens of this land, that carry their undeniable identity for all to see at all times? That, which constitutes who they are, their individuality, humanity, all put in question. Their physical and other characteristics declared undesirable, to state it gently. That they are good, hardworking moral people notwithstanding.

Empowering
DIFFERENCES

Race

Race is one of the most visible differences that we can see. Race largely determines the way that we are seen, how other people interact with us on a daily basis, and how we are treated by society at large. The color of our skin and the clothes that we wear are two key things that we look at when we see a person, and we create our own stereotypes in our minds subconsciously about the person based on those two things. If you are walking down the street and you see a young, white, college kid in swim trunks, a surfer shirt, flip-flops, and sunglasses, you might assume that they are there for the beach or are on spring break. Another example is if you see a middle-aged, white woman who is carrying her chihuahua in her purse with big rimmed sunglasses, you might assume that she is pompous and arrogant. Seeing a young, black man with a hoodie and sagging pants, you might assume that he is 'ghetto' or dangerous. The list of examples goes on. Oftentimes we don't even recognize that we are subconsciously putting people into boxes, judging them based solely on the color of their skin and how they appear.

Every day, we are examined, questioned, and judged by the color of our skin. We are granted certain privileges, or discriminations, based on how light or dark our skin tone is. The way that we are treated in an office environment can vary depending on race. If you are one of the few people of color working with a team of with white people, you have to work twice as hard as the white people on your team in order to be recognized for the work that you are doing. A person of color's voice is often overshadowed by a white person in the room who says the exact same thing. This is because of the unconscious bias that many people have. Unfortunately, as a society, we tend to value and listen to white and lighter skinned people more than people of color.

This is why it's important to empower people of color to speak out, to boost them up, and give them the confidence that they need to stand up and voice their opinion. Empower them not be apologetic for the color of their skin, and to not try and hide it either. Encourage them that their race is something that they should highlight in important meetings and interviews. Their race can be their greatest assets in key moments and can help them connect with multiple communities. More companies are trying to diversify the people that are in higher level positions because there are proven returns for a business that hire people with diverse backgrounds. [10]

Nowadays more companies are jumping aboard the inclusion wagon. They recognize the changing work field and the growing need to show that they support diverse initiatives that represent all people. Your organization may have started or implemented a number of different initiatives, which is great. If your organization hasn't, then strive for change and present the data that shows how inclusive work environments help propel profits.

Be careful not to tokenize these initiatives. By tokenization, I am referring to the practice of putting one person of color on an all white team and calling it diversity. Another example would be moving a person of color into a higher position in order to claim diversity among leadership. It's a patronizing move that can be used to claim inclusion without doing much else to create change in their organization. In cases like these, or if your organization has no initiatives, be the person who points this out, strive for systemic change in your organization, find allies who support you and your efforts, and work collaboratively to create real change. Create a business plan and present the data to back up the changes, even if only small steps are taken at a time. Keep striving to make sure that no one is excluded or tokenized.

In working to create a more inclusive culture, you need to understand the accessibility issues that people of color face. As mentioned, many people carry an unconscious bias towards people of different races. There are typical job associations for every race. Those associations frame the way we perceive others. An Asian person is typically seen as someone who excels at math or science, and someone who would be good with computers. A black person is typically seen as a lower income worker, someone who works at a Walmart, or fast food chain. A brown, Hispanic person is typically seen as either a cleaner/maid, or a construction worker. A person of color who is born into a richer family may look down upon other people of color because of their class background and their own internalized racism. It's because of this that certain people are either granted or denied certain opportunities.

In an interview room, if a person of color doesn't wear the right clothing, doesn't seem professional enough, or doesn't speak in a professional manner, then they can be overlooked for a lighter skinned person with the same qualifications. People who aren't Caucasian have to fight against the harmful stereotypes that many people put on them in the first few moments of meeting. People of color have to showcase, beyond a shadow of a doubt, that they are the best person for the job. It was easier for me to rise to a management level position at Boston Market because I'm white. The environment that I was in was also filled with other white people, which made it easier for me to fit in. White male's were who others expected to see in a higher corporate management position running the stores. As such, it was not surprising that the extra work I put in was noticed by my superiors. Catching the attention of my supervisor was not my intention at the time. For me, I was simply trying to survive.

This leads into the importance of investing in the people of color on your team. Having a more diverse team who is leading the different management positions is not only good for the people in the office, but also for the organization as a whole. Listen to their perspectives and the concerns that they have. There is a good chance they will offer a perspective that you may not have been able to see and allow you to identify areas in your office space and in your organization that can be improved. If you are in a position to influence management positions, work to create a more inclusive work environment, bring more people of color who you recognize can excel in a management role, and invest in different training and programs to help them get into higher executive positions. Committing to a more inclusive environment, and bringing different voices into the conversation, you will see the benefits in the long run.

Do your part in educating yourself. Understand the systemic obstacles that people of color and marginalized people have to overcome in order to hold the same position as someone who is white. Learn the struggles that people of your race have to go through. Get to know why a person may be struggling, held back from higher positions, or lacking recognition, all because of their race. Use what you learn to influence the other people in your office to be more inclusive, and why it is important to invest in people of color. Use your position if you are in higher management, or part of an inside group, to influence the people around you about the importance of inclusion initiatives, and what insights different people of color can bring to the table.

Listen to the stories of people of color, what they have endured, and how they have to come to the position they are in now. Listening to their stories can enlighten you and others about how the world treats people of color. In some instances, you will hear how the world is able to lift people of color up, and in far too many cases, push them down. Their stories can also reveal which areas in your organizational culture can be improved, policies that should be changed, and offer a fresh perspective on problems that you have been facing. Telling stories can also inspire groups of people to take a stand and demand that change is created. One person speaking out can inspire another person to speak out and share their story. Sharing your own story can inspire another person to open up and share theirs with you.

Similar to language, recognize that our society doesn't take well to people of color. They are constantly being put down because of their skin color. There is systemic discrimination against people of color in organizations, schools, and businesses. Be there for someone who is struggling, the person in their corner who cheers them on and checks in on how they are doing. Small bits of motivation can make a difference in someone's day and push for them to keep striving for more in their job. Understanding a person of color's concerns and struggles, they are more likely to open up to you and take your words at face value. Do what you can to keep them motivated, whether that's checking in on them, being a guiding hand, informing them of new opportunities and pushing for them to take them, or trying to influence people around you to help create a more inclusive environment.

Being a marginalized person who is in a higher position, mentor a person of color who may be struggling to make an impression in their field and rise to a position that they know they can perform in. Take what you've learned throughout your career, and the lessons that you've learned through reading this book, and empower them to live and speak truth to power. Be an ally that pushes them forward, teach them the key things that they need to be doing to get to those crucial meetings and what they need to say to make an impression. If you've been struggling to get noticed and aren't sure what you need or can be doing, be purposeful in seeking a mentor. Finding an advocate will give you the advice and lessons that you need in order to succeed.

Someone who has used his position and power to empower others and speaks to inspire others to share their truth is Paul Ashley. He showcases his authenticity and tells his story to show other people that they can be themselves and thrive.

Race - Paul Ashley, BMS

I make it a point that I am as authentic as possible not only for myself but also for others. When people see me, being a black male is obvious, me being gay isn't. I am authentically black, authentically gay, and authentically Christian. All of these are what make up my identity and who I am. I have been through a lifelong journey of self discovery, perseverance, and have chosen to live fully as myself with the hope to inspire and influence others through my journey of Inclusion.

Too often in history, multiple facets of a person's identity are left out and the intersections that people have are not seen at first glance. If you look at the history of LGBTQ+ movement, that movement was led by trans women of color: Marsha P. Johnson, Silvia Rivera, and Miss Major. Even now, the Black Lives Matter movement has several LGBTQ+ people leading the movement. So the question for me and many others, is how we, in this unique time, honor all of the intersections of a person's identity. This doesn't mean that it is easy. There are many times that I feel too black for gay spaces and too gay for black spaces. Some of these feelings are based in the reality of the makeup of the spaces that inhibit, but many times my uncomfortableness stems from decade's worth of internal struggles to accept the totality of who I am. I realize that I have to continue to make myself and others uncomfortable because that's where growth, equality and equity can occur.

As my voice in organizations like The NGLCC, the National LGBT Chamber of Commerce[11]; my fraternity, Alpha Phi Alpha Fraternity, Inc.; and The Boys and Girls Club of America grow stronger, I realized that I have the ability to both inspire and influence the next generation. One of the things that I've discovered is that the more authentic that I've become, the larger my platform to share and inspire has become. Often times when I'm at events, people would come up to me, especially young gay black men, and talk about how surprised they are to see me as an out gay black man so publicly, and how inspirational that it is. I can't tell you how humbling that is. Hearing comments like that, is what keeps me going. That's why I continue to speak up and share my authenticity, to inspire all people that they can do the same.

Empowering DIFFERENCES

Religion

Religion is a difference that you may not notice as much in the office environment. Outside of a necklace, clothing, or someone bringing up their faith, it's likely a difference that you probably haven't paid too much attention to. Oftentimes we hear about religious differences when people are being discriminated against, either verbally or physically. For religious minorities, fearing that discrimination can be a daily concern.

Even within religious communities, many people have faced discriminations because of other identities that they have. For example, a bisexual person in a Christian community can face persecution from their community because of their sexual orientation. Empowering someone through their religion means understanding their concerns and also what struggles they have faced. They have likely experienced discrimination by both those with differing religious beliefs, and by those within their community. Empower them and help them feel safe and authentic in their spirituality and their religion, and help them overcome the struggles that they are facing.

Let another person enlighten you about their own experiences with their religion. What led them to their religion? What keeps them practicing? Have they faced any persecution as a result of their beliefs? They can shape the way that you perceive a community or religion, and reveal preconceived notions you have about people who are religious, or who practice a religion other than your own. There are stereotypes and preconceived notions about what a religion says about a person. If you are a religious person, be the one to enlighten others through your own story and educate another person on what your religion means to you and what you've had to endure because of it.

Not every place of worship is the same. Each person who is attending and speaking has their own background, their own perceptions of what their religion means to them, and their own perceptions about other people. People can share a common religion but that doesn't mean that they agree on the same theology or have the same understanding of the world as you. Each person's story can enlighten and educate others about what another person's religious experience has been like.

Educate yourself about misconceptions you believe, and check what biases you may have when you encounter a display of someone's religion, even through something small like a necklace or a headscarf. Take inventory of your thoughts and emotions. What assumptions are you making regarding the individual's background? Do you have any offenses that come to mind? Some people are more strict in their religious attendance or in their practices. One person may feel led to pray multiple times a day, while another may feel content attending a few services per year. Religion looks different for everyone, even for those who practice the same religion. The most important thing to remember is that however a person chooses to practice, it is their choice, and it is valid.

Find another person who has a different background than yours. Get to know their story. Find out if they have faced any discriminations because of their identity within their religion, or by others outside the religion. To give a personal example about my spiritual journey, both of my grandmothers grew up Jewish. Customs and traditions were imparted onto them, and then onto me, even though we weren't an extremely devout family. We followed some of the traditions and holidays, but we didn't necessarily attend sessions every weekend. We recognize Jewish faith and customs, but my parents also exposed us to Christianity. By exposing us, I mean having us attend Bible schools and various other events held at places of worship. As I grew up, I began to not really have one strong tie to any one religion. With that said, I have always grasped my knowledge of a higher spiritual power. Of course, I recognize that others may disagree with me, and I find that totally okay.

As I mentioned in my about me, I had a tumultuous time of being a teenager and I latched onto my high school sweetheart, Whitney. In the summer of 2000, for her 18th birthday, I decided to take her to New York City to celebrate. Little did she know that I had planned to propose. She thought I was just going to give her a promise ring. We decided on a longer engagement, that way we would be a little older before we got married. We decided to marry in the Catholic Church because Whitney was raised Catholic. Since our wedding was happening in the Sacred Heart Church of Tampa, we had to have the church's stamp of approval to get married. This included enrolling into their classes. For me, love was uniquely tied to my survival, so if that meant I needed to be involved in the Catholic religion then so be it.

Later on in our relationship when I began to start living authentically, we were going to services at a Christian church, but they started to exclude me at every turn from attending anything that involved religion or spirituality. There were times when I was asked to leave churches, and not be involved or allowed to volunteer. The lack of inclusion hurt me greatly. I was denied the ability to participate in any religious practices because of my gender identity. I was treated as an outsider and unwelcome in the community. A community that's built on the

110

foundations of love and acceptance turned a blind eye to those principles when it came to loving and accepting me into the church. This isn't to say that there aren't more diverse and accepting churches and places of worship, but this hurt me at my core and this ultimately led to me not being involved in the Christian religion at that point.

On the flip side, I had an amazing inclusive experience connecting back with my original birth religion, Judaism. A few years ago my cousin reached out and invited me to attend her son's bar mitzvah. I was really nervous and not certain what to expect. I wasn't sure how they would treat me because of my gender identity. Because of this, I decided to bring my oldest son with me, thinking that he could act as a buffer in case it didn't go well. Upon my arrival I was greeted with open arms. Family members that I really hadn't spoken to since announcing my gender transition were excited to see the real me for the first time.

Then the night before the bar mitzvah we went to service at the temple. I was invited alongside my sister to open the ark, where the Torah was kept. I was surprised to even be invited into the temple, and even more so be asked to participate in the service. After the service, the Rabbi came up to me and gave me a minute-long hug. She told me that I was exactly where I belonged, then she shared that I was not the only LGBTQ+ person present. Her sharing about herself was very eye-opening and it made me feel accepted in myself, my religion, and this community that I felt more connected to now. Though the major moment happened when she was telling me that not only am I accepted in the Jewish faith, but my boys both are accepted as full-born Jewish children because I am one of their mothers.

It meant the world to me to hear those words and to know that, not only me, but also my kids were included. That I felt like I found a community and a place that I felt accepted and loved. It allowed me to feel more confident in myself, and my identity as a Jewish person and allowed me to connect on a deeper level with my spirituality. This is the positive benefit that being in an inclusive environment can bring to a person. I felt this level of identity and community that I hadn't before in my spirituality, and I was able to channel that into more positive energy in myself and the work that I was doing.

Not having that inclusivity in a community makes a person feel like they aren't religious enough, or that there is something wrong with them and that's why they are being excluded from their community. Regardless of whether you are religious or not, you can help create a more inclusive environment for the people that feel excluded in their religion or because of it. Be there as a supportive ally and friend, and remind them that they are religious enough, that other people's interpretations of scripture and difference shouldn't deter them away from believing that they are worthy of being a part of their religion.

Inclusivity also means being the positive influence on others by putting down microaggressions and discriminatory behaviors that a person might be doing to another person because of their religious background and beliefs. Enlightening others about your own personal experiences, and the experiences of people close to you, will open up conversations and give you the ability to influence others through education and storytelling. Create positive change in a work environment, or in someone's life, by changing the way that they perceive people of different religions, or how a religious person perceives another person's differences.

Putting it simply, people make assumptions about the people that they see. Especially when it comes to people who publicly 'wear' their religion. Whether that's a necklace that has a religious symbol, a religious headscarf, or even a pin worn on a business suit. These are markers that symbolize a person's devotion and religious background, but they can also create an obstacle when trying to get into the workforce. People have their own misconceptions about what a person's religion means, and that influences the way that they think and interact with that person. For example, there is the stereotype that Jewish people hoard money. There's also the outlandish conspiracy theory that they are the ones who are controlling things from behind the scenes on a global scale.

These stereotypes can create a negative impression before they even know anything else about the person, which can lead to them being denied starting opportunities or the ability to advance within an organization. Learn what accessibility struggles and hurdles a person who has a religious background may face, and what you can do to alleviate some of those struggles. Some people may just need someone to lean on and confide in, while others may want support in trying to implement change within an organization.

The Bill of Rights prohibits discrimination on the basis of religion, whether that is harassment or not meeting their religious accommodations. Title VII of the Civil Rights Act expanded those protections to be more encompassing in an organization. Unfortunately, that doesn't mean that it's as easy as submitting a complaint and then everything is fixed. The person who files the complaint may face retaliation and backlash from co-workers or supervisors, simply for voicing their concerns. This is why it's important to listen to the concerns of a religious person, and follow their lead with any desired actions. First to be sure they are supported, but also to ensure they do not file a lawsuit.

Access also means within a person's religion. Looking back at my own experiences, having the ability to marry my wife Whitney was a matter of access. I had to be granted access to the church and the community in order to have our wedding. I was granted access to the community because of the way that I was presenting and the way that others had perceived me. Once that perception had changed as I started to be more authentic, I was barred from accessing the Catholic Church. It was demoralizing and it hurt me at the core to know that this was apparently a consequence of being authentic. Luckily, I was able to reconnect with my Jewish roots and now I recognize that how I was treated before isn't the same for every place of worship, but it still left a mark. If you are part of a religious community, stick up for a member that you notice may be discriminated against and work with them to find a place that they feel safe and able to practice their spirituality among people who share the same ideal of inclusivity within the community.

Empower religious people to speak and show their truth in the face of a nation that would seek to destroy it or shame it. Encourage them not to hide who they are, but to be proud of their spirituality and authentic with their religious background. For me, part of empowering my religious background came with feeling safe and comfortable in the environment I was in and feeling accepted by the people in the community. Having the Rabbi say that I was a part of the community, and that my kids were also a part of it as well because I was their mom, gave me the confidence that I needed to say that I'm a Jewish person. To feel connected in a way I hadn't felt before, and through showcasing my religious background I hope to inspire others to feel confident with their own spirituality.

Empowering one person can create a chain reaction where one person gains the confidence that they need to be themselves and that confidence shines through for other people to see. Through empowering one person to live their truth authentically, they can inspire others to do the same and be comfortable displaying their own religion. To know that they can also be authentic and unapologetic about who they are and their spirituality. Also, that they have a place in their religion despite what other people may say and how other people may treat them because of their differences.

Motivate a person who has a religious background to not give up and put down their religion. If you are a religious person, or if you know someone else who is, share your story or theirs to help motivate them to keep moving forward and inspire them to live authentically. It's hard getting harassed and discriminated against because of your spirituality, but it's even worse to get the same from people who share your religious background. Having an ally and advocate in your corner helps alleviate some of that pain, knowing that at least there is one person who supports and is cheering you on to keep being unapologetic and confident in yourself and your spirituality.

Invest in a religious person, getting to know them, their struggles, and what you are able to do in order to help them. You don't need to know and learn everything about the person's religion in order to support them. Focus on getting to know what they need and what accommodations would be helpful to them. Invest in accommodations that people with certain religious backgrounds need, in training that teaches cultural competency when it comes to religion, and in making sure people feel safe in the environment that they are in. It's hard to devote time to working in an office environment that doesn't feel safe and comfortable; having to constantly worry about a certain person harassing them or saying some off-handed comment.

Being a person who has a higher position, and especially a person who has a religious background, be a mentor for someone who is in a lower position than you. Educate them about what they need to know in order to excel in their role, and be their advocate and sponsor. Teach them the tips and tricks that you've learned along the way and how you were able to navigate through the office environment to rise throughout your career. Being a person who is stuck or is starting out in your career, be purposeful in seeking out a mentor. You will be able to advance a lot quicker in your field and your career by listening and applying the advice that people in higher positions have to offer to you.

Empowering DIFFERENCES

Sexuality

Lesbian, Gay, Bisexual, Transgender, and Queer people (LGBTQ+) people have been getting more and more mainstream media coverage from different celebrities coming out via social media, expressing their sexuality publicly. Despite the publicity that LGBTQ+ people have been receiving, there is still a long way to go, both legally and socially, before there is any semblance of equality. From a lack of protections, to being denied opportunities and having rights restricted, there is still an enormous struggle across the country for LGBTQ+ people to be seen and treated equally. There are still targeted hate crimes and discriminations against the LGBTQ+ community that don't get local or national spotlight and are swept under the rug. You most likely know someone who is LGBTQ+, whether you know it or not.

There are still many misconceptions about what a person's sexuality means, misleading stereotypes about identifying who's LGBTQ+, and in most states, companies have the ability to fire an employee for simply being LGBTQ+.[12] As much as people would like to think that the struggle for LGBTQ+ equality ended in 2016 when same-sex marriage was legalized in the U.S. via the supreme court case, Obergefell v. Hodges[13], there are still tons of hoops that LGBTQ+ people have to jump through to get to the positions we are in and there is still a concern of even letting another person know our sexuality. Don't entirely rely on an LGBTQ+ person to tell you every lingering question that you have about what it means to have certain sexualities, and do your own research. You don't have to know everything that an LGBTQ+ person has to deal with and know every struggle, but have a basic grasp of what it means to be LGBTQ+ and what we struggle through on a daily basis.

Understand that not everyone wants to come out. Some will wear their sexuality proudly as a badge of honor, their sexuality being a huge part of their life and culture, while others choose to remain more quiet and choose not to disclose unless there's a need to. If you are heterosexual, learn the privilege that you have in terms of your sexuality. You never have to come out, disclose your sexuality, or worry about getting fired or harassed for being who you are. You do not have to fear talking about your partner's gender identity, saying she or he in casual conversation because people already perceive and accept you as heterosexual. There's never a doubt that you are heterosexual because that is the normal, and we typically perceive most people as being heterosexual.

Learn what your company's policies are, how they affect LGBTQ+ people, and the rights that they have. Find out if there are any protections from being fired for being a LGBTQ+ person, or if LGBTQ+ are barred in any way from accessing any benefits or services that your organization offers to its heterosexual employees. Research the policies that other companies have put in place and the lasting benefits that those policies have brought for their employees and their business. There is the Human Rights Campaign's Corporate Equality Index[14] that looks at the policies and protections that a business has in place for LGBTQ+ people and gives them a grade based on those policies. Your organization might be listed on the index and it can give you a good place to start as to where your organization is in terms of protecting its LGBTQ+ workers. Even if your organization isn't listed, this is something that you can bring up to your bosses as something that your organization should be a part of. It will give your organization

As of SCOTUS ruling in June, 2020, Bostock V. Clayton County
While this officially protects LGBTQ+ workers from being fired by adding sexual orientation and gender identity to Title VII of the 1964 Civil Rights act under the premise of gender discrimination. At time of publication, this has not been enforced or challenged.

introspection and transparency for employees and customers, and help identify policy areas that need improvement.

Educate yourself on what you can do to create a more inclusive environment. Part of creating a more inclusive office environment is to have inclusive training for your team. Teach them what it's like on a daily basis to walk throughout the world as an LGBTQ+ person. Illustrate what it's like to be worried about holding a partners hand, disclosing their sexuality through casual conversation, having to constantly worry about coming out to people, and having to explain your identity for the hundredth time to someone. Training that teaches the basics of what it means to be an LGBTQ+ person helps to cultivate a more inclusive work environment so that when a person comes out, the person or people they are coming out to at least have a basic understanding and are more accepting of the person.

Learn if there are any cultural competency training around LGBTQ+ people in your organization and if there aren't, then you can look into specific training that other people have been doing. Look into consultants who can come in and educate your team. Invest in different training sessions with your team and your co-workers about LGBTQ+ people. Having a more diverse and educated team creates a more inclusive work environment and boosts not only cohesion in your team dynamics, but also boosts revenue for your organization.[15] Being a LGBTQ+ person, you can do what I've done through my interviews and be an educator. The one who is leading the training and educating people on their biases, misconceptions, and what LGBTQ+ means. If you are able to, take the initiative and either push for training to be implemented in the office space, or be the one organizing/leading them.

Being a heterosexual person, invest in getting to know an LGBTQ+ person and learn what you can to do to be an ally. Think about the privileges you have and what you can do to support your other co-workers who are LGBTQ+, or co-workers who have their own negative preconceptions about LGBTQ+ people. Whether that is sticking up for the LGBTQ+ people when they are facing discriminatory language or actions, working with them to try and create and implement inclusive policies, or simply checking in on them to see how they are doing. If there's one thing that LGBTQ+ people need, its allies in the workplace and in their lives. Someone that they can turn to and trust with the struggles that they are dealing with, and someone who will actively listen and help do what they can to remedy those struggles.

A lack of education, lack of an inclusive work environment, and lack of protections for LGBTQ+ people, lead to a perfect storm that denies access; either to a job, advancement, and recognition within an organization, or to even being fired for being LGBTQ+. It is perfectly legal in most states for an organization to fire a person based solely on their sexual orientation, which is why many LGBTQ+ people are reluctant, to say the least, to let someone know that they are LGBTQ+. Even if the person wouldn't be fired, they can still be refused opportunities to either excel in their role, or try to advance to a higher position. Stereotypes and unconscious biases about a LGBTQ+ person can lead to a manager refusing to see the work that they are doing, or seeing their work as less than the work of their heterosexual co-workers.

Access also includes the ability to attend certain functions. Whether that is work trips or conferences, a trip for meeting certain goals in the organization, or a training event that is being hosted by your organization. LGBTQ+ employees are often denied access to these different functions under the guise of "not being a good fit", or "training being at capacity". Actions like these lead to LGBTQ+ people having to work twice as hard in order to be seen and recognized as an equal to others, even if they have the same qualifications.

We have to overcome the preconception of being seen as lesser, that by being LGBTQ+ our work is less valuable, or that we don't know what we are talking about. That and having to deal and work with people who are generally homophobic and have their own biases against LGBTQ+ people. Educate yourself on the accessibility barriers that LGBTQ+ face and what you can do to help alleviate some of those barriers, like basic access to healthcare. LGBTQ+ people are repeatedly denied healthcare because of their sexuality, or their perceived sexuality.[16] You can help alleviate this by referring a LGBTQ+ to a trustworthy healthcare provider, or recommending other resources. If you are in a position of power, then you are able to lower accessibility barriers and help educate the people who are in a similar position as you, or higher, about the hurdles that LGBTQ+ people face.

Companies like to have the public perception that they are inclusive without having to change their own policies and examine how their organization is treating their LGBTQ+ employees. Typically, they change their logo to rainbow when Pride month comes around and only boost the voices of their LGBTQ+ employees during this month to garner support from the LGBTQ+ community. More companies are realizing the buying power that the community has and is trying to reach the LGBTQ+ community without catering to the needs of the people. This is why it's important to hear the truth from LGBTQ+ employees, to listen to their stories, and let them enlighten you about their truth. What they have had to experience working in the organization, and discriminations that they may have faced working on a day-to-day basis.

Listen to their stories and what hurdles they have had to jump over, or what hurdles they are still trying to surmount. Their stories will help you gain a more solid understanding about what changes need to be implemented, what you can do to help create change, and what you can do as an ally to support the people on your team. If you are an LGBTQ+ person, find an advocate or ally and enlighten them with your story. Open up to them about what you have had to go through and what you need from them. Share with them the policies that aren't in place, and the protections that you need in order to feel more secure in your job and your workplace.

Influence others through storytelling. Enlightening gets a conversation going and gets people to realize the inaction of some companies. Enlightening can guide people who are able to create change and influence the way that they think about the organization, and can be an eye-opener to the way that their organization and many others have been treating LGBTQ+ employees. Getting people to realize the lack of protective policies, and the need for training for the organization, coupled with learning the lived experience of a LGBTQ+ person, can create more allies and advocates. Being an LGBTQ+ person, use your story and your background to influence the people who can create change and educate them on why change needs to be implemented.

Often, people who speak up and share their story are the ones that people look towards as confident leaders. They speak their truth and inspire a crowd of people to think about their own place and what they can do in order to help create positive change. Share your story to enlighten others. In doing so, you may inspire other people to speak up about their own experiences, what they have gone through, and what discriminations that they have faced. It only takes one person who is confident enough in themselves and their story to move a group of people to speak out and work collectively towards a more inclusive environment.

Speaking out and living your life authentically also empowers others to do the same. It shows that other LGBTQ+ co-workers aren't the odd one's out and that there is someone else who is able to stand out and be fearlessly authentic as themselves. Being visible and speaking out, you become not only a leader, but also a role model for others to live their life authentically. Empower and encourage other LGBTQ+ colleagues to speak out and be themselves if they feel comfortable doing so. Work to provide the foothold that they need in order to excel in their position as themselves.

If you are a person in a higher position, consider mentoring an LGBTQ+ person. Take them under your wing and teach the techniques that they need to know in order to succeed in their role and in the organization. Teach them the techniques that you have learned through your time working and what leadership lessons you feel would have been beneficial to you when you were in a similar position. You can also be an ally for them, letting them know who you think would be a potential ally, and whom to reach out to. Take the lessons that you will learn throughout this book and impart what you've learned onto them. Build them up, and they will come back to support you and potentially be a mentor for another person as they rise throughout the organization, and in their field.

Being new to the field or stuck in a career, seek out a mentor. For me, going through Boston Market, I did my best to learn as quickly as I could. When I started in my management role, I struggled for a bit trying to learn everything I could about what it meant to be a manager, and what I had to in order to excel in my role. In my second career, I learned from my past career and was purposeful in seeking out a mentor. I found mentors who taught me what I know now, and they are some of the people who helped push and drive me to climb for a higher position and put myself in roles I didn't feel completely comfortable in. Because of their guidance, I was able to rise to the position I am in now, where I am able to work to create change in the organization and in my communities.

Change unfortunately doesn't happen instantly. It can be months to years before real change is implemented, and even longer before positive results are visible. It takes the work and voice of many to create change. It also takes time, energy, and a constant push to create forward movement within an organization. Voices and concerns can fall on deaf ears for far too long. It isn't until the right person listens and is able to influence those in power to implement more inclusive policies and practices. This is why it's important to motivate people to keep going. Whether that's motivating a person to keep striving for a higher position, being there if they face any discriminatory behaviors, or standing with them when trying to push for change in an organization.

This is why it's important for more people to speak their truth, to be open and authentic about who they are so that others can feel that they can do the same. What follows are the words of Todd Rice, a leader in his field and a strong advocate for change. Todd is someone who fully supports people being their authentic selves.

Todd Rice, Lead for Supplier Diversity at American Airlines

I try to inspire others by being my true, authentic self. As an openly gay cis man in corporate America, I hope others can see they don't need to hide to be successful. Life is too short to pretend to be something one is not. By showing that to others, hopefully, they too can be open about who they are. If you're working in fear of being discovered as "different" at work, you won't be as productive or creative. You won't bring your honest ideas and opinions. You won't add your valuable insight. You won't be you and that ultimately may lead to being unfulfilled, unhappy and unsuccessful. By being out and proud, I hopefully inspire others to do the same.

Researching Your Differences

Get to Know Yourself

Having a solid baseline for understanding people's differences, and getting to know the basics of how to empower your own, is going to take us further into the first ground rule: understanding yourself. Part of that is taking a deeper look into yourself and knowing how different aspects of your identity affect you on a daily basis. The ten differences that I've outlined are only a baseline for you to start with. These are common differences that are either visible, or can come up through different conversations. There are other differences that are significant to you and impact your life in different ways such as military status, whether you have children, if you have a passport, and where you were born. These are differences to take pride in, to view them as strengths. Part of researching is learning how your differences affect you in the eyes of a co-worker, a stranger, or your boss. Having a solid understanding of your differences will help you to build confidence in who you are. With that confidence in yourself, you'll be able to walk into any room and own it.

In order to gain that confidence, you will first need to research your differences. You need to learn about yourself, your unique position, and what communities you are a part of. Be aware of what privileges or disprivleges you have because of certain identities, how your identities intersect with one another, and how people perceive you on a daily basis. Cultivate the connections and relationships you have in a community, and use those connections to help you in your career. These are all things that you need to be thinking about and what can help you understand yourself and the people and communities that you are connected to.

I will lay out the baseline of how I've researched my differences, where that research led me, and how I was able to bring together what I've learned in a meaningful way. My research allowed me to stand out and make a strong impression on the people who were hiring me. For me, I focused on the differences that were the most visible and the ones that had the most impact in my life. From the ten differences I've laid out, my research focused on gender, sexuality, education, class, age, and religion. I became familiar with what those identities meant for me and how I could best use them in different situations.

You may come up with different ways to research your identities and want to learn about other aspects that aren't listed. That is perfectly fine and I encourage you, once you've gone through and read this chapter, to dig deeper where you are most interested, and learn more about yourself. Researching and understanding not only our identities, but ourselves, is a lifelong journey that is filled with discovery and rediscovery. As you continue throughout your career and your life, you will continue to learn more about yourself and others that you can research and dig deeper into.

Start with the Basics

To start your research, I want you to take a sheet of paper and write down the differences that you have, using the ten differences that I've listed as a starting point. The list can be formatted however you like, but really think deep into what separates you from others. There may be small differences that you may not have given much thought, or something that you think may not matter in a professional setting, I want you to put those differences down on paper. Don't think about how these differences can be researched or applied in a work environment right now, just focus on creating your list. Put this book down for a few minutes or a few hours, however long you need, but take some time and come back to this once you've created your list.

Now that you have compiled the list of your differences, I want you to research each of them. Conducting research will help you in the process of highlighting you and your story. Thinking back to 2008, I was still discovering parts of who I am. I really needed to look holistically at myself. I needed to not only know who I was, but also build confidence in myself. Walking into any room, I was immediately put under a microscope and I needed to show my value to the people that would give me the time of day.

How people communicated with me was hugely different before and after transition. I didn't realize that I had privilege until I started going to those interviews as Ashley. Going to those first few interviews I thought, "wow, I must've had a lot of privilege if this is the way that I'm getting treated now." Some of the dialogue that I had with some of the employers and what they said to me floored me. I know that I would not have been treated so poorly had I been presenting as a male. I was looking through the world with the same pair of eyes as I did before my transition, but the world looked back at me in a completely different and hurtful way. Perceived sexuality also played a huge role in the way people would perceive and judge me. A common assumption from others was that what I was doing was based on sexual differences. I learned the hard way that many people, and society as a whole, treat others poorly who express any difference other than the perceived norm. I had to learn how to explain who I was and teach the people that were interviewing me how I could bring more to the table because of the identities that I had.

In order to do that, I had to "research" myself. Think of it like a journey of self-identification. My research was centered around the LGBTQ+ community, and more specifically the transgender community. Your research may differ based on all of the things that make you different. Some of the best places I went for research were from basic online searches. This is where I found the Williams Institute at UCLA. They have tons of studies and research for many things including LGBTQ+ studies and understanding law and public policies. They have information and studies for people of color, and different generations. All of this was amazing information to have and this was only the beginning of my search.

I found information from data, numbers, statistics, and studies. My research went as far as even trying to understand how much of the population had red hair. Even my hair color was a unique identifying difference that I wanted to highlight. And no, I don't mean that I was highlighting my hair by changing the color. I felt my hair was something unique about me, and that I needed to bring attention to that.

Now armed with all this research, I went into my job interviews as the one controlling the conversation. Not only was I going to be able to speak and educate about information pertaining to me, but every time I went to do that I could highlight some of the information that I had researched. This really ended up being a game changer for how I was going to execute interviews. I was able to address the huge pink elephant in the room: the identities that I have, along with all of the data that I had researched. That included the reasons why the pink elephant exists, and how it's going to help their organization.

Conveying My Research

In addressing the pink elephant in the room, I realized that I also needed to learn how to connect with people on a more personable level to get them to be more open to the facts and data that I was presenting. Regardless of how much information I put forward, if they weren't willing to listen and learn from me then it would be nearly impossible to get my points across. One of the quickest strategies for catching their attention was to talk about my family.

I would guess that roughly 90% of the people I would come in contact with who didn't know me would make the assumption that I do not have kids. When I would bring up my children, it was a night and day switch. Family and parenting are very humanistic things. They are common ground items that make it easier to connect with another person to grow a relationship. It is likely that you either have kids, or

131

know someone who does. My family quickly became something that I would highlight and something that would help create a connection with the other people in the room.

Now that I had a baseline for how to connect with people, I needed to know if I was going into a conversation with someone who is anti-LGBTQ+. If I got asked, "why would I do business with you?", I needed to know how to best respond. I had to learn when it was the right time to talk about different studies and data, and when it was the right time to educate the person. I also had to know how I was going to be able to convey that information, especially to someone who was anti-LGBTQ+. I know best how to position myself in business, that included me talking about my family, and that helped normalize myself in their eyes and helped increase the chances of us doing business together.

It took a lot of trial and error. Every person is different, and every person has their own background, their own biases, and their own priorities. However, every person that I talked to, both through those interviews and further into my career, they were each learning experiences. There was only so much that I was able to learn from googling online how certain people are treated, and it's a stark difference between reading about statistics about a certain population and seeing it for yourself. Online is a great place to start but your research should expand beyond that.

Expanding What You are Researching

I encourage you to be like a sponge. Soak up information from all different sources. Whether that is online, talking with other people about their experiences, or noticing how other people talk to you because of your physical appearance. Notice how the dynamics change depending on who you are interacting with. Be observant and notice the small changes that people make when talking to different people. Why do they change their behaviors when interacting with certain people? You likely do the same without even realizing it. Question and examine why and when a person changes their behaviors, check another person's and your own biases, and take every experience as a learning opportunity. The more that you are able to understand yourself, the more self-aware you will become and you'll be able to take control of the conversation.

As I moved throughout my career, I needed to continue my research. I suggest that everyone continues to keep researching their differences, especially as those differences can change as you grow personally and professionally. When I was working as a banker, my needs to research communities became different from when I was just looking for employment. To make myself more valuable to the organization, I needed to better understand the communities I was serving, and the business owners I was helping, and research was a key element to that success. One example of this relates to credit scores. Personally, my credit has fluctuated between very high and quite low due to life circumstances. Early on in my first career, I had excellent credit. Some things happened in our lives that were beyond our control and my credit went from excellent to really bad, very quickly. From there, with

133

hard work and calculated steps, I was able to rebuild my credit. I had first-hand knowledge of how to fix my credit, but I needed to do more research before I could actually help others in their mission of improving their credit score.

Credit advice was not a direct job function of my role as a banker, but I saw it as a way to differentiate myself and provide more value to my client base. This in turn helped to create more loyal partnerships and client recommendations. Because of the success I experienced with gaining knowledge about credit and how to teach others, I expanded my research to varying sections of the financial industry community. Though all of this information greatly helped the community I served, it ultimately benefited me as well. It wasn't necessarily about my diversity anymore, it was about me seeking knowledge and then using the platform to empower others. The end result was me still being true to myself and empowering others at the same time, and it led to a larger scale message of empowerment.

Another thing that I uncovered while I was doing a lot of research was how many non-profit organizations existed across each diverse community. This became an opportunity to engage with these organizations, partner with them, and learn more about the communities that I'm a part of. These nonprofit organizations provided an opportunity to make me feel extremely connected to my diverse community. Many of these organizations also provide research statistics on the demographics of the people that they serve. Some of them also conduct their own economic impact studies. It became apparent to me that volunteering with these organizations provided extensive partnership opportunities.

Step by Step on How to Research Your Differences

1) Taking The Self Assessment -

Now that you have the background of how I was able to research and understand my differences, I ask you to follow and repeat what I've done. This includes doing your own outside research into who you are, understanding what communities that you are a part of, and what these identities mean to you and the people around you.

The first thing that I'm going to ask you to do is a self assessment. The following questions are meant to get the gears in your head turning and get you to critically think about yourself. Think about some of the things that you are already doing, how some of your identities are visible or invisible, and your social position. You don't have to have a concrete answer for all of these, and this is by no means meant to be a threshold test to compare you to others. These are questions that I've asked personally that have helped me lay the foundation of getting to understand myself. There are a million other questions that you may ask yourself, these are meant to act as a foundation or starting point.

What are the visible differences that you have? When are they the most visible?

What are the invisible differences that you have? When are they the most invisible?

For these first questions, I want you to take the list of your differences that you've created and I want you to put them into these two

135

categories. There may be some identities that fit into both of these and that's okay. Some differences are only visible or invisible at certain times. For example, educational background is an invisible difference until it is brought up. Race is a visible difference walking down the street, but invisible to others when we are speaking on the phone. Language is an invisible difference when speaking online, thanks to the existence of translators like Google Translate. If you pass someone in a hallway, you can make an assumption about the language(s) they speak, but it is impossible to know without having a conversation with them, and even then you may not be able to grasp the whole picture. They may be fluent in 5 languages and you would have no way of knowing unless they bring it up. Take into consideration how often an identity that you have may come into play in conversation or how a person interacts with you. Which ones don't get mentioned or noticed as much? What is the dominant identity that people see you through?

Do you have the ability to travel, either to different states or out of the country?

Where have you traveled to and how were you able to afford traveling?

What have you gained from other cultures?

What other experiences took you out of your comfort zone?

The next questions ask you to reflect on what certain privileges you may have, as well as how far out of your comfort zone you've gone. Having the ability to travel is a privilege in and of itself that not everyone has access to. Taking a vacation to France, or to New York City, is something that costs a lot of time and money and is a lot harder to do when you're working 60 hours a week working three jobs to provide for a family. This question also asks if you've gone out of the comfort zone of where you live. It's easy to get adjusted and only know what is around you and your immediate area, there's nothing wrong with that. It is beneficial to get out of that area of familiarity and learn from other people and cultures who don't fit into that comfort zone. Oftentimes, we learn more about ourselves through learning about another person and their background.

Do you see yourself as having privilege? If yes, what privileges? If no, why not?

What is intersectional about yourself?

How does your privilege or lack thereof influence others?

These next questions ask you to look at the difference list that you've created and examine which one might lend you privilege in multiple situations. The first question asks generally if you think you have privilege, while the follow-up one asks what could lend you that privilege or disprivilege. The other questions ask for you to again look at those identities and think about yourself in a more specific lens. Which of the identities that you've listed can intersect with one another? As well as in a social situation, which of those can come together to influence a person?

Have you ever been empowered?

How often do you empower others?

For these questions, it's okay if you've never been empowered, or empowered another person through the examples that were given in the previous chapter. Remember, empowering another person means to give authority to; meaning giving them the authority and the ability to achieve what they want. Empowering a person can be as simple as boosting up a person and telling them that they are more than qualified for a certain position. Supporting a friend or a family member as they speak to a group of people. Empowering a person can be small actions that support a person in helping them get to where they want to go.

Do you donate towards diverse non-profit organizations that empower others?

What communities do you see yourself a part of?

These questions are general questions that are about your actions and engagements in terms of community. What communities do you feel you are a part of and are you putting in anything towards those communities? Donating can mean time, treasure, or talent. How you choose to donate is up to you and what the donation looks like is also your decision.

How do you showcase your authenticity?

What do your differences mean to you?

What do they mean to the people around you?

Where do you fit into society?

These questions ask you to look at yourself through the lens of another person. Think about what other people notice about you, and how you stand out in their eyes. This could be something simple like a necklace or a pair of earrings, a certain piece of clothing that you're wearing, or the way that you are interacting with other people. We all showcase our authenticity through different actions. Sometimes we do it in private for those who are closest to us, and in other times through grand displays of who we are.

What identities would you want to highlight vs wouldn't want to highlight? Why?

For this last question, take a look at the list that you've created and list which of those identities you'd want to highlight in a conversation. The conversation doesn't have to be with a co-worker or a boss, it can be with a friend or acquaintance that you've recently met. Which parts of yourself are you more likely to showcase, and which parts are you more likely to be more reserved with? When you are thinking about which identity falls into each category, ask yourself why you would or wouldn't want to highlight a certain difference.

Reminder: these questions are to get your gears turning in your head and to help you start thinking more critically about what your identities mean to you. You have to do your own part in understanding what your combined differences mean for you. Which ones do you want to highlight, and in which situation you will bring them in to focus?

Step 2 - Digging Deeper into the Identities You Want to Research - The Most Prevalent

Now I want you to take a look at the self assessment and the list you've created. Highlight which of your identities you feel are closest to you, and which identities you want to empower. These are what you want to do more research on. Dig into your differences, getting to know more of your background; understand what your identities mean for you and the history that comes with having a certain identity. This could include how people of color have been treated historically and in our society today, the ways that we lift certain LGBTQ+ people and put down others, or how businesses value bilingual people but culturally we shame those same people for not speaking English in public. These are all things that, as a society, people do. They may be visibly apparent for some, but for others, they may not have noticed how certain identities can affect people on a daily basis. These each carry a historical tie in. There's a history of treating or favoring a certain group of people compared to another, and understanding that history is a first step in countering the negative associations and stereotypes that people have about certain identities.

For me, it became apparent how people treated me in those interviews, and it wasn't until that point that I started to understand how much easier my life was prior to transition. That isn't to say you need to undergo a massive physical change to understand how you are treated, but instead, be more aware of the differences in how you are treated versus another person. That could be the way your co-workers and bosses treat and interact with you, versus how they interact with someone else who has different identities than you.

Being in a meeting with your co-workers, notice which one's are doing the most talking. Which of your co-workers are bringing the ideas to the table and who in the room is getting the most attention? Becoming aware of the behavioral patterns that you and your co-workers have is something that takes time. Overtime, you will start to learn the habits of certain people and their tendencies in favoring a select few. Usually, it is those that are favored that get the most "spotlight". Two important things to keep in mind. The first is to not immediately jump ahead and accuse someone of a behavior. The second is to take in multiple accounts of people's behaviors, especially people that you interact with on a regular basis.

Part of researching your identity is to learn from other people's experiences who share a common identity as you. What have their experiences been like compared to yours? Ask yourself why they might be similar or different. What is it about your identities have led you both to having the experiences that you've had? Let them enlighten you on what their story is, and enlighten them about your own. Just because two people share the same identity doesn't mean that they share the exact same experiences and walk throughout the world in the same way. Learn from other people about their experiences, especially if they have a different identity than your own. Oftentimes, we are able to learn more about our own experiences by understanding how others are treated. For example, if on your list you wanted to research your religious differences, get to know a person who has a different religious background and how their experiences differ from your own.

Though I will note, do not be intrusive. Some of this research you are able to do on your own and could include videos, documentaries, reading, gathering data, and even public speaking talks like Ted Talks. All of these are ways in which you are able to better understand a collectively shared experience of a group of people. Not everyone wants to divulge their personal experiences, or educate someone else about their oppression. A lower class may not want to educate an upper-class person about the privilege that they have and what they should be doing better. It is important to learn from other people, but that should only be when they are willing and able to recount their stories and personal experiences.

This leads into doing your research into statistics based on different identities. Doing my research into the LGBTQ+ community, and the buying power that the community has, gave me the foothold that I needed for interviews, and it was how I was able to move up rapidly through my career. On top of the work that I was putting in, trying to do as much as I could to get as many hours as possible, I was able to put what I had researched into an action plan that I then presented to my bosses. Along with the statistics that I found on buying powers, I also found different research studies about the importance of having more inclusive environments. There is data and numbers to back up the reasons why it's important to have an inclusive environment for any identity. Having that in the plan I presented helped solidify the reasons to have a diverse person move up in the organization.

Step 3 - Understanding Which Communities You are Apart of - Community Tie Ins

The third step is to take what identities you want to learn more about, learn which communities you are a part of, and which communities you want to be more connected with. Community tie-ins, and community relations are a big part of the selling point that I had when it came to talking about what I brought to the table. It's one thing to say that you have a certain identity. It is a whole other thing to put yourself out there in those communities and build relations with the people within them.

The importance of finding communities and being a part of them is, one, to learn more about yourself and your identity by listening and learning from other people's experiences. Two, community tie-ins bring a sense of belonging; being a part of a community, you are able to build relationships with the people in them. As mentioned before, talking to other people who share your identity can also share similar experiences and can teach you important lessons about how you are able to walk throughout the world. Something that I had to consider when I was starting to get acquainted with the trans community was how different my life and experiences have been because of the privilege that I have. That isn't to say it lessens the experiences and the hardships that I've endured, but that I'm able to recognize that I would've endured worse if it weren't for certain privileges. Being a part of my community, and listening to the voices and stories of others, has helped me understand my position and where other people stand because of their differences.

If you are already a part of a local community, that's great! If you aren't and are wondering where to even start, you can look up your local communities online. It could be your local chamber of commerce, or other similar local organizations that people show up to support. There are probably a ton of communities in your area that you've never even considered or thought would be in your area. You can do a simple search online to see if there are any that you are interested in getting to know more about, and if there aren't any local one's, than there are also national level communities and organizations to be a part of like National Association for the Advancement of Colored People (NAACP)[17], the Human Rights Campaign (HRC)[18], National Organization for Women (NOW)[19], and so on. Thanks to the internet, there are also online communities that you can find and join. They can be online forums, discussion threads, websites, and groups like Facebook groups.

Establishing relationships and getting to know people in your community also has community tie-ins that you can use in your career. I made sure that any event, meeting, or group that I went to was connected to the work that I was doing. Whether that was through networking to get more connections in my field, seeking people who could give me insight and advice into what I could be doing more of in my career, or bringing people to use the services that the organization was providing. Working in a financial services organization that supported the LGBTQ+ community was a sticking point that I mentioned, and was able to draw more clients to come to use the organization's services. Through networking with my communities, I was able to draw a massive influx of new clients and get their wisdom and advice through their experiences. All of this culminated when I

144

applied for higher level positions. I was able to present the work that I was doing within my communities and the extra business that I was drawing in for the organization. This showed the extra work that I was putting in, and it put me in a more favorable position because I had connections to a community and was drawing in business from them.

Participate in local and national events, and be a part of a community while keeping the mindset of your interactions being networking and learning opportunities. You're going to connect with people from those communities who are in your sphere. The people there each have their own unique perspective that you can learn from, and engage with, to build your network of connections. You can market your position and what you do within communities, especially business groups that thrive on networking and local support.

Step 4 - Framing it All Together - How to Use This Research at the Right Moments

Putting this all together, researching your differences is not something that is done once. We are all constantly learning more about ourselves and the people around us, and researching is a lifelong process. Throughout your journey and your career, you will continue to discover and rediscover different things about yourself and who you are. You will find more about yourself through the research that you conduct and the people that you will meet or have already met. All of the steps and tips that are listed here, serve to act as a baseline of what steps you need to be taking to understand yourself and build the confidence you need in yourself to empower the differences that you have.

Before you are able to build confidence in your identity and why your differences are something to highlight, you need to understand what they mean for you. Understanding what it means to walk into an office with the identities that you have, and what those identities mean to you and the people around you. As I mentioned, it's easy to say you carry with you x, y, and z identities, but if you don't know how you can leverage those identities and what they mean for you, then they will only exist as a list simply describes you, or worse, they will be seen as a barrier. The research and outreach that I'm asking you to do form the foundation of how I was able to come to know how to leverage my identities and use them as factors to highlight. Connecting with different kinds of people, and learning from each of them, was the pathway I used to advance my career. It also helped me build my authenticity and confidence. I needed to hold my own and speak my truth when no one expected I'd say a word. Having this baseline of understanding is the foundation that you need for building your confidence in yourself and your identities.

Chapter 5

Building Your Own Confidence

Note: If you haven't already, take some time to research your differences and who you are. You don't need to have put in hundreds of hours into researching your differences, instead be sure you have a solid baseline of yourself before delving further into this chapter. For this chapter, you are going to be working on building your confidence in who you are, being outspoken and unapologetic in how you present yourself.

Being Confident in Your Differences

Understanding yourself is the foundation of empowering your differences. Have a good grip of knowing how you are able to walk throughout the world and how the world sees you. Having that foundation, you are able to start building confidence in yourself. It's terrifying at first, putting your differences out there unapologetically, especially when those differences often times are faced with disdain and discrimination. There are certain identities that we subconsciously, or consciously, try to put down as to not draw attention to them because there are oftentimes negative repercussions; a rude, off handed comment that's made, the way that people behave around you or avoid you, and even verbal or physical harassment. Putting yourself, especially your differences, out there unapologetically is hard. I won't lie about that, but I will say, for as hard as it is, it is worth it. Having confidence in yourself, your identities, and the way you carry yourself with them, is how you empower your differences and move forward, faster in your career.

Take it from me, I did not have the slightest bit of confidence when I was starting to understand myself. I was terrified of what people would think of me and my family, and how they would treat me differently when I walked in a room. It took me years to come to terms with myself, to say, "I am who I am, and no one is going to take that away from me". I may walk into a room, get looks from the people there, but I am going into that room and I'm going to rock it because that is who I am and I won't apologize to anyone for being the confident person that I am now. If I didn't walk into each and every room thinking that I was the most confident person there, then I would get steamrolled and looked over constantly.

To put it simply, if you aren't comfortable with who you are, then how the hell are other people around you supposed to be comfortable with you? If you walk into a room uncomfortable and feeling out of place, then it will show. We tend to show our confidence through our body language and our actions, oftentimes unconsciously. If you've ever been in a classroom and not sure of an answer a teacher has asked, you keep your head down and avoid eye contact so that the teacher doesn't call on you. The confident person in the room raises their hand straight in the air and locks their eyes with the teacher to get their attention. Unconsciously, we do these small actions depending on how confident we feel in the situation.

Confidence is something that takes time to build up and believe me, I know that it's not the easiest thing to build. Something that I've held true to myself and throughout my journey is, "fake it till you make it". It may seem simple but it does work. Walk into a room filled with executives thinking that, "I am the most confident person in the room", even if it may not be true. It will help you get in the right headspace in order to act confident. Make eye contact, use hand gestures when you are talking, walk and talk like you know exactly what you're doing and what you're talking about, and other people will pick up on your confidence. People tend to gravitate towards seemingly confident people and who speak with conviction. They are seen as leaders, and they are the one's that turn heads in a room.

Rising Above Negativity

Confidence is key, not only in your survival, but in teaching yourself how to thrive. People often approach me and mention how confident I am. In many ways, I don't think too much about being confident, I just think of it as a way of rising above constant negativity. Many people in the trans community face this, but also other intersectional minorities as well.

In order to rise above that negativity, you have to showcase a level of confidence. It didn't happen overnight for me, that's for sure. I think getting negative reactions from people, and having employers laugh at me were, ironically, instrumental in me building confidence internally. I took each negative remark made about me and used it as a building block. Instead of using those building blocks to assemble a wall to protect or hide myself from the world, I decided to use them to build a platform to constantly stand on. This allowed me to mentally be seen as larger than life.

One of those comments that I got was, "Are you a drag queen?" Someone actually asked me that while I was working as a teller at the bank. That comment was extremely hurtful to me in the moment, but after that exchange I made it a point to remember that comment and I decided to use it as fuel, as a building block for the future. Everyone that laughed or put me down in any way, I used them all as fuel or those building blocks for my platform to build myself up. I also used those statements in my mind to prove them wrong, that I could perform, and succeed in the role and position I was in. I used their negativity to break the stereotypes that were in their head, and also to prove to myself that I could do it. I could make it in this world, and I was able to go after the dreams that I had, and meet the goals that I had set for myself.

Just showing up was difficult because I knew that someone was going to say something cruel or demeaning, but I had to take the high road because I knew that if I didn't, and I flipped out on the person and caused a "scene", then that would only sink my career in the long run. I had to swallow all of the negativity that I would receive on a daily basis, and shrug it off. I worked on what I could and that was to focus on myself, and making sure that I was doing all that I was supposed to do in my job function, and so much more. This way, when it came down to it, I was the one the in the organization they looked to when advancement opportunities came up.

I knew that if I kept building my platform, I would be able to display my confidence and my best attribute, my authenticity. I knew by doing this I would allow my authenticity to shine and allow people to see me, the real me, from far and wide. You have to keep turning negativity into fuel so that you can use it to boost yourself further and push yourself along in whatever you want to achieve. If we don't reflect on the good, the bad, and the ugly, how are we going to be better and have the passion and the drive to continue being better?

Keeping Motivated And Inspired By Leaders

Though something here to keep in mind; your courage won't be everlasting, you will have to keep drawing it from somewhere. Having inspiration is another way of building your confidence. Life is too short, you need to fight for your fair share and more. I want you to make dreams that others would say are impossible, into a reality. I think you can do it, you can do anything. Find inspiration from others that you can draw from. Inspiration can come from anywhere or anyone. Do research on inspiring people from your diverse community. You should know how they empowered their differences, and if you are able to connect with them, please do. You will draw courage just from attempting to talk to them. I would challenge you to really connect with someone in this sphere, as there are only upsides.

How I was able to meet some of the leaders I was following was by writing to several of them in my community, or by attending an event they were speaking at or just attending. I made a point to try to introduce myself, and then thank them for their contributions. I used this connection point to take a picture, if possible, without being pushy or overly aggressive. Sometimes I would only get the picture and be able to remember the moment, while others I was able to connect and talk on a deeper level on the direction an organization was heading, or simply build a personal rapport with the person. Whatever the outcome was, I put myself out there to meet the people who were inspiring me and I'm able to look back at those moments when I need inspiration.

Bold leaders I followed and learned from:

Justin Nelson - I have had the pleasure of following Justin for more than 8 years now. When I became involved in the local LGBT Chamber of Commerce, I noticed his passion for leadership. Then I was able to learn more about how he co-founded the National LGBT Chamber of Commerce (NGLCC). He's the type of inspiring leader that shows humanistic qualities. One of the things I love about what he does is keeping things real. My first interaction with him in person was at NGLCC's conference one year. I didn't actually recognize who he was at first. I started a conversation with him and was sharing my honest feedback on how their organization needed to be more trans inclusive. During our discussion he sat there with such grace and compassion and allowed me to vent about everything that I felt was wrong. At the end of our discussion he then thanked me for my comments, and agreed that they needed to do better. He then promised to engage with me more, if I was willing, which was a smart way of looping my leadership qualities to help his organization.

This led to us working together to create the NGLCC Trans Inclusion Task Force. The first task force that's part of the NGLCC network. Together we decided to have me co-chair the task force alongside

152

Sabrina Kent. Sabrina works for the team at NGLCC, so the bond was very strong. Over the past two years I've had the distinct pleasure of working to create change economically for the transgender community. Sabrina and I have had our friendship blossom throughout this as well which has been truly amazing. The growth in transgender and gender non-conforming businesses who are working to get their business certified has been nothing short of amazing.

Strategic leaders are always thinking, sometimes multiple steps ahead of the game. One other thing to note that I've noticed in my interactions with Justin through the years, has been his ability to share openly what his strengths are, and where his weaknesses exist. You'll notice that in speeches he gives around other intersectional diversities, he is very quick to point out his privilege as a white male. I love how he takes the time to build up and invest in other diverse communities because everyone can own the outcomes to move inclusion forward.

Debbie Lundberg - A mentor of mine connected me with Debbie. This mentor was very instrumental in helping to find the money in the budget to pay for professional coaching for me. Debbie is incredibly plugged in through the local chamber of commerce, and other various nonprofit organizations. So, it was amazing that we hadn't met before this, but I'm really glad that we were able to connect and build a relationship.

I had the pleasure of benefiting from access to the leadership development coaching from Debbie. This was one of the key things that helped me build confidence. She helped me channel my emotions to be a more engaging thought-provoking speaker. By the time I met

153

Debbie, I was displaying a ton of confidence, but might not have been directing it in the best way. I was presenting as a highly excited speaker, and was not necessarily as focused or controlled as I could have been. I needed her coaching way more than I even knew I needed it. Her coaching opened my eyes to what I was still struggling with emotionally. There were experiences in my past that I hadn't gotten to the root of, but having the leadership development coaching helped me work through some of those experiences and taught me how to channel my emotions into the presentations that I was giving.

Another great takeaway from my experience in working with Debbie, was the implementation of a 360° feedback review panel, which included external community stakeholders and internal people within my work team. Before interacting and working with her, I didn't know that I could've been able to objectively look at feedback the way that I was able to during my time with her. She made me realize that I needed to be considering everyone who could be affected by the work that I was doing, and that I needed to get their feedback. Having their feedback made it so that I was always putting my best foot forward and was looking out for all of the stakeholders involved.

Working with her made a huge difference in how I was able to showcase my confidence and leadership together at the same time. If you get a chance to check out her story and her book, it's pretty inspiring. You will love how she overcame obstacles working in a male dominated industry, and now how she presents powerfully! Her book is titled Presenting Powerfully.

Sarah Kate Ellis - Sarah Kate was one of the influential leaders that I did a lot of research on over the years. Watching her mannerisms, and the words she uses in her speeches, were just some of the key aspects that I drew from. Being able to go on a major news network and stick to your talking points and showcase confidence, leadership, and compassion at the same time, are the skills that not many people possess all at once. Watching her do this time and time again made a huge impact on how I would present and learn from my experiences.

Over the past four years I've had the pleasure of attending her events through GLAAD[20] (GLAAD is the international LGBTQ+ advocacy organization working to amplify and protect LGBTQ+ voices). I had the honor of meeting her two years ago during the GLAAD Media Awards Week in Los Angeles, CA. Though we had only met briefly during that time, this past year I went through vetting and was voted on to GLAAD's national board of directors, which was a dream come true. She's inspired me through the years, and now I get to help her in our mission to amplify LGBTQ+ voices is such an honor. I had the first pick of my seat at the table for my first board meeting in November of 2019, and subliminally I somehow chose the perfect seat directly across the table from her. I was able to soak up everything that she presented on, and the way in which she presented it. Now as a personal donor, and someone who raises funds and awareness for GLAAD, it's pretty exciting to be able to soak up as much as I can in the leadership space from her each and every meeting. This is the best return on my investment that I could ever receive.

Being a Confident Speaker

I look up to all of these people. I'm always blown away at how they speak to an audience and the way they carry themselves in front of a crowd. Many times, those who give public speeches may seem like the most confident person in the room. They know what they're talking about, speaking with conviction, and not stumbling on a single word. The truth though, for a lot of those people, they are terrified of being in front of a crowd. Just because a person speaks with complete confidence does not mean they do not feel anxious or worried at all speaking. Instead, they are able to push past those feelings to deliver. For the audience, they only see the speaker flawlessly executing their speech. For the speaker, even if they are nervous, they don't let it show because they know that if they are uncomfortable, or if their voice waivers, then it may affect how their audience receives the message. They choose to push through their fears because they are confident in what they are talking about, what they need to say, and who they are.

Most public speakers spend hours and days preparing what they need to say. When they finally take the stage, the floor, or the microphone, the room listens. Nobody comes out of the gate being an outspoken, confident person. It takes time, training, and even therapy for the most confident speakers to build up that confidence. They've put in the time that they need to build themselves up and know exactly who they are. My driving force was to prove the other people wrong. I knew internally who I was, and I was able to work up my own courage. I drew from the silently disproving people. I used the exceptional work that I was doing to slowly become more outspoken about my identity and finally became completely unapologetic. It took a lot of time and

156

support from the people around me to build myself up and be confident in who I am. Having supportive people around you who cheer you on and are there for you when you need it will help to build up your own confidence.

One Brick at a Time

Take small actions to build your confidence. Remind yourself that you are worth the time investment. That you are doing great things. Small affirmations that you can give yourself, or even ask a friend or a family member to help build you up. There will come a point where relying on your own self-confidence will only get you so far in feeling good about yourself. Having a group of supportive people around you will help lift you up higher and help you build yourself up. These people who will raise you up, can be a group of co-workers, community members, friends, or family members. Knowing that someone is cheering you on whenever you are doing something major like a job interview, or something important to you, like presenting at a company meeting, it can mean the world to know that there is someone in your corner.

Something I want to note is that this isn't a simple, "put these tips into action for a few hours and bam! You're so much more confident." This is something that takes a lot of time and practice. It is something that people work on every day and it's something that I'm still building within myself. There is no defining pinnacle to reach where you can say, "I'm the most confident person now!" Like with researching yourself, it's something that will continue throughout your life. Whether you are consciously working on yourself, or unconsciously building yourself up, building your confidence will take time and there may be times when you stumble.

It's okay to have your confidence waver in a situation, whether that is when giving an important talk, or just in day to day life, being confident is something that takes constant work. You can be the most confident person one day, and not feel the same the next. That doesn't mean you're any less confident in who you are or what you are talking about. Some days you'll have more confidence, and others you'll have less, but overall and overtime, you'll slowly start to grow more confident. That's where you turn to other people for support and to help you push past those points.

The biggest tips I can give you in being more confident in yourself are: be loud, unapologetic, and courageous. It's okay to fear speaking out, but don't let that hold you back from saying what you need to say and speaking your own truth. Too often we feel that we need to apologize for who we are, for the differences that we have. Thinking that because some aspect of our identity may be different from the rest, that we should lower our voice and not step on any toes. Worried about what might happen if we speak up and voice our concerns or even showcase our identities.

Your identity is something to take pride in. It's a part of you and what builds on your own uniqueness. Regardless of what other people think, regardless of how society believes you should think, your identity is something that you should take pride in because it's who you are deep down. You are worth it. Your voice matters and what you have to say matters. Voice your opinion, speak out where you can, and when you feel like it's needed. Have the courage to speak up even in the face of your own fears, even if you are faking it, and don't apologize for who you are. If you have the confidence in yourself to know that you can do this, whether that's speaking out in a meeting, raising your concerns, or speaking to an audience, then no one can take that away from you.

Step 2

Knowing Others

Privilege

What is Privilege?

Privilege is defined as a special right or advantage that is granted or available only to a particular person or group. These are typically granted to a person at birth, but there are some privileges that can be gained, such as class privilege. I won't be going into every single privilege or disprivilege that exists, as that could be its own book series, but I will be talking about what privilege looks like, how to recognize it, and how to check your own privilege. As with the other chapters, I am going to be asking you to do some of your own research into your own privilege. I can't be the one to explicitly tell you all of the privileges that you have, you have to be able to recognize it within yourself, others, and how privilege can shape a person's perception of people.

An important note; privilege is not something to hide or be ashamed of. It can be hard realizing all the disadvantages that other people have in comparison to your own, but by no means should you feel guilty about privileges that you have. Use the privileges that you have to help raise and lift up people who don't have the same advantages you have. That is how you use your privilege; for positive action that uplifts and empowers both people and a community through action and ally-ship.

Understanding culture is also important in understanding what makes you diverse, and what makes you privileged. In The United States, it is generally understood that the dominant culture is white, male, straight, cisgender, Christian, with a high income or economic status. That culture will be different in other countries. In any society, the dominant culture will have the most privilege, but anyone with these traits also has privilege. Privilege is not something someone has or does not have, it is on a spectrum. It's not as cut and dry as saying, if you're white, you have privilege, and if you aren't, then you don't have any. A combination of the identities and socio-economic factors determines how much privilege you have.

Privilege can take shape in several ways: in the way that we interact with people and the world, the opportunities that we have, and how we are able to live. The more privileged a person is, the easier it is for them to have their basic needs met. This could be things like a roof over their head, or having an easier time accessing, navigating, and interacting with people and society as a whole. Growing up with privilege affects people in ways that we oftentimes don't even see or understand. To say that someone has more privilege doesn't automatically mean that life is magically easier, but that there are more opportunities that are given to you because you have more privilege.

Ashley's Privilege

Thinking about before I transitioned, I had a ton of privilege, though at the time I didn't even realize any of it. It's like I lived in a bubble, and none of the problems that existed in the world rarely ever applied to me. I was just cut off from the world and blind to see the advantages

164

that I had from birth, compared to what other people had to struggle and endure through. Born as a white male, into a middle-class family, I never understood how much worse other people had it until I started to explore and understand myself and people around me.

The blessing in disguise was that it allowed me to try to survive what I was going through in battling my gender dysphoria. I kept to myself and only focused on what I needed to do in order to keep surviving. I didn't want to "cause a scene" by voicing my concerns or opinions, and looking back on it, I wish that I would have used my privilege differently back then, and chose to stand up for others. I wish I would have used my position and my power to help uplift others who had no support and no one else to turn to.

When you really start to analyze yourself and think about how many advantages you may have vs another person, you'll realize it runs deep, and things you took for granted, another person may never have. Oftentimes I think about how lucky I am to have so much privilege. I feel like that statement is something that sometimes needs to be said louder for those in the back of the room.

The transgender woman just shared about how privileged she is. Hopefully, that will resonate as you've been reading this book. Even though I've faced my own struggles, I still recognize the different privileges that I have. Of course being aware of my racial privilege is the easy one to quickly mention and address. Would I have been hired and promoted in my two careers if I didn't have white privilege? Maybe. Maybe not. I do know that my race is an advantage that I have that has allowed me to rise faster to the position that I'm in, and has opened doors that wouldn't have been opened if I wasn't white.

I also have privilege in terms of me "passing" and my hair. Passing is a term in the trans community for how well a trans person looks as either male or female. I know that hair seems like a small item to have privilege about, but there are so many people from my trans community that struggle in the hair department. Plus red hair seems to be highly coveted. For anyone, hair is one of the biggest indicators that we look towards in identifying someone's gender identity. If someone has longer hair, we typically see them as feminine, and short hair as masculine. For trans women in particular, growing hair long is a struggle, and many have to resort to using wigs while their hair grows, or if they are experiencing hair loss.

I also have a huge amount of ability privilege. I think it's important to recognize my ability because it helps me to think about others when I'm hosting an event. I have the privilege to see the text on the screen, and I can hear the words being said. So many people I come in contact with don't have awareness for people who may have differing abilities. This is an area our society needs to make major movements to be more inclusive.

Somebody once asked me why I made the choice to transition my gender. I thought for a moment before I responded. When I did respond, I mentioned that I didn't actually make the choice to transition, I made the choice to survive. I knew that this was what I needed to do in order to keep living; to wake up each and every day and feel like it's worth it. Over time throughout my transition, that surviving has turned into thriving. The thing that I keep in mind though, is that I actually had the privilege to begin transitioning. Many in my community don't get that moment because they may not have the ability or privilege to survive.

There are a number of reasons why a person can't transition, whether it's a matter of money, having a family, coming out to the people closest to you, and even the amount of hate and violence that's directed towards trans people. There are vast amounts of reasons as to why some people can't or choose not to transition, but the thing to note is that it's never a matter of willingly "giving up" male privilege. No one would ever want to choose to give up so much privilege. I must have dropped about twenty social economic levels when I went from a white, cisgender presenting male, to being a white trans woman. The decision that I made was to live, then next was to move forward in my life. Even though I lost some of the privileges that I had, that is nothing in comparison to the happiness that I have now in my life.

Checking Your Privilege and Others

Think for a moment about the identities that you listed in Chapter 4. One of the questions from the self assessment was asking if you felt like you had privilege, why or why not? Take into consideration the dominant culture in your community and how those identities compare with the ones that you had listed. You may have privilege in one part of your identity while being disprivileged in another. As I mentioned, privilege is on a spectrum. The closer your identities line up with the dominant culture, the more privileged you are.

On the list of identities that you've created, compare them to the dominant culture. For some identities it's easy to understand if it is privileged, for example being in the middle class, you may not be as privileged as an upper-class person, but you are able to live somewhat comfortably without worrying about food on your table or a roof over your head. Comparing your own identities to the dominant culture is only the first step to take in understanding how you move throughout the world because of your identities. You have to come to understand what privileges your identities grant you in different situations.

It is important to conduct a privilege check frequently. If you think about when someone is hosting an event, they typically do a microphone check before the event. Making sure that it's working and that everyone can hear them before they start talking. That's similar to what I'm proposing around a privilege check. It should be a fundamental thing you do, sometimes even multiple times a day but at least daily, especially before you interact with others. Think about all the things you may have access to that others may not, whether through birth or acquired. Do you have a college or other type of higher education? Are you able-bodied? Do you have a roof over your head? Are you seen as equal through the eyes of the law? The answers to these questions and many others can impact even the most basic interactions.

They can impact how another person interacts with you and how people treat you. If you dress in a suit and tie, you will be treated with more respect than if you were dressed in sweatpants and a t-shirt. The same can be said based on your race; systemically, the darker your skin tone, the more poorly you are treated by societal structures. White people are treated and respected more than people of color in job interviews. When applying for loans people of color are often saddled with a higher interest rate.[21] There is a certain dialect that people talk in when they want to sound "professional". Those who don't talk in a "professional" voice are looked at as less educated and less knowledgeable. These are only a few examples, but the common thread is that how we look, not just what we wear, but the complexion we have, the color of our skin, and how we talk are all factors that lead into how much privilege we have.

Think for a moment about the type of education you've had growing up. Did you have the opportunity to go to a magnet or private school? Were you able to go to college, and if you have, did you have to take out student loans or was it paid for by a family member or scholarships? If you didn't go to college, why? Was there some external factor that prevented you, or did you choose to go a different route?

Now think for a moment about the job that you have now. How did you get to the position you are in? Did you find out about it on a major job website, or through a recommendation from a friend or family member? If you have experience promotion, how were you able to rise through your position and were there any factors that you think allowed you to rise faster than others? The point in asking all of these questions is to get yourself to examine whether some of the opportunities that you had were because, or partially because, of the identities that you have. These are questions that you need to be asking yourself to understand how much privilege you have, and what those privileges have granted you.

Only when you understand your privilege, can you begin to understand how to use it to empower differences. The questions and examples that I've laid out are only a few that I have asked myself in order to better reflect on how much privilege I have. One of the practices that you can do to understand your own privilege is to put yourself in the shoes of someone else who has a different identity than you. Think for a moment about each of your identities that you have listed individually, and when they most likely could come up and play a role in how you navigate the world. The easiest example is to think about how much money you have in relation to someone living in poverty, how they are trying to make ends meet, and what they have to endure in order to survive. Even having this book right now, and learning about how to empower differences, is a privilege that not everyone can afford.

I can't list out all privileges and disprivileges that people may or may not have, as that would take several more books to simply list those out. Part of understanding your privileges and where you fit into the spectrum is doing your own research. Learn from history, and from other people and their experiences. I can't be the one to explicitly tell you that you have x amount of privilege because I'm not speaking to you face to face. What I'm asking of you is to take a moment each day, with an open mind, and learn more about why certain people have, or don't have, certain privileges. Something as quick as educating yourself by looking up something new about a different community every day, or taking a moment to think about how an interaction with someone would have gone if you were in someone else's shoes. Think for a moment about an important conversation you had, or an interview, how differently would you have been seen and interacted with if you had a different race or gender.

An important part of understanding your own privilege is to listen to the experiences that other people have. Hear their stories and experiences and let them enlighten you about your social position and the privileges that you have. That doesn't mean to ask every single person you know to educate you on your own privilege because in and of itself is a privilege, and not everyone is willing to divulge and tell you how you walk through the world. It's not the job of marginalized people to educate the more privileged people about their own privilege. If you know someone who is willing to help you learn, or know someone who has shared their story, that's great, but if you don't, there are a ton of resources online that can help you. There are speakers, books, and people talking about their daily lives on social media and what it's like to go throughout the world carrying a certain identity.

Be open and receptive to what they are saying, and the stories that are being told. There may be some that are shocking and horrifying to learn, and some that don't seem real, but do not discount them or another person's lived experiences. The stories of others may challenge your own personal beliefs, and that's okay. Absorb the information and be open to hearing it. Take a moment and place yourself in their shoes, and think how differently a conversation or an interaction could have gone. People look and treat you differently based on how they perceive you, especially if you are not a part of the dominant culture.

Even in smaller interactions, like going to the bank or talking over the phone, a person's perception of you can alter the privilege that you have. Speaking in perfect English on a phone interview will create an image of how people are going to see you, and based on that image they will treat you differently. How differently would a person see you and interact with you if you can't speak English that well, or understand what the other person is saying? Would you be in the same position you are in now if you had a different gender, race, or ethnicity? This is part of a privilege check that I regularly do. I know that because of my white privilege, I was hired and was able to rise to the positions that I've held. That doesn't mean my white privilege is an inherently bad thing that I should feel ashamed of. I am able to use my privilege to empower other people who don't have the same privilege, and help provide a platform for them to speak their truth and their story.

Where the Most Privileged People Fit in

The key thing about this book is that it's not just for individuals to take their differences and use them as an advantage. It's also for individuals who may feel like this does not apply to them. I have a unique perspective having presented to the world as a white, cis, straight male. Oftentimes when I give a motivational speech, I get approached or asked a question afterwards about where white straight cisgender males fit into the shift of diversity and inclusion.

Typically, when I get a question like this, I want to, in the nicest way possible, put it back on the person asking that question. I know that the question itself comes from a place of trying to understand but I know that there may also be fear behind this question. The idea that white, cis, straight, males are somehow getting phased out and replaced by diverse people.

The place that the most privileged people fit in is to be there as an ally for others. To recognize, not only the discrimination that occurs, not just in the workplace, but also in systemically in this country. I want someone in that place, who is asking that question to be thinking about how they can be a better ally; what they need to be doing in order to educate themselves on a subject that they don't understand, to immerse themselves in a culture and people that they are unfamiliar with, and get to know their struggles and their needs that they have. I want them to question how they are best able to be an ally and advocate for others.

Having worked in a workplace environment for twelve years, presenting as a cisgender, white male before transitioning, I wish that I would have known and experienced the things that I've experienced now living my life authentically. Seeing firsthand what women in the workplace have to go through, seeing firsthand how extreme minorities are treated. Knowing this now gives me the thought that all individuals, regardless of identity, should be looking to empower others and build them up to make the world a safer place for everyone. That the people who have more privilege should be using it to uplift and help pave a road for those that don't have the same advantages.

Using Your Privilege

There are numerous ways that you can use your privilege to uplift and empower other people. The simplest of actions, like inviting someone who you wouldn't normally invite to come with you to an event, can make a difference in someone's life. There are more specific actions that I've highlighted previously, like speaking up in a meeting to allow a co-worker who's been constantly overlooked to share their viewpoint, mentoring someone who you noticed has been struggling to break through the mold or if you're in a higher management position, using

173

your voice and your power to provide a platform for those who can't speak to share their concerns and stories. That is exactly what it means to empower others.

Using your privilege as a tool to be an ally and to help those that are underprivileged is about access. Privilege grants you certain access to tools and people, and it opens doors that would have been closed off. Utilizing your privilege through allyship means holding that door open for other people to enter, and/or giving others the tools that they need in order to open the door themselves. Writing a letter of recommendation for a higher position, creating or advocating for leadership development training, and speaking out in support of your co-workers, are all ways of utilizing privilege to create opportunities for people and to foster a more inclusive environment.

Intersectionality

What is Intersectionality?

Intersectionality is a concept first introduced by Kimberlé Crenshaw: it is the interconnected nature of social categorizations such as race, class, and gender as they apply to a given individual or group, regarded as creating overlapping and interdependent systems of discrimination or disadvantage. In simple terms, think about an intersection. Each line is one identity and where those lines intersect creates a person's unique individual experience. For example, from my own experiences when I lost my house in 2010, the way I was treated and how other people viewed me was through the intersection of being a poor, white, trans woman. The intersection of my identities shaped how I was able to interact with the world and what discriminations I faced.

Intersectionality sits in the heart of all of our differences and should be empowered every moment. This theory takes a variety of contexts into account when looking into an individual's experience. Think again about who makes up the dominant culture in the USA. Understanding intersectionality means realizing that people who are in social categorizations other than the dominant culture can experience discrimination in multiple ways. Think again about an intersection. Having several lines, they may not all intersect at the middle, and some of them may intersect with one or two different lines. This means that all of your identities may not intersect at once at all times. For example, your gender and religion may intersect and determine how someone interacts with you, or your class and race intersect and affect how an organization makes their decision on hiring you for a job. Your intersecting identities affect you on a daily basis, whether you're able to see and recognize them.

Why Understanding Intersectionality is Important

Part of understanding yourself and also other people, comes with understanding intersectionality. In order to create a more inclusive environment and to empower those around you, you have to understand how multiple, intersecting identities affect yourself and other people on a day-to-day basis, as well as interacting with different societal structures. Part of empowering another person through the ways listed previously in chapter 3, is knowing what struggles they face. You will need to think critically about the ways you are able to help, whether that is through one of the empowering action words, or even just listening to their concerns. Even for yourself; how are you supposed to go about empowering your own differences if you don't realize how they affect you in multiple ways?

Understanding intersectionality means looking at the identities that you have, and realizing how they shape your interactions with other people. Look at how you access different societal systems, such as going to the bank, interacting with someone at a store, how your boss treats you differently versus your co-workers, etc. There are numerous examples of societal systems, these are only a few examples. Think about your race, class, and gender. These are some of the most visible identities that we have and that affect all of our interactions. How you are perceived is not just based on one of those identities. For example, a white man isn't seen as just white, a lower-class woman isn't just seen as a woman, and an upper-class person of color isn't just seen as upper class. All individuals are seen through a combination of identities. It is at the intersection of these identities that you and I are judged by society. It is this judgement that determines what barriers, or lack of barriers, that we face.

This leads back to privilege. You can have intersecting identities, some being privileged, while others being disprivileged. A white middle-class woman has the privileges of being white and middle class, but still faces the barriers of being a woman in a male dominated society. The identities that you have, and the intersecting privileges and disprivileges that they carry, shape the unique perspective and lived experience that you have.

Ashley's Intersectionality

I think about my own intersectionality constantly because it's important in how I view myself and how the world sees me. That is one of the main reasons why I decided to write this book. Connecting differences and then highlighting those differences by empowering them. Exactly how I came up with the name of the book. Being a woman, being LGBTQ+, being trans, and having a diverse religious background, gives me my own unique lived experiences. This is my intersectionality identity unapologetically.

When I come in contact with people, I have to objectively think about how they're receiving me and which layer of my intersectionality they are judging me on. For example, one time I was in line at a sandwich shop, apparently that day my transness was in full effect, i.e., I must not have been passing very well. One of the workers pointed me out in the line and then I saw them as they were mentioning to other co-workers and then pointing back at me. This created a domino effect of the other workers all pointing me out, and it felt humiliating. When it came time for me to order as I was waiting in the line, suddenly there wasn't anyone there to serve me. The manager came out and asked the workers what was going on, and then I left. I decided to spend my money elsewhere. That day was one of the moments that I started making conscious decisions to practice economic equality. The foundation of economic equality is to only spend your money where you know that you're being valued and where they appreciate your differing background and the contributions that you make to society.

The way that the people working at that sandwich shop perceived me was based on more than just my gender. I wasn't just the trans woman who was just trying to order a sandwich, I was the white trans woman in that shop. I had the privilege of being white in that situation. They kept their comments to themselves, not approaching me directly by saying anything, or worse. There have been numerous occasions where a trans person who isn't passing, or "clocked", as it's commonly referred to, is verbally harassed or physically assaulted. That isn't to say that if I was of darker skin tone that would have surely made the situation worse, but the odds are that me being white helped me evade worse reactions. It was a moment that my intersecting identities brought me both privilege and disprivilege.

178

Recognizing intersectionality in others is vital in being able to empower them. Personally, I try to see others for who they are, without any preconceived notion about who they might be based on a first impression and the identities that I can recognize. People will surprise you, and people have a multitude of identities that you would never have guessed and a story that you never would have imagined. I look at it like how people view me. People will have their own assumptions when they see and hear me, and as much as I try to correct any misconceptions, there will always be assumptions made. Comments that are passed around like I'm the purple elephant in the room who doesn't know that I'm being talked about. I never want a person to feel the same way that I did, to feel judged based solely on their identities and who they are.

I think that our unconscious biases sometimes get in the way of doing this on a regular basis. This is why I'm purposeful in getting to know other people. There are somewhat easier identities that you can look at to understand a person, but working to champion and empower someone's differences requires looking beneath the surface. This requires you to get to know people on a much deeper level in order to empower them. Invest in getting to know the person and understanding how their identities inform both their decisions and how they walk through life, and also how society forces them to walk a certain way by putting up obstacles that must be overcome because of the intersecting identities that they have. Getting to know their struggles, hearing their stories, and letting them enlighten me expands my world view and allows me to put myself in their shoes. It is then that I am able to understand their intersectionality, their lived experiences, and what I can do to empower their differences.

179

Using Intersectional Experiences to Advance Career

More organizations are starting to understand, more than ever, that a diverse workforce yields more productivity and better outcomes. There is a growing trend of major companies and organizations embracing more diversity and are trying to do what they can to make sure that people are working in inclusive workplaces. Many are looking at education other than a college degree, including life experiences. Think about how you can convey your experiences, make it measurable, and transfer it to the organization, whether you are looking at a new position, or an advancement in your current role. Be the catalyst for this in the organization. As someone who has persevered through a lifetime of overcoming the challenges related to not being a part of the dominant culture, you can bring a fresh perspective along with resiliency- both of which cannot be taught on the job.

You can do this in many ways, here are some examples:

Lived Experiences Climbing the Ladder

 Part of my intersectionality and what makes me diverse, is being a high school graduate, and using that to help me in my day job. So many people who work in the human resources are college graduates, whereas most people view my intersectional diversity as being trans. My biggest thing that differentiates me from my co-workers, and people in my field, is the fact that I only have a high school degree. I've managed a Diversity and Inclusion program for 5 years, versus a certified diversity professional with a bachelors in business administration. I bring in the perspective of having to work up from the bottom of the ladder. I know what it's like to be a bank teller, what my needs were when I had that position, and what the needs of my colleagues were. I could see that the organization was starting to be more diverse in who they were hiring, but that there was still more work to be done.

Since I had to work my way up the ladder, I'm more connected with the people and the systems of the organization, and can advocate for what change is needed. This versus someone who only joins the company with limited knowledge about the culture and can only see things from "an outside point of view". This is on top of how me rising through the ladder rapidly showcases my resiliency. The hurdles and barriers that I've had to overcome in order to get to the position that I'm in now. Not just as a person who has a high school diploma, but as a white, trans woman, with nothing but a high school education having to figure out how she was going to survive and provide for a family. All of these pieces come together to form my experiences and further show a fierce commitment to rising above challenges.

Using Privileged Intersectionality to Help Empower Others

As a person who has worked up through management and hasn't had traditional education, my lived experiences when working at Boston Market were both privileged and disprivileged in different ways. I took up the shifts that I did in order to survive, but I managed to move up partly because of my white, male presenting privilege. Sometimes, I had a hard time seeing things intersectionaly. I was sometimes too close to all of my co-workers, I didn't go to college, and neither did many of them. They were presenting as more diverse, I was presenting as a white male. My lack of diversity was haunting. I had to invest in my co-workers, educating myself, understanding, and listening to what they were going through.

During that time, I was also battling with my gender dysphoria, and I couldn't verbalize or communicate any of those things. I was hiding my true self while trying to be compassionate and understanding of other people as a co-worker and a manager. There are a wide range of intersectional people in the restaurant industry, but I couldn't communicate that I could understand what other people were going through, they only looked at me and saw privilege.

I could only attempt to immerse myself and try to get to know the people I was working with. There were employees that only spoke Spanish, so I tried to learn as much Spanish as I could. Working as a manager, I set aside time for everyone that I was managing to come talk to me about any concerns that they had. I wanted to use the privilege and position that I had and invest that back into my employees and give them access to me, to make sure that they were being seen, and that they had an ally who was doing what I could to hear people and try to create change.

Being A Part of Multiple Communities

I asked back in chapter 4, when researching your differences, to look into what communities you are a part of and how you can be more connected with them. Whether that is a local community, a business organization, or even an online community. Working with people in your community, whether that is volunteering time at a local nonprofit, or being a member of a community organization. These are life experiences and connections that you are able to highlight about yourself and showcase how your intersectional background makes you a more well-rounded candidate. Someone with intersecting identities, or who has diverse intersections relates to a larger segment of the population on various levels. When mapping out your identity map, and ultimately, how you will use your differences to empower yourself in your career, think about how your connection to these groups will drive collaborations and the change of dynamic that you can bring.

I was making sure that when I was starting to put myself out there into different LGBTQ+ organizations, that I was forging meaningful connections with people. I was, and still am, investing in a community, and those investments have seen numerous returns, not only for myself, but also for the community. From the identities that I have, I've been able to be a part of numerous communities and organizations, and even for some that I don't share a similar identity, like people of color, I've been there as an ally. I have been there as someone wanting to learn more about what I can do with my own intersectional background. I've also been able to provide feedback from my own point of view to help make sure that other people and organizations have an intersectional lens, and are hearing from people that aren't usually heard from. Much like my experiences as a manager, I was making sure that the organizational leaders were hearing my concerns, and that they were making improvements and committing to ensure that everyone's voice is heard.

Making Sure Your Organization is Intersectional

Intersectional leadership should be an organizational culture building imperative. Choosing leaders who bring more intersectionality and diversity to the organization will inspire others to grow in their career, create more workplace cohesion, and attract more diverse talent to your organization. People want to work at an organization where they know that they are being valued, where their voices are being heard, and that they don't feel like they are being tokenized for the sake of trying to appear more diverse. I certainly don't want to be the only trans woman in an organization, I want to know that where I'm going to work isn't going to feel like I'm on an island by myself. It gets to the point where I feel like I'm an elephant in the room where I'm "the trans employee"; the one that people go to for all trans related concerns. I don't want to be the only resource or representative for the LGBTQ+ community. This is the reason why I am selective about the organizations that I work for, being intentional that they are inclusive and that they have a diverse workforce.

Organizations have to make sure that they are walking the walk. It's easy for them to project the image that they are a diverse workplace, showing their support with carefully crafted messages, or changing their icon to show support for a specific time or event, like changing logos to be rainbow during pride month. These gestures show support, but with the internet and diversity statistics about organizations being widely available, it's easy to see which ones are projecting the image of being intersectional, and which ones are actually doing the work.

184

I've had events where I was asked to speak on a panel that didn't represent an intersectional lens, where I was the most diverse candidate that they had speaking at the event, with the rest of the speakers there being all extremely privileged. I've gone back to the organizers and communicated to them that I can't have my brand associated with an event that doesn't align to my personal value. There were times when they switched the panelists and listened to my feedback. There's also been times when I had to decide to walk away, even from a paid engagement. We all ultimately have a choice every day to choose to do business with organizations that value intersectionality, or not.

There needs to be concrete actions and steps that are being taken in order to create a more intersectional workplace and business. An empty message will leave more people in disdain for the organization, rather than driving in new business. This is where having a strong understanding of people's needs and intersectionality are able to come into play. You're able to showcase your knowledge of the needs of the organization; bring in statistics from different sites like HRC's Corporate Equality Index, the National Business Inclusion Consortium, and Bloomberg indexes, and make the case for why your organization needs to be more inclusive and intersectional. Smaller actions that you can also take are listening and getting to know the lived experiences of intersectional people. Show you're an ally and use your voice when you can to voice your concerns and amplify concerns that other workers have.

Intersectionality in Marketing, Images, and Publicity

Something that I want to make note of here is that being intersectional extends to more than just policies and people, but also marketing and speakers. To ensure communication is well-received, you have to make sure you have specific diverse communities speak about themselves. For example, if you are talking about people with differing abilities, then someone from that community should be speaking on that topic. When someone is planning a LGBTQ+ event, you can bet that chances are they're going to reach out to someone like me to gauge my opinion on their flyer, or other information being communicated. The last thing I want to see is a flyer or graphic promoting an event that's supposed to be reaching my community that doesn't represent my community.

Getting different viewpoints and having people speak for themselves When planning events or conferences, I recommend that you make a list of all your speakers and then put an intersectional lens on each person and their content. Looking at the identities of the speakers, their backgrounds, and the perspective that they bring. Making sure that the people who might be speaking to a diverse workforce aren't all white and male, reiterating the same talking points that only resonate with a fraction of the audience. This will help to transform your event to be a leading agent for inclusion. Content should be vetted by different intersectional people as well. This will ensure it has a double lens viewpoint. The more lenses that something has, the more intersectional it becomes. The same can be said for promotional and marketing material. Making sure that it is viewed by multiple perspectives will make sure that the message is on target and that the material is mindful of all people.

Every place you go, and everything you do requires you to work incredibly hard in making sure that you have an intersectional lens, and consider who is being represented. Representation matters in a major way for intersectional communities. Working to make sure that people are included, and that you recognize the barriers that people face because of their identities, sets you as a leader. By investing in intersectionality, you are building support for all parties involved; yourself, the organization, and the diverse intersectional communities.

Chapter 8

Political Differences

We Need to Talk About Politics

Let me start by saying that Empowering Differences is apolitical! Regardless of your political party, you can use the lessons in this book and the 10 empowering actions to help empower differences, both yours and others. I wish that was all I needed to say in this chapter, but as can be expected, that's not the case.

Sadly, politics gets in the way of so many issues that diverse communities face on a daily basis. Whether that is governments that draft legislation directly targeting a community, or the politics that another person has about an issue or group of people. Politics is one of those topics that, as much as we try to carefully navigate when communicating in a professional setting, is personal when it directly affects your life and the way that you're able to live.

Personally, I can tell you that I have had elected legislators attempt to craft legislation that targets my identity. So-called bathroom bills have been presented in numerous states as of 2017 and the only one that has been passed and then repealed is in North Carolina, the infamous HB2 bill.[22] These bills are proposed to "protect restrooms", especially in municipalities that pass human rights ordinances (HRO). HROs are designed to ban discrimination based on certain characteristics, usually different identities. The myth is that HROs allow for anyone to access any bathroom. But the facts don't support this myth, the facts say that in the states that prohibit discrimination in public accommodations, there's been no reported increase in any violence statistics in the bathroom.[23] The fact is trans people are the ones who are terrified of using a public restroom. Speaking from personal experience, I can't count the number of times that I've feared for my own safety. Worried that I'd get a look from the other people in the bathroom or harassed for just needing to use the bathroom. These bills are specifically designed to target trans people, create a culture of fear around the trans community, and hide the true meaning under the guise of "public safety".

Now that I got that out of my system. The lesson here is that as much as we may not like to talk about politics, they affect our everyday lives, especially when the political discussion is about our identity.

How Do You Navigate a Political Conversation in the Workplace

I feel that this is usually a given, but the best course of action is to maintain political neutrality when you aren't sure of the political affiliations of the person you're talking to, or the people in the room. There is an art to being apolitical, and I'd be lying if I said that I've mastered that art. It takes a lot of time to develop that skill and be able to direct a conversation to be productive and meaningful. One strategy I have developed is to stay away from wedge issues. These are issues like abortion and gun control, things that people have a divisive stance on, that can turn a friendly conversation into hostile, meaningless dialogue.

It can be hard to avoid politics in discussions though, and it's even harder not to say something when it directly affects you, or someone you care about. As I said, trying to be apolitical is a skill that I'm still trying to master and there have been conversations that I've had to walk away from, or not say anything because I was talking with a client or a manager. When I'm able to have a political conversation with someone, what I have learned is to try and find common ground in those situations. To try and bring the conversation back to things that should be neutral. I think inclusion and equality should not be a wedge issue. People from all parties should want their community to do well. Try to move away from assuming the polarizing positions and try and bring it back to things that everyone cares about. In talking about gun control, no one wants more mass shootings to happen. Bring the conversation to where you both can agree and also be curious.

Something that helps in finding the common ground is trying to understand where the other person is coming from, and why they believe what they do. Don't approach the conversation with an accusation or assumption, invest in getting to know why they believe what they do. Once you know why they hold certain positions, you're able to educate and enlighten with personal stories and statistics, how a policy or political topic has affected you or someone you care about and how they affect a community of people. I've had to explain to people, in regards to the bathroom bills, that while on the surface it claims to care about people's safety, they could essentially restrict me from using a public restroom. If I did, I could either face a fine, or verbal and physical harassment.

Another thing I do in this space is just make it about the numbers. For me, the nature of politics, one way or another, should always come back to the finances. Of course when I say finances, I'm talking about the economic output for your diverse community. If I'm talking about something that should be non-partisan, then mentioning the NGLCC economic study should be great. If I'm talking to someone who refuses to do business with LGBTQ+ people, then I'd bring in the statistic that LGBTQ+ have a buying power of 1 trillion dollars.[24] I'd talk about how that number has continually been growing and the economic power that the community has which makes a huge impact. Oftentimes, once we bring the conversation to something that both parties can agree on, is when the conversation moves forward.

Having Political Conversations with People You Don't Know

There have been times when I've had political conversations with complete strangers and have been able to educate them about some positions that they held. Working my way up at the financial services organization I had to travel a lot to different events or functions. Oftentimes I'd be seated next strangers and I'd keep to myself or try to have some light conversation. There was a time that I was sitting next to someone who was clearly a Trump supporter. Even though we likely had differing political views, I thought to start a conversation with them. I wanted to understand what it is about Trump that made this person support him.

I started the conversation and I asked them for their honest answer. Their response was that it was his focus on the military, so I asked how the administration actually takes care of the troops. They asked what I meant, and I told them that I come from a military family. My father and grandfather were in Vietnam and WWII, respectively, but under the administration's rules, I would not be able to serve. They have enacted a trans military ban that would effectively remove about 15,000 healthy and fit people from the military just because of their identity and I would never be able to serve if I wanted to.[25] Everything that I was telling them was non-partisan, these are just the facts of the situation and the policy.

When I left that conversation, they were appalled that there were troops who were healthy and were actively being kicked out of the military. That conversation was like any other conversation that I may have had. I listened first to what the other person had to say so that I could understand what was important to them about politics. I can agree and disagree with whatever their viewpoint is, but I can present factual information that supports my agreeing or disagreeing. That goes back to finding common ground. You have to be able to artfully and craftily present what you are talking about so people understand your position. I didn't make it about polarizing views. I made it about the actual policies that make a difference for marginalized communities and how they should be non-partisan.

This is why research is important. It is important to know to bring up in conversation so that you can back up the claims that you are making. When I was proposing the idea of why we needed to have the role I have in diversity and inclusion for the organization that I work for, I brought statistics and data to that conversation about diverse communities to make the business case. That is what tipped the scales and allowed the position that I have now to be created. Changing that person's mind about how the Trump administration treats our troops, was due in part because I had the numbers that helped show the severity of the issue and provided evidence behind my words.

Breaking Through the Mindset

Too often there are assumptions that people are stringent in their point of view. That no matter what we say, there is nothing that we can do to find common ground and change a person's mind. That has been exacerbated further with social media and trying to have a conversation online with a random person, but people are more open than you might think. Throughout all of the conversations that I've had, a majority of the people that I have talked with are open to changing their minds, but it does take time. There have been only a few people that I've encountered that are stuck in their way of thinking, but that doesn't mean they won't ever experience a shift. It takes several conversations and tons of educating. It is possible to change a person's viewpoint, but you may not even need to get to that point. It's not your job to change a person's mind on a particular issue.

You don't have to invest the time and energy into everyone who disagrees with your political beliefs! If I did that, then I'd be burnt out right away. It's exhausting work getting a person to change their mindset on a particular topic and it may not be beneficial for you to put in that investment with certain people. Instead, focus on the 96% of the population who are open-minded and willing to listen. The reason I share these stories and lessons is for when you are working with someone you want to educate and/or invest your time in. It is when you are investing in someone that you will need to understand their viewpoints, and try to find common ground. It is beneficial to find common ground so that you can work more cohesively together. These people are the ones that you have a closer relationship with and likely include: networking partners, managers, mentors and mentees, and business partners.

Politics in Mentor Relationships

When talking about mentor relationships, you don't always get to pick your mentor, so you have to go into this relationship with an open mind. I've had mentors that have been across multiple political parties. The key in working with each of them was that I would always try to focus on the end goal for this relationship and not let things get political. They have each taught me a lot, and while I may not have agreed with all of the positions that they have held, that doesn't devalue or take away from the skills that I learned.

Now of course if you are building a relationship with a mentor, I would think eventually you may talk about something that could be seen as political. To me, this was one of the main reasons I wanted to address this in Empowering Differences. This is where education is the key. I've had several sponsors and mentors who didn't understand what the infatuation is with politicizing of the transgender community. The key thing that I've done here in this space was to always take time and educate them about my community. Their questions came from an honest place as they were genuinely confused as to why trans people were constantly politicized. I would take the time to explain history and enlighten them about my own lived experiences. Great change has come as a result of having several conversations with my sponsors and mentors. To me, it's all about changing hearts and minds. When you educate one person then that one person has the opportunity to educate other people, which creates a domino effect of change for your diverse community. I think this approach holds true for all layers of diversity.

Something that I also did here was utilize the access that I have to them. When you have access to someone who is in a position of power, you have to take that opportunity and seize it. That means doing more than just taking in the lessons that they are imparting on you. Use the opportunity to network with people who are also in a position of power. Make your name and ideas known to the higher ups. Your mentor can help amplify your voice and concerns to make sure that they are being heard and addressed within your organization.

Another key point here is to make sure that the education that you provide is non-partisan. For example, I'm not going to go into this conversation with a high-level sponsor of an organization and talk about how many Republican people from Congress have been arrested in a bathroom versus the trans community. There is a statistic that's being kept on that, but this is neither the time nor place to share it. Especially if I don't know their political leanings. That could potentially ruin a sponsor or mentor relationship.

Look at Things From Multiple Angles

Politics in general is always a touchy subject in the workplace. If you are empowering your differences, you need to be certain that you're being true to yourself. I say this to mean that you don't have to sacrifice or put down your beliefs in order to come off as more agreeable to another person. There is a fine line to understanding the other person's perspective and where they are coming from, and staying true to yourself. There will be times, and likely have already been times, where you have disagreed with what another person has said. That person being your boss, a friend, a co-worker, or family member. You don't have to agree with what they are saying in order to gain their support or even empower them. Seek to understand where you both can stand on equal ground and work to achieve the end goal of the relationship that you have in mind. Whether that is seeking out a sponsor, making a connection, or pitching an idea to someone.

The thing that I immediately think has one of the biggest impacts when discussing political differences is access. Access is key here because it's what can ultimately change when you begin to look at things more holistically. I can tell you that personally having been a registered member of two different political parties, that the majority of the people believe what they are being told. When you are a member of a party, you are often guided to certain news sources, specific podcasts, and radio show personalities. I would never try to get you to change those, or change your political party regardless of what it is currently. What I would tell you, would be to expand your access to more news, more speakers, more podcasts across multiple parties. It will help you see things from multiple levels, and increase your ability to be more culturally agile.

Cultural agility is the ability to understand, incorporate, and successfully work within and between multiple different cultural contexts and locations. The more culturally agile you are, the easier it is for you to understand another person's differences, and be better equipped to empower people who come from completely different backgrounds from yourself. You're able to put yourself in their shoes, and see how they interpret the world with their differences.

Seeing things from another person's perspective and having more cultural agility, you're able to see how a person's privilege and intersectionality shape that person's worldview and why they have their political background and viewpoint. There are a number of factors that go into understanding a person's political viewpoint but the foundation is their privilege and intersectionality. How privileged a person is and how their identities intersect, shapes how they see the world, and how the world treats them.

For many of the people that I've educated about the trans community and how it is perpetually targeted by governments, those I am educating have the privilege of not having to question their gender identity, transition, and live as a trans person, thus they have never faced the same barriers the trans community has had to face. They are unaware of the struggles that trans and LGBTQ+ people face because they have never had to face them. They could've chosen to remain ignorant and ignore the lived reality of the trans community, but they didn't. They wanted to learn more. They wanted to understand the background surrounding the politics of my identity and what they can do as an ally. The same principle applies to being more culturally agile when it comes to working with people who have different political views. The easier you are able to put yourself in someone else's shoes and get their perspective, the better able you are able to find common ground and work through the differences that you have with the other person.

Knowing Your Audience

You have to sense the moment in the room, know when to talk about certain topics and test the waters. The conversation with the person on the airplane was seeking to understand rather than me attacking. You have to have social awareness of when it is the right time, especially in the workplace. I am selective about what information I share with people, making sure that what I'm sharing is both appropriate for the situation, and that the person may be receptive to what I'm going to be sharing.

I may be able to discern a piece of a person's identity based on their identities, or something that they are wearing, but that doesn't paint a complete picture of what their beliefs are and what lived experiences they have. It takes several conversations with the person and probing questions to get to know where they stand, and what I feel comfortable sharing with them. For many, it's not even necessary for me to divulge certain things about myself because that doesn't lead to anything. If I'm talking with someone casual in the office that I have just met, I don't need to tell them my entire life story. That takes more time and energy out of me that I could be investing in other people that will yield a return on my investment.

You have to pick your battles carefully, not everything is worth diving into. You have to decide whether it's worth it to raise your voice and try and meet someone halfway. What is the end goal that you are trying to achieve, and what is the nature of the relationship you have with the person you are talking to? These are two questions to keep in mind

198

when having political conversations that will help you navigate through them.

A good example of recognizing your audience is my family. Having conversations with family, I have to choose where I chime in and make sure that my voice is still heard, since a majority of my family is republican, including my in-laws. I have to educate them on how political parties engage in identity politics like bathroom bills.

That is when I will make my voice heard the most. When the political conversation shifts to news where the trans community is attacked, whether it be a physical attack or a legislative attack. Those are the times when I will share what's going on and present it in a light that makes them question, "what if that was me?". What if the news report of a trans woman being denied a claim to change her gender marker on her driver's license was denied just because she is trans? What if the article about a LGBTQ+ person being physically assaulted on a subway ride home was me? Putting it in a context that they are better able to empathize with makes it easier for them to understand how it affects me and my community at large.

They truly don't want to see me hurt in any way, or restricted from using public services because of my identity. That is the common ground that I'm able to find with my family. Unfortunately, that doesn't work with every political topic, and trying to explain and educate them on a variety of issues would be immensely draining on me and would take years to get to the point where we can fully agree on certain subjects. However, political conversations aren't the defining point of my family relationships, and at the end of the day we still care about each other. We have our differences, but we are able to navigate and work through them. I will continue to be my authentic self, and if it clashes with my family, then that is on them to work through and understand. I can and am only willing to do so much.

The same should be applied when navigating different relationships that you have with your co-workers, managers, mentors, sponsors, etc. Regardless of the differences that you have,
there is a point where you can work through the differences and accomplish what you're working towards. Navigating that will look different for every person and relationship but at the end of the day, there will always be a common ground that can be reached.

Chapter 9

Investing in Others

Mentoring and Sponsoring

For this chapter I want to convey the importance of paving the way and giving back to others. I have to take a moment to cover mentoring; I think our society is getting complacent with it, and that it's more of a required item than something we invest in willingly; a company program that people are required to go through instead of something that people willingly seek out. One of the biggest misconceptions is what a mentor/mentee relationship can look like, as well as the additional importance of sponsors.

Mentors provide valuable support and education, but sponsors provide a voice when you don't have a seat at the table. To be mentored, you need to be present in some way with your mentor, but being sponsored can happen without you present. The real thing people should be working towards, in addition to mentors, is finding a sponsor, rather multiple sponsors. Like a business banker who had a seat on the employee hall of fame selection committee, or the bank president, or the human resources executive. These are people who are able to speak on your behalf, bring your name up to attention when discussing awards and/or promotions, and share ideas that you have with the executives that are able to bring them to life.

Finding and Cultivating Sponsors

Having a variety of sponsors should be one of your ultimate career goals. These are people who will be there when you need them the most. They are strategic leaders in an organization or community. They are the people who have a seat at the table. They will be there to speak your name when you don't have a voice.

One of the questions that I've gotten when I tell people this is, "well how do you find a sponsor?". I found it easy to find sponsors when I offered to take something off their plate. Volunteering to lead an initiative for them in their market or line of business. When it became me doing a favor for someone else, trying to help them in some way, there were times when I'd ask for their support when it came to putting my name out there but oftentimes, they would recommend me without me even asking. I opened the relationship with helping the other person and continued to deepen it, and thus they networked my name and who I was when I wasn't even in the room.

Another method I use in conjunction with taking work off of an executives plate, is becoming a top producing employee. Let the work that you are doing speak for itself. Offering to take on extra tasks or responsibilities, while already performing exceedingly well, shows initiative and a drive to do everything that you can in order to benefit your team and organization. This is also paired well with community service. Community service is a great way to get noticed by the leadership in the organization. As I mentioned in previous chapters, make sure that the community service that you are doing has some tie-ins back to the organization, and keep a record of what community service you have been providing. You have to keep track of what you've been doing and business that you are drawing back to your organization. These are things that you want to bring up as you develop and foster relationships with potential sponsors. This data shows the added value that you are bringing through the volunteer work that you are doing in your community.

I highly recommend doing all these if possible, but be sure not to burn yourself out, work with what you can fit into your schedule. For me, in the beginning I was going out about three nights a week. These were all about strategically working to gain access to sponsors at the organization, but also sponsors in the community. The problem was that I was trying to be everywhere at once. I stretched myself too thin amongst multiple organizations and commitments that I wasn't building up the connections I was making and over committing to too many events and meetings. Going out three nights a week was a good place for me to start, but I should have concentrated my efforts with one or two organizations for a set period of time before working with another.

Being a Sponsor for Someone Else

When creating an environment to invest in others is part of your goal, you will also want to think about how you can sponsor other people. It may be a situation where you encounter someone in your organization who is at the same career level as you, find a way to build up and empower them because if they move up it can benefit you long term. Also, consider how you have been building personal relationships in the community where you live. Finding time for youth and others that you can provide leadership education towards can make a major difference.

I try to give back time each week to sponsor someone who is from my diverse community. Sometimes it's as simple as reading their resume, then providing feedback. Also, I can share their resume with a hiring manager; this is a simple sponsoring action that can happen very easily. Of course, there are times when it can be much more involved. I might have to really invest more resources. Usually at that point, I will loop in other contacts I have that would be able to help sponsor the person that I'm engaging with. But the end result is working to empower others, and my community, which will have a lasting impact after I'm gone from this world.

Being Mentored by Someone

Let's go back to mentorship now because this is as important as sponsoring someone. How many people have you seen and wished that you could have a sit down conversation and learn from them? What lessons have they garnered, and what advice and wisdom they could impart on you? Many people want the most successful person in a company, or community, to be their mentor. We treat this almost like a badge of honor, but what I'd ask for you to do is to try to approach this a little differently. Anyone on any level can mentor another person. I know bank tellers who taught me so much about life and many other things. It doesn't always have to be the top flight executive.

Whoever you consider or decide to be a mentor, keep in mind that it should be a partnership. You should be providing something to your mentor in the relationship as well. Both parties should actually receive mentoring from each other; just because someone is established doesn't mean they can't learn from someone else. My best mentorship partners were the ones that were collaborative. We bounced ideas off of each other, taught each other what we've learned in our careers, and enlightened each other about our personal experiences.

Something to consider is the time commitment before ever asking someone to be your mentor. While many mentor/mentee relationships are seemingly month to year long relationships, they can also be much shorter. Being mentored by someone doesn't have to be over a long, extended period of time. In some cases, it can be a sit down conversation that you have for a few hours, once or twice. How long the mentor/mentee relationship lasts, varies depending on what the two of you agree on, and what you both are able to commit to. Time is a resource that, for many, is not in abundance, and you need to consider the amount of time that you and your potential mentor have to put into the relationship. This will shape what the relationship will look like and if you create a more rigid, or free flowing schedule.

Mentoring Someone Else

Now that you understand mentoring and sponsoring, let's now think about how you can help to invest in others coming up after you. The best way to build up diverse communities is to invest in them by passing on what you have learned throughout your career and life. There is nothing that can stop you from being a mentor now that you understand these principles. I would recommend beginning with your diverse community. For me, I started sharing my experience of hunting

205

for a job with other people from the transgender community. I would network and meet with the student groups at my local college campus, talk with people in my chamber of commerce, even talk with people online. This turned out to be an extremely helpful experience that I could immediately share with others who would value what I was giving back to my community.

You should do the same thing for your diverse community, whoever that might be. There are people in your community out there who would appreciate your knowledge and experience. For many people up and coming, this isn't a tell all guide about how to operate in the business world and what they should be aware of given their diverse identities. College and training can prepare a person to perform a task and execute a job, but the real world experience as a uniquely diverse individual is taught through storytelling, sharing similar experiences, and mentoring someone. Think about all the things that you wish you would have known when you were starting to get into your career. What do you think would have been valuable to know when you were starting in your field and in your job? These are takeaways and lessons that you are able to impart on someone who is in a similar position to you when you started working and experiences to enlighten others about what you have had to personally overcome to get to where you are.

You also don't have to have recurring meetings with them either, sometimes mentoring might only be one or two meetings. Best course of action is to agree to what you have time for so you maximize the time you have to donate. Like I mentioned before, mentoring someone doesn't have to be a weekly, hour long session that lasts several months. They can be a sit down conversation that you have with someone at a meeting, talking with someone after an event or meeting, even talking with someone online. These can be as long as the two of you agree or as long as a conversation lasts. Mentoring someone takes shape in all different ways and varies based on each person.

Organization Mentorship Programs

If your organization has established mentor programs, please take advantage of them! Those are going to usually be the best because the mentors are already agreeing to a partnership. They know the time commitment in advance, and they have experience mentoring people. They likely already have a schedule in mind, or agreed to meet and check in with you. The mentor also knows the topics that they want to cover with you on a regular basis. It's important though to come with organized goals of what you hope to gain from a partnership, and how you can help your mentor. Take these meetings very seriously, take notes, keep track of deliverables, and the progress being made in the program.

This is also one of the best ways to be highlighted in a crowded mentorship program, keep track of progress, and the return on investment. I can tell you that if you turn in an impact report on each of your mentorship partnerships, the organization running the program will want to highlight you as a success. Each organization is always seeking a way to quantify measurable results from engagement programs. You will become the hero overnight, and gain great exposure in the program. Another piece of advice is to keep an agenda of what you want to cover in each meeting. This will help you maximize the time that you have with your mentor and cover what you want to learn. On that note, be very time oriented, ready to start and end each session on the agreed upon time frame. All of these small things add up in a big way, and the smallest things can help you stand out.

When entering a mentoring relationship you need to also check your mentoring program for inclusiveness. A non-inclusive program can lead to the more privileged people in the room receiving more of the focus, time with mentors, and more opportunities that can arise from the program. You want to make sure that if your organization has a mentoring program, that they treat and view everyone one in the room as equal, and that there aren't a select few in the group that have more opportunities because of their privilege.

There are a number of ways to check and see if your program is inclusive, even seeing how inclusive your organization is, through different reviews, metrics and data. Depending on the size and type of organization that you work for, they might be required by law to submit Equal Employment Opportunity Commission (EEOC) metrics and a breakdown of the identities that the company has. Glass door reviews, exit interviews, and talent metrics will help you get a better overall glance at the inclusivity of the organization. Diversity Best Practices, National Business Inclusion Consortium, and Diversity Inc, provide great resources on how to bolster inclusivity, and part of what they do is come in and conduct a review of where your organization stands, and offer best practices and suggestions of how to move forward.

Remember all the key ways to invest in others. Mentoring and sponsoring are each slightly different. These two tools help you along the way to advancing your career. The last thing to remember here is that mentoring and sponsoring should be done both ways. Not just with your mentor/mentee relationship, but that you need to be a mentor and a mentee. Meaning two separate relationships operating at the same time. Same thing with sponsoring covered here in this chapter; seek out, engage, cultivate, and develop sponsors both for you personally, and for others from your diverse background and your community.

Trust

The Importance of Trust

When working to empower others, and even just getting to know others, you have to build trust with them. Trust that you can share sensitive information, personal stories, and take constructive feedback. Relationship building is one of the biggest things in the world of trust. There are things that I can communicate with others once I feel and know that I can trust them with what I'm about to tell them. When I know that the person is willing to listen and make changes, either in their behaviors, opinions, or beliefs, is when I am able to voice my concerns, share my opinions, and invest more time in the relationship.

Building relationships and trust leads to a more inclusive environment where education is more valued and obtained. We take advice and listen to the people that we trust. Whether that is another person, a community of people raising their voice, or even a news reporter. If we don't trust the person or people who are speaking then we don't take what they have to say to heart. If you didn't know and/or trust someone to help oversee a project, then you wouldn't listen to what they have to say or advice they try to give. Trust is at the foundation to getting to understand and empower others.

Building trust and being able to educate another person leads to enlightening them. Remember that enlightenment is directly tied to getting to the heart of the matter; the emotional trust of others. Being able to share your personal story and the perspectives of the people around you is key to this process. We tell our stories and take our time to educate others we trust who want to hear our story and know more about us. Oftentimes, by putting that level of trust in someone and sharing a part of ourselves with them, they are willing to do the same. When someone is vulnerable, open, and honest about what they've been through, it can get other people to open up about their own lived experiences, allowing you to learn from them as they have learned from you.

The importance of building enough trust stems around the importance of cultivating allies. Much like sponsors, allies help create a more inclusive environment, educating and enlightening others with what you have shared and taught them. Allies working in tandem with different communities is what can drive systemic change for the betterment of everyone. Every community needs allies to help them achieve their goals and missions, and the same can be said for every person. We all need allies who are there to help support us, either in our personal struggles, or in driving more community wide or systemic changes. Building trust with communities and people cultivates allies, and it's through allies that we are able to create change.

How to Build Trust With Someone

When I think about ways that I can build trust with others, I tend to focus on educating them. Knowing that while talking to a stranger, no matter what, we're still both humans. We each have our own perspectives, but there is common ground that we can both find. Starting from that point, I bring my facts and lived experiences to the table, teaching them about the positions that I have had, and why I hold the positions that I do. I also focus on listening to the other person and their own perspective. Letting them enlighten me as to why they see the world the way they do. Education and being a good listener; these are two points that build trust with someone. Though I do want to make a note that even after finding that common ground, I have to decide whether to continue building that relationship. What is the cost-benefit that will come about through this? If it's not worth the investment, then I walk away from the situation. Trust works both ways in virtually every interaction.

Another way to establish yourself is something that I've already mentioned previously around cultivating allies, which is helping out where you can. If you notice that someone is struggling with a task, and you're able to, offer to help them. Small acts of generosity that don't have any strings attached, gain people's favor and trust. Use those moments as an opportunity to get to know the person, and for them to get to know you. Be a sponsor and ally for them in what they need, and they will do the same for you. When you are trying to build a relationship with someone, continue to talk and get to know them. Find out what they've been through and what challenges they face. Trust is built with a person as you continue to get to know one another, either personally, through your work, or experiences. Don't just help someone out, get to know them and let them get to know you.

The other thing here is to follow the steps earlier in this book around research. I have to be trustworthy in order to build relationships. I have to make sure that what I'm saying is factual; that the information that I bring to the table, and what I am sharing with others is factually accurate. Throwing around fake statistics and numbers that anyone can fact-check is not a good idea. Presenting false information would only hurt my position when trying to build a relationship. I've mentioned several times so far to come prepared with statistics and knowledge on hand in case you need them, but in the event that you don't or can't remember specifically, don't lie. That will only hurt your credibility and your relationship with the other person. Building allies and cultivating trust with another person needs to be built on honesty and authenticity. When thinking about trust, also consider what you showcase and who you choose to surround yourself with. In essence, you better practice exactly what you are asking your supervisor and other people to do, constantly. If you don't practice what you preach, that will be noticed and called out. Being two-faced will only bring more distrust on you, and distance yourself from people who could be potential allies.

Breaking Through the Mold

You need to use trust in multiple ways to break through. Remember that it's not just in the way in which people view you, it's also in the way that you view people. Trust should be one of your ultimate navigating tools within the workplace. When you think of a supervisor who is about to assign an important task, think about all the things that go through that person's mind before choosing someone to complete that task. They have a certain level of trust and confidence that the person they choose will complete the task without any major issues. How that trust was built is largely through work ethic, past performance, and work experience. What also influences many decisions though, is unconscious bias. Unconsciously, we tend to trust people who look similar to us, have gone through similar experiences as us, and people who are more privileged.[26]

By people who look similar to us, I don't literally mean people who could be our twin, but rather people who share similar characteristics with us. They share a common identity with us that we are able to relate with, and it's that similarity that leads to us tending to trust them more. Upper-class people are more likely to listen and trust the word of other upper-class people. This isn't something that's necessarily a bad thing, but it's important to recognize it, and realize the reasons why we trust someone more or less given our identities compared to theirs. The same thing can be said for those with similar lived experiences. We relate to others who share common experiences, and because of that, we trust them more intrinsically because they're better equipped to understand what we've gone through and our lived experiences.

Privilege plays a large part in who we trust throughout our lives. Think back to who makes up the dominant culture in the U.S. They are typically people who are white, male, straight, cisgender, Christian, with a high income or economic status, and they are seen as more trustworthy because of their privilege and status.[27] Speaking for my own personal experience working in the corporate environment, men, and especially white men, were given more opportunities, more tasks to handle, and more responsibility. Going back again to my rise through Boston Market; I was able to rise as fast as I did because upper management trusted me. They saw me as a white, straight, "man", working extremely hard, and trying to maximize the amount of work that I was doing. They trusted me, not just because of my work, but also because of my privilege at the time.

Sometimes trust is something you have to break through, especially when the person assigning tasks might not know much about you and your background, or your diversity. In many ways, you have to take your own level of marketing and trustability to people. You have to find ways to showcase what it is that you do, and how your differences bring such an element to their team that is undeniably important. By trustability, I mean how likely a person is to trust you. All the factors that weigh in a person's mind, from your appearance and work performance, to unconscious biases that people have from others with your similar differences.

This is where the importance of sponsors comes in to make a huge impact. They are able to influence the managers and executives about the value that you bring, and why they should trust you. When having a sponsor that has the trust of high-level managers, those managers will listen to your sponsor, and therefore extend some level of trust with you basically by proxy. They are also able to help break through unconscious or conscious biases that a manager may have by vouching for you, and helping you gain opportunities that you wouldn't have been able to get before.

In the case that you don't have a sponsor that can do this, follow the lessons from the past chapter. Offer to take work off of a manager or co-worker's plate, take initiative in tasks, and highlight the work you're doing outside your company that has tie-ins back to the organization. It may take building up allies and sponsors with your co-workers before higher ups take notice and recognize the work that you're doing, and become a sponsor for you. As mentioned with cultivating allies and sponsors, this can be done by enlightening people through your story and influencing others to be an ally and support you, it can be through the work you do, listening and getting to know the people on your team, and letting them tell you their story. The important thing is to have, and/or cultivate, a central group of people that you trust, and who also trusts you. From that central group, continue to grow and establish yourself within your organization as someone others can trust when they need help, and position yourself as a team leader.

Leveraging Education to Build Trust

Gaining trust with someone, especially those who have a higher position, accesses the doors of possibilities for you. Once they know who you are, and what you bring to the table, a certain level of trust develops that you are able to perform in a role or complete a task. This was especially true for me when I was working my way up through the financial services organization. There are many misnomers or fears about trans people; who we are, what our experiences are, and what we go through on a daily basis. There were co-workers who I could tell wanted to ask questions, who wanted to know more, and seemed to be uncomfortable approaching me or asking me for anything. They didn't understand my identity, know who I was, and were afraid to ask out of fear of saying something insulting or crossing a boundary.

People fear what they don't know and in order to break through that and get people to trust me, I educated those around me so that they would feel more comfortable around me by getting to know me. I would answer the questions that they had, and then share information about myself with them. There are more shades to me than one identity. By bringing up different aspects of myself, like my family, or my educational background, people got to know me for who I was outside my gender identity. Since I was willing to be vulnerable in those moments, I was able to have real, honest conversations with people; meeting them where they were at and I was able to build trust with them. Being authentic with someone and educating them opens up a relationship where you both can speak your minds and trust is formed.

I do want to make an important note that it is not your job to educate someone on your diversity or identities. This is a way to cultivate trust with someone, but that doesn't mean that you have to always be the educator. It is not a diverse person's job to educate someone else on their diverse dimensions. Whether you or someone else chooses to educate another, is because they have chosen to invest the amount of time it takes to educate them. It is also not a diverse person's job or responsibility to educate another person on their privilege. Too often I've seen both of these take place, where a more privileged person wants to be educated about a person's identity and wants to learn about systemic issues, but wants answers from a person directly affected. Instead of doing their on research, they are relying on the person who has to deal with discrimination to explain the discrimination that they face to others. If someone is willing to explain, then that's great, but there are many people that don't want to explain a person's privilege to them and how socio-economic systems can benefit them.

A quote from Audre Lorde, a black woman, poet, feminist, theorist and writer,

> "Whenever the need for some pretense of communication arises, those who profit from our oppression call upon us to share our knowledge with them. In other words, it is the responsibility of the oppressed to teach the oppressors their mistakes. I am responsible for educating teachers who dismiss my children's culture in school. Black and Third World people are expected to educate white people as to our humanity. Women are expected to educate men. Lesbians and gay men are expected to educate the heterosexual world. The oppressors maintain their position and evade responsibility for their own actions. There is a constant drain of energy which might be better used in redefining ourselves and devising realistic scenarios for altering the present and constructing the future."[28]

It is from this that educating yourself is one of the most important things that you can do to build trust with diverse people and communities. It's okay to not know every single community's struggles, but if you want to know and help, take it upon yourself and do the research. There are books, articles, documentaries, magazines, papers, and other resources that will help you get a better understanding of any community. Come with that knowledge and be an ally constantly. Already knowing what you can do to help as an ally, putting those ideas into actions, and knowing the struggles that people face will help to build and foster trust.

It requires a certain amount of trust that you can educate and enlighten other people. This also goes back to political differences, and feeling safe in that they are receptive to what you have to say, and are willing to hear you out. Educating and enlightening doesn't always have to specifically revolve around a person's lived experience. In some cases, it's speaking up and asking for a change in language that's being used, or even how something is presented. For example, if I'm on a conference call, or in a meeting with a community leader, and I hear them use the word "guys" in reference to multiple people, then I have to have enough trust with that leader to tell them why they should refrain from using that word (It being that it is a over encompassing word that assumes everyone in the room is a man). If I don't feel comfortable, or have enough trust that the person will both listen to my suggestion and take it seriously, then I might not say anything.

The importance of that level of trust can be a key component for anyone in your network. If you feel that your voice, and what you have to say isn't going to be valued and listened to, then oftentimes we choose not to say anything because what's the point? If our ideas aren't going to be executed, then why bother saying anything? This is part of the reason why building trust with others is crucial to empowering others and yourself. People are more likely to open up to you, share their stories, support and sponsor you, as well as offer you mentorship on where you can improve. It's a mutually beneficial mentorship that you then create with multiple people. As you continue to grow and learn more about the people around you, continue to foster the relationships you have, and become someone who is a trusted ally and sponsor for others. Also, please remember to follow up with others whom you have not yet built enough trust with yet, because eventually you will want to empower them and others through education.

Step 3

Developing Your Strategy

Chapter 77

Strategic Engagement

Putting Yourself Out There

Throughout this book so far, I've emphasized the importance of getting to know other people, and building relationships with others. I'm going to continue to emphasize that, but you should also be considering how other people view you, and who is part of your audience. Who are the people that you are reaching out to, what is the best thing to highlight about yourself depending on who you are talking to, and how are you going to gain access to larger communities? These are all crucial components to put the lessons from this book into action.

Remember to use your differences as an advantage as often as you can, even multiple times each day. This is the ultimate game changer in creating a path of influential access. You have come a long way in this process to find who you are, and now it's time to create your accessible opportunities. Considering all that you have identified and researched, now let's put it into action. Take your largest perceived weakness from your differences and begin there. Perception is not reality in this case. This "so-called" weakness is your ultimate selling point. I want you to begin to highlight this item in every way possible, it's at the central core of empowering your differences.

Let me speak from example, as it relates to my personal journey. Many people that I know see being openly transgender as a huge disadvantage because so many people are afraid of the unknown. The first moment I realized this was in 2010, I remember it like it was yesterday. I was sitting in a job interview, and I was asked the bare minimum number of questions and then got the obligatory, "we will call you". I left there thinking, I wonder what I could have done differently.

Well, for one thing, I didn't address the metaphorical big pink elephant in the room. I was so afraid of not getting a job offer that I was not being authentic. So, I decided to take the scariest step for me. This is when I accidentally made the move to be my own advocate for my diversity, and my community. The following week, I showcased my decision in full force during another job interview. Upon answering one of the standard questions… "Ashley, where do you see yourself in 5 years…." I decided to let it go, and worked my diversity into my response. "Well, professionally I plan to have been growing with your company, and personally, I am excited to continue my gender transition from male to female". What followed next was way more shocking to me, which was a follow-up question. The hiring manager was just like any other human and was curious to learn more about my diversity, since I brought it up it was fair game.

I apparently opened the floodgates because each interview seemed to include an educational session, some of them were almost an hour just talking about my community and how we are all just people. By about the 10th interview like this, I was starting to get discouraged. I was thinking that by now I would have found a job that wanted to hire me on my merits, my openness, or my authenticity, but that was not the

224

case. This led me to begin to doubt my approach. Then I started to think as if it were my own business, and I began to believe that I would want all my employees to be authentic, but I would want to make sure that it doesn't deter from the mission of generating more revenue and profit for my organization. This enlightened me to amend my approach another time, and this leads me to one of my favorite takeaways. Celebrate your diversity and authenticity, but at the same time link it to something that will increase revenue and profit for the organization. For my next couple of interviews, I drove the conversation about my authenticity to not be just about education for my community, but education about the buying power of my community, how many people in my network needed to know about their organization, or how more productive, authentic employees are in the workforce.

I had the pleasure to discuss with my original hiring manager, Nicole Fielder, what she thought during the last section of my job interview approach. She shared with me that when she initially saw me, she thought that I was a man wearing a dress. This is one of the biggest heart wrenching nightmares that exist for trans feminine people. We never want people in society to view us that way, ever. Then she said that after she got to listen to my responses, her thinking was that I was way too overqualified to be a part-time bank teller. After highlighting my community, and the return on investment that I was going to provide, her last fear was that I was going to find a better job, and leave pretty quickly. During the interview I addressed that as well when I told her that I plan to move up very rapidly in the organization. Nicole also told me that she's learned so much about the trans community upon our years working together, but I've noticed how she has been a huge ally who advocates for all diverse communities constantly.

If you are thinking that an organization doesn't want you, then you need to show them the value you bring, and when I say you, I mean all of you. Your whole self should be every part of what you do, and how you grow your career. Come prepared with the research that you've been doing about yourself, others, and then consider how to frame your inspirational story alongside who you are deep within yourself. By this, I mean what parts of your story are the best to share with the people that you are talking to, within the allotted amount of time. Trying to connect with someone at a large event, you may only have a few minutes to make an impression so you need to come prepared with an elevator pitch. Ideally, you'll be able to have a longer conversation with someone, but this is always a good thing to have ready just in case.

When I was working to build up myself and my own personal brand, networking was such an important step in that process. It allowed me to meet people who do incredible things and expand both of our networks. I have had access to many opportunities in my career, and in my own business that have been made possible by leveraging the connections in my network. By working purposely to interconnect people, you are then lessening the degrees of separations of people. The six degrees of separation theory is that we are all six people or fewer away from everyone in our community. What I'm asking of you is to work towards making your network one degree of separation. To actively get to know more people in your community, your field, and your local area. This is a networking strategy to open your world to a new set of possibilities, increasing the access to more people.

Building Connections

Access as a principal is one of the most important things that you can leverage in your career journey. Early on in my second career working for the financial services institution, I was focused on being everywhere. Gaining access to all people at every event, trying to be where everyone was, and constantly putting myself into different social and professional circles. This style of networking proved to be very toxic, I was everywhere, and didn't have a centered focus in my mission. I was basically overusing access and it was causing me to have too many events and too many people to connect with on a regular basis. After a couple of years, I realized that I needed to be more strategic in the way that I was thinking about access to others. I reduced the amount of networking that I was doing and made sure that I wasn't just networking at different events, but also investing more of my time into specific organizations. Whether they were non-profits, chambers of commerce, or volunteer organizations, dedicating more time to a smaller number of organizations led me to forge stronger relationships with key people, compared to knowing a ton of people but not making meaningful connections. These new strong levels of connections proved to be very important in my journey.

Gaining access to key communities can be done in a multitude of ways. Networking events in person, virtual events online, joining associations and clubs, and my favorite, volunteering with local non-profit organizations. All of these example events are great ways to gain access to your community. Remember that the main solution here is strategic influence. Be very smart about the time that you invest in these groups. Be sure that you build significant partnerships with others and not look to collect the most business cards or contact info. There is an art to networking properly, I feel that it's best captured by empowering other people. Remember when you meet someone, regardless of their title, always offer to help them first thing. Many of my friends refer to this as servant leadership.

Of course, networking is super important overall, but for me, the biggest thing that made a huge impact in my career was when I was thinking two to three steps ahead of each event and subsequent interactions. For example, I would make sure to choose the event that was going to provide me the most access to the people that I wanted to get in front of, versus attending the most populous event, or the one with the best guest speaker. By doing the research and knowing who was going to attend, and participate, this made this choice a lot easier.

People Research and Community Awareness

Each time you engage with new people you should know as much about them before engaging as you can find. With how easy it is to look up information in this day and age, it is imperative to take advantage of this tool. Take social media for example. You can look up a person's background, where they've worked, and details about themselves, which is a great tool to research who might be at an upcoming event. Look for people that are attending that would be good for you to meet, but also think about why you want to meet them. What do you hope to gain from having a relationship with said person? What can they educate and enlighten you about, and vice versa? Are they a community leader that can be a great connection to get to know more leaders and establish yourself in a community? Leverage what your research says, and focus on maybe two or three people that would be good for you to meet.

When coming up with reasons for meeting someone, you need to think about what positive aspects you bring to the table, so they can make an impact for that person. Consider a way that you can actually help them with their business, or maybe take something off that leaders plate. When I'm out networking at an event and somebody comes to me and offers to help with a nonprofit organization that they see me involved with, I would be excited to work with them or offer them support. This is a great way to show how motivated you are to help and learn about someone, their company, or their non-profit organization they are affiliated with each day.

Think about this in reverse as well. Individuals and organizations conduct tons of research on people they consider hiring, promoting, or partnering within any capacity. Do you think your potential employer is not looking up your entire digital footprint? Even if you are private and not friends with anyone at work, trust me, they know all your social media handles because social media is a place where you showcase yourself. Entities understand the risk involved with each person they do business with, for good reason. The point is, you need to operate just like a business would, you should do an appropriate amount of research to prep yourself for a planned "interview", or even a chance meeting. Think of this also in the model of opposition research, get to know your competition as well.

Part of the research that you should be doing also needs to be about the community that you live in, and everything that might be relevant to others when you're out networking. Being aware of all the things that happen locally, including relevant news stories, and in my case, even Netflix series like Tiger King[29]. Yes, I did just give a Tiger King reference because I live in Tampa, which is the home to the Big Cat Rescue. As you can guess, the topic of discussion comes up often in meetings, so it's important for me to be culturally aware of this documentary. Being culturally aware allows me to be an active participant in those conversations and engage further with the people I'm networking with and I have the access to build a stronger connection.

Your community awareness should also include sports. Sports are a vibrant part of communities here in America. Please make sure that you are culturally aware, and you invest time in knowing which of your community teams wins and loses, at a minimum. There have been many times that I've gained access to a longer conversation with an executive because I was able to encapsulate what happened the night before in a sporting event. This has also opened up the door for me to gain access to the corporate suite during sporting events. I'm assuming that most people know who has access to the corporate suite during a sporting event, a majority of the time it's owned by a senior leader in an organization. Through sports, you now have access to them and the people around them as well. This creates a cascading domino effect of influence for you to soak up. Opportunities like this don't come every day, so you have to be very poignant to capitalize on them. Think in advance which of these empowering actions you are planning to use, and which are the most effective for you to use at each given moment. Do your research as to who they are, what you might be able to relate to, and determine the best approach for each individual person.

Situational Awareness

 Something to take into consideration is the event or the situation that
you are walking into, and how you present and carry yourself in
different situations. One of the things that I pride myself on is adapting
to each situation. Whether that is the way that I dress, talk, or the way
in which I carry myself. I read the room and adapt to what the situation
calls for and I recognize that my passing privilege plays a huge part in
this. If I'm attending an event that is more conservative in nature, I am
not going to wear the highest of high heels, or dress as loud. I might
give my pink blazer the night off. Given my intersectionality, I'm going
to do what I can to make sure that I'm not the elephant in the room. I
don't want to walk into a room and already have eyes on me because of
the way I'm dressed. I want to make an impression based on what I say
and the ideas that I'm bringing to the table, and not my stylistic
choices.

This all boils down to strategic influence. I don't want to dilute myself
or my voice, I want to continue to empower myself and others, but
influence here is key, and how you garner strategic influence based on
the audience that you're presenting at or speaking to, makes a huge
impact. In a setting that would be more conservative in nature, I'm
going to highlight all of the financial investment impacts that I bring to
the table. I'm going to focus a conversation on the monetary impact.
Keeping the conversation focused onto something that tailors both of
our interests will shift the conversation from identity politics, to how
each party can help benefit each other. This is going to help enlighten
others to my diverse community, and the kind of influence that I can
bring to their organization.

The settings and the situations that you are in will shape how you want to highlight your differences, and which aspects that you want to bring up in a conversation. You're going to have to read the room and judge based on the conversations and the intersectionality of the people in the room, which is the best part of your diversity to highlight. This also goes back to navigating political differences, finding common ground with the people that you are conversing with, and what's important to them. In many cases for me working for a financial services organization, a lot of the ties to my diversity are linked to the buying power of my communities. A good strategy is to consider what ties you can link with your diversity and how to connect that into conversations you have with leaders and managers. These strategies are only the beginning of putting everything that you've learned so far together to make an impact for yourself and those around you every chance you get.

Learning From Your Mistakes

Mistakes Are Going to Happen

Throughout your journey, career, and even working through this book, it's important to understand that you will have shortcomings; not everyone is going to excel in everything. When I asked you earlier in the book to do the self-evaluation, did you make any mistakes while doing that? Was there anything that you left out, either intentionally or subliminally? Have you made missteps in your job or career? The important thing is to be honest with yourself when answering these questions. Mistakes can seem like a stain, but they are also how we grow as people.

Mistakes are bound to happen, that is the fact of life, and no one is perfect. Mistakes in general are a fundamental foundation for where you need to improve and a tool for motivating yourself to make changes. A good practice is that you address what happened and learn from it. Recognizing where you went wrong is the first step. Oftentimes we're aware of our own blunders, but there are many cases where we don't know that we've made an error, that we've misspoken, or done something wrong, and other people point out to us where we messed up. If someone is trying to explain where you made a mistake, they have enough trust in their relationship with you to try and educate you about what they have noticed. Listen to what they have to say and take in their mentorship. It can be hard to hear and realize that you've made a mistake; no one ever wants to do something wrong, but use this as a moment of reflection and use it as a building block.

For me, it is eye-opening and enlightening to see where I need to improve. Make a shortcoming something you can build more education around. Mistakes can be a real, live, self assessment that shows us where we can improve. It's important not to dwell on the mistakes themselves, but on how we can do better for the future. Throughout this chapter I'm going to share some of the lessons that I've learned through mistakes that I've made in my career journey.

Invested Time In Wrong Organization

I've invested time in an organization that eventually did not align to my personal goals. Looking back in the past, I was so excited to serve on a board for a non-profit organization that I didn't even consider looking into their finances, or past history. This was one of the first opportunities that I had to be a part of a greater change. To make a more profound impact and elevate, not only my voice, but also those around me, and in my community. I don't want to go too deep into the details about the organization, but to put it simply, there was a bunch of work that needed to be done.

I didn't follow my own advice in this book around researching organizations and learning about their backgrounds before building my plan to engage. The opportunity to be on the board seemed like it made good career sense, which led me to believe everything was golden. I

234

was naive, and while opportunities like these don't show up every day, I realized during that I needed to make sure they were the right opportunities for me. Being on the board, I was now put in the position of being responsible to help to fix any issues that were uncovered.

The takeaway from this mistake was to make sure that I do my research into who I'm working for, and who I'm investing my time in, as well as learning when it is best to cut ties. There is certainly an art to this, I'm still working to improve this skill in my capacity but remember that your time is one of the biggest investments that you can make in yourself or in others. By others, I'm referring to nonprofit organizations that you could potentially partner within your community. So be sure to maximize your time investment, and do as much research as you can to make sure that you're making an equally beneficial investment.

Undervalued My Volunteer Contributions

Honestly, I am always excited and thrilled to give back to my community, and volunteer in as many places as I can. I'm also no stranger to fundraising for non-profit organizations, though there have been times that I've made a mistake in undervaluing what I actually bring as a volunteer for a community nonprofit organization. This is also not just in the realm of nonprofits, but undervaluing what I can bring to an organization as well.

Throughout my 10 years of community volunteerism, engagement, and working closely with organizations, I have continually thought that what I have to give, the experiences that I've had, and the work that I do, isn't that great, or it isn't as good as other members. I'd put myself down constantly, focusing too much on what I need to be doing better, instead of recognizing the amazing work that I was doing for multiple organizations and communities. While self-improvement and reflection is important, it's also good to keep in mind and remember the successes that you've had. As much as you take stock of the mistakes you've made and what you can do to improve, keep a similar list in mind of the amount of positive things that you've done. Those need to be the fuel to inspire you to do more.

Keep in mind as well, all of what you bring to an organization each day. What you have to contribute may seem like the most mundane thing, but can actually provide a ton of value and insight for them. We each have our own unique lived experiences that shape our perspective of the world and each has a place at the table. My diverse lived experiences are highly sought after, from a capacity of having lived experiences in both genders. This type of lived experience brings an inherent amount of value for whoever I'm partnering with each and every day. The biggest lesson I learned around volunteer commitments is recognizing the investment value of my time, treasure, and talent all equally.

Educate Others but Only to a Certain Degree

Upon receiving more recognition in different communities, I was asked to speak and share my story more often. I was excited by the opportunity. The idea of being recognized as a speaker and being able to share my thoughts was something that I never thought I'd be doing. I was so entranced by the idea of speaking that I didn't even consider charging a speaking fee. From a marketing perspective, it was great being able to do a free speaking engagement with a big name to build up my credibility at the beginning. I wasn't about to jeopardize the engagement by putting a price tag on it. I didn't even consider charging businesses and organizations until I had already spoken multiple times.

This is another example of where I feel I made a huge mistake in undervaluing what I bring to the conversation from a financial perspective. In this day and age, you could easily build up your credibility by showcasing your speaking and training ability by hosting video sessions online. The prospect of being able to share your experiences and speak to a larger audience can be extremely appealing, but many organizations and businesses will try and skimp out on giving you financial compensation. Through my own experiences, this is unfortunately a common thing. Many businesses want to have diverse speakers come into their offices and conduct training, or have the person speak, but don't want to compensate them. Many people that I know have had the same mentality that I once had, they didn't want to jeopardize the possibility of educating others, and did it for free, or for how much the business or organization was willing to compensate.

The takeaway from this was to always be SMART (specific, measurable, achievable, realistic, and timely) about who I was giving my time and energy towards. Depending on who I'm talking to, I'm going to focus on specific topics and share specific points of my story. Now when I'm asked to speak, I weigh all of the factors including how much I'm being compensated, how much will it cost me to speak, and how long I'm being asked to speak for. I also have to consider what I'm hoping to gain out of a speaking engagement, other than financial compensation. Who am I educating and what networking opportunities can come from this that can boost my name and business in different circles? Is this a worthwhile opportunity for me, or is it just an idea that a business has but wants me to speak for free because they don't want to make the financial investment for their team? Lastly, do I have the time available to travel to a business's physical location to speak? I have to be real with myself and my schedule. As much as I would love to take every opportunity that shows up, I've learned to not stretch myself so thin to the point of not performing at my best where I need to be.

My main point is for you to limit the amount of free education you offer to organizations that you do not work for. Educate others, absolutely, but be SMART about who you are educating, know what you hope to achieve from it, gauge if you will be able to meet your goals, and assess how much time it will take for you. Much like speaking engagements, trying to educate everyone will leave you burnt out with limited results. Be strategic about who you are educating and why. This will maximize your time investment and ensure you are influencing the right people. In terms of speaking on a larger scale, don't do it for free for a company, when it could undercut people. Nonprofits, sure, depending on the size and scope of it, but high dollar universities and organizations need to pay up. Your voice and your story have value, and it is a privilege for other people to be able to hear it.

Choosing the Wrong Difference to Highlight

Let me first start here by saying that none of your differences are wrong. However you choose to highlight your differences is your way of inspiring and empowering others. Though I do advise a word of caution when highlighting certain differences in calculated situations. This goes back to researching where you're about to be present, and who is attending. There have been times when I've talked about LGBTQ+ rights at an event, and had people walk away during a discussion. I can't control what others do, say, or think, but I had to take a moment for myself after seeing that. It's disheartening and I certainly don't feel great when someone walks away when I'm trying to highlight a part of myself, but I've learned to not let it get to me, regroup, and take in what I can.

The biggest thing here that I want to bring to light is that you have to be stoic and inspirational. If what you're presenting is actually inspirational, then the majority of the people will continue to listen and be educated on what you have to say. Though there may be times when you have others who don't listen, who don't get it, and just walk away from the conversation. What I've learned is to not give up, and keep motivating yourself. If you're at a cocktail party for instance, and you're talking with a group of people and there's an adverse reaction by some because of a difference that you've highlighted. Take a step back, excuse yourself from the conversation for a moment, maybe go to the restroom, and remotivate yourself. Don't give up and try to not let it get to you. Focus on being a listener in that situation and soak up what knowledge you need to know before trying to re-engage in the future. Don't focus on what you should have done in the moment, instead, direct your energy to what you can do in the next moments moving forward. Once you are able to consider what happened or what you could have done differently, you can cultivate a plan on what you should do in the future.

Storytelling and the Importance of Mental Health

Early on in my career, I wasn't able to communicate effectively about what I was going through, and what I needed personally, including the type of support and mentoring I needed. I was able to articulate facts and wear my identities as a proud badge of honor, but I was still developing how to communicate what I was going through on a day-to-day basis. From that, I wasn't able to express what I needed from other people and help them understand what I was going through on a deeper, connected level. Bringing up statistics and research is always a great tool to have, but being able to communicate your personal story is a game changer that can sway people and increase their level of enlightenment.

Data and research can point to larger societal issues that diverse communities face, but personal stories are something that people can relate to and empathize with immediately. Sharing a difficult moment, or part of your journey with someone can build a relationship and trust with that person, but you have to be able to communicate it clearly. I was struggling emotionally and I thought that I could solve my personal struggles on my own because that's what I've been doing for a majority of my life, it's all I knew. I would personally choose to try to combat things myself, often internalizing them. Individuals raised as boys are often taught not to display emotion which had a major negative impact on my life. Lucky for me, having the love, compassion, and support of Whitney and the boys is what ultimately helped me survive. I realize now, I should have sought the help of a mental health professional to help me work through some of the things I was dealing with.

Talking with a mental health professional is something I recommend everyone do. It can be helpful to talk about a difficult period in your life, or even work through a stressful time. Communication can help many people by having someone they know that they can talk to openly about anything. It's about being able to be honest and real with yourself about what you're feeling, and work through it with someone who has been trained to help. I know now that by not seeking out a mental health professional, I was set back by about a year or two. If I had been working with a mental health professional earlier in my career, then I would have been able to better foster relationships, and be able to put myself in the position to make better connections. Working with a mental health professional helped give me the confidence that I needed in order to excel as my authentic self.

I wish that people would take care of their mental health as much as they maintain their car, cell phone, and other technologies. There shouldn't be such a stigma about talking to a mental health professional, or even talking about mental health. I know that not everyone will have access to afford a mental health professional, or may not even have one in your area. What I will suggest is that you find someone who you are able to talk to about your well-being. Find a close confidant that you can talk to openly about what you've been struggling with and what you need, even if it's just work related stress. Having someone in your corner who you know you can trust and speak openly with, is invaluable and will help keep you motivated and inspired through highs and lows. Maintaining your mental health is just as important as maintaining your physical health.

Following My Own Path

The road less traveled is one of those things I think about when I consider my career journey. I often wonder what my path would have been like had I taken the typical track into branch management. I certainly had the management experience. I had multiple conversations with leaders that said that they could put me on the track to be a branch manager because of my past experiences, but I wanted to focus on being an individual contributor. At the time, I was still trying to understand the best way to empower my own differences. I was still learning more about myself and I knew that managing a team of people wasn't what I needed at the time.

As I was trying to understand more about myself, I partnered with every unit in the organization as a way to soak up as much knowledge as possible. From investments, to wealth management, I wanted to know as much about my surroundings as possible. I had numerous conversations with people, I had cross mentoring relationships, and through those relationships I also taught people about myself and my community, and they taught me about theirs. I was curious. Through all of my research, I decided I wanted to become a registered investment adviser, though some of my mentors saw the path that I was taking as a mistake. In their minds, they saw a perfectly laid out plan, especially given my work experience. It made sense in their minds that I should follow the path that was seemingly laid out for me as a branch manager.

I appreciated and took into consideration the advice that my mentors gave me, and it did give me perspective on the career trajectory that I could have. I knew that if need be, then I could continue that track. When I decided to become a registered investment adviser, I didn't fully know what the path I was taking entailed. It was not projected for me to be the Vice President of Diversity and Inclusion within five years of starting as a part-time bank teller. There wasn't a clear-cut path for me, but I do know that getting my Series 7, and Series 66 investment security licenses, led me to the next great stepping stone in my career journey. It was a risk, absolutely, but the payoff was enormous because of what I decided to do with the licenses. It was because of those licenses, and the investments that I had made across numerous different branches, that made me a much more valuable candidate, and allowed me access to multiple opportunities I wouldn't have had without my extensive expertise and background.

The point I want to make here is that sometimes you need to follow your own path and do what is right for you. There may be others in your career, like mentors or sponsors, that think you are making a mistake in your career path. It's important to hear them out and assess amongst your closest confidants. This will give you a sounding board so that you are not making this decision alone. Whether or not you decide to listen to their advice is up for you to decide. No one can make the decision for you.

Take into consideration the advice of those around you, but if you are set on something, then go for it! Even if it ends up not being what you expected, or wasn't the path that you should have gone down, at the very least you learned what doesn't work. Trying something new never has any guarantees, but you can learn from the experience. Expanding how much you know and your experiences is never a bad thing. I don't think that there are ever any wrong career paths that a person can take, there are simply trajectories that some have, and some paths will take you to widely unexpected places.

Separating Church and State

Cultivating your brand from the beginning is a tricky item to navigate. This is probably one of my biggest mistakes I've made in my journey. I had to play catch up in many ways from this mistake. I wasn't thinking about the brand I was building, but was just focused on performing at my job. Making sure that I was doing the best that I can, and the result of that was my employee brand, and my personal brand, blending into one another. I wasn't seen as this diverse person with my own lived experiences, or the leader that was active in my communities, I was more so seen as just Ashley, the hard worker. While it was great that I was getting recognized in that way, the other shades of myself weren't as widely recognized and it became hard to tell the difference between all the facets of my brand as a whole.

I like to call this separating church and state. Much like how the U.S. separates religion from the government, you have to separate the different roles and titles that you have obtained. As you begin to empower yourself and others, you will be cultivating leadership qualities and people will start to recognize you in that way. It's important to realize that people won't simply view you as, for example, just a project manager. Yes, that's an important role, but you want to make sure that your entire self doesn't get blurred into just that role. Being confined to one role limits the recognition that you can have, and reduces your identity to just that role. It is by no means easy to separate the different parts of yourself, but it is something that is important to do and consider when you begin putting the lesson in this book into action.

I love the word persona here. I feel like we all have to maintain the personas of what we're putting out in the universe in order to empower others. This is in the same vein as code switching. We all have different personas depending on who we are interacting with, and the positions that we hold. For example, there is Ashley the mother, Ashley the VP, Ashley the author, and Ashley the community leader. These are all different personas that I have, and how I interact with others depends on which persona is at the forefront.

It did take me a while to separate these personas and make it known to those around me that I wasn't just a hard worker for an organization, and that I had different roles and different parts of me that were starting to shine. The hardest was trying to figure out how to separate personas in social media. Early on, I funneled anything social media related, and anything brand related, through my personal account and I wasn't getting the recognition that I could have gotten if I didn't blend all of myself together into one account. When I realized this, I created multiple accounts, my personal account, another as a professional account, and a third for the promotion of my business. It is difficult to maintain all of these accounts and manage the health and wellness of each of them. I have to be selective about where I post certain things, where I share certain thoughts, and make sure that my professional ones are kept up to date and stay relevant.

All of this falls into strategic positioning; putting yourself and your brand in the spotlight so that you can showcase all parts of yourself.

You need to make sure that you maintain that strong separation between an organization and yourself. Like I've said here, it's not easy. You'll have to motivate yourself to be disciplined to develop the separation of identities, but it is worth it. If you want to be a company person and rise through the corporate ladder one step at a time, then keep performing and you will move into a higher position. However, if you want to leap up multiple steps of the ladder at once, to go from a part-time worker to VP of a major organization, then you need to do a whole lot more.

I was performing well in my positions and sales, yes for sure, but that alone wasn't what was going to put me over the top and get me to where I am today. To get to where I am, I had to use all 10 empowering actions. I needed to separate church and state, and highlight everything that I was doing, and all of the skills that I brought to the table. I think about this in terms of basketball; yes a sports reference. Layups are worth two points, and are relatively easy to make. Layups are like small steps that you can take to help your career, you should absolutely take them. Three pointers are harder shots to take, and they yield more of a reward than a layup, but you want to be strategic in using them. These are larger choices that you can make in your career, and to give an example, for me, it was deciding not to follow the career path of being a branch manager.

If you want to make bigger moves and bigger changes in your career, you need to be aiming for those three point shots. Yes, you might miss sometimes, but you need to keep going, keep trying, and don't stop. Set your eyes on where you want to be, and do everything that you can to make that a reality. You may miss, you may get injured, but nothing really ends until you let it end. An opportunity may be missed, or something could have been done differently, but you have the power to make another opportunity for yourself. Whether that is leveraging the influence you have with other people, continuing to expand the work you've been doing, or even access to meeting the right person. One door may close, and you may make a mistake, but there will always be another way; whether you create that yourself, or an opportunity arises because of the work you've been doing. Continue to recognize mistakes so you can have the motivation to not only overcome them, but have the inspiration to climb back even higher the next time.

Chapter 73

Navigating Personal Communication

People's Perception of You

From the last chapter, one of the things I mentioned was social media, and how managing and shaping your brand to give it its own identity is important. By managing your persona and brand online, you are able to manage the perception that people have about you. If you are posting about the events that you are going to, volunteer engagements that you've been at, and things that you are doing to help others, you cultivate an image of being a community leader. What you put out on social media, and how you present yourself, affects people's public perception of you. It's your own messaging which is all tied to communication and how you leverage it every moment.

How people interact with you, and if they choose to listen to you and your story, partially depends on how they perceive you. The ultimate goal with keeping these things in mind is to cultivate advocates, sponsors, and crucially, allies. Oftentimes, I like to say that allies are golden. The terminology of allies is used often in the LGBTQ+ community, but honestly all diverse communities need, not just allies, but also advocates. Allies are people that are supportive of you and your diverse communities. They will listen and understand your personal story, and help you in the ways that they can. Advocates are people that go a step further and are the people who are driving systemic change. Whether they are taking actions politically, through a company, or through a community, they are the people that leverage their influence to create change on a larger scale.

Throughout this book, I've mentioned the importance of gaining the support of people around you. In the last chapter I mentioned the importance of being able to tell your personal story. How you choose to share your story, and what parts you are willing to share, are decided by you, but the impact that your story can have can shift a conversation. For example, with my family, when they were talking about a political conversation, and I was able to bring up how certain policies will, or have affected me personally, is when they were able to reflect and understand my point of view. They may not be complete allies, but I consider it a win if I'm able to shift the conversation and get them to think critically about what they are saying, and then feel differently about my community.

Framing Your Story

Think about how you're feeling during your communication of what you've gone through and your lived experiences. That emotional connection needs to come through to gain the enlightenment of others. Oftentimes we undervalue the stories we have, or the things we've learned, which are worth sharing with others. Telling people what you've experienced doesn't have to be in the form of a speaker talking to an audience. It can be simple things that you've gone through, like a story of how you got a job, a time in school that you've grown from, or how a relationship that you had with someone affected you personally. Your interpersonal stories don't have to be the most life-changing events to create change for others. The important thing is to think about the lessons that you learned from what you've gone through, how certain actions, policies, and people have affected you, and how this can continue to enlighten others.

Another approach that I like to use when painting the narrative for my story is to make it super personal. When I first became an inclusion advocate, I didn't verbalize the discrimination that I was facing on a daily basis. I didn't know how to frame it, what to focus on, and how to effectively share my story. As much as I would like to give the whole scope of my story so people can understand my background and the discrimination I face, people don't have that amount of time to listen and understand, and I don't have that amount of time to tell everyone I interact with each day. It'd take hours to go through and explain each intricacy, and because of that, I have to frame parts of my story to the conversation.

What specific points, and what challenges I face, depend on who I'm talking to and what the context is for that conversation. For the person in the airplane, I tailored my story to the military experience in my family, and how, if I wanted to, I wouldn't be able to serve. When talking about a political conversation on legislation, I'll tailor the discriminations that I face to laws and how they can affect me on a daily basis. When telling your personal story, you have to curate it to the conversation that you're having. Think about the main points of your story. What are the takeaways? What do you want people to gain from your story? What can other people do in order to help? These are only a few questions to get you thinking about how you are going to tell your story. Throughout this chapter, keep in mind the impact your story can have on other people.

Control the narrative so people understand what it is like to walk a day in your shoes, which is the best way to ultimately inspire someone to be an ally. In some ways, you have to think of it like you're running your own public relations firm. Constant media messaging, and persistent education creates more inclusion. You have to gain other people's buy-in, and in order to do that, you have to utilize all 10 empowering actions and be able to communicate your message consistently. When I think of controlling the narrative, I think about juggling all the balls at the same time, and at the same pace. If you happen to drop one of them, potentially you could drop them all. That is why framing your story really matters, it will allow you to recover or pivot if an issue comes your way.

Using Your Story to Gain Allies

As I said earlier, I didn't always control the narrative in the way I could have. I had to learn to access influential people, share my story, and work to inspire more allies. All of those things together are what helped me leverage communication, to move up rapidly in the organization. That was how I built solid relationships with senior leaders in the financial services organization.

The first part was gaining access to them. I let my empowering results speak for themselves. You have to deliver on results in order to get people's attention. Once I was on their radar and able to have a conversation with them, I brought in my personal story. I focused on the points that were the most relevant with who I was talking with, and crucially gave them my recommendations for actions they could take, or things that could be improved. Upon communicating my story, I was able to change their perception. In many cases, they became allies; sympathizing with what I've gone through and commending me on how far I've come. They helped toss my hat in the ring when positions came open, and helped spread my name to the executives in the organization.

Sometimes though, it's not going to be good enough just to have someone be an ally. You're going to have to take things even further with building an advocate. You may come across systemic barriers that create a glass ceiling effect. This is where you need to have advocates and sponsors; someone, or ideally a group of people, who understand who you are, your story, and use their influence to cultivate change. Understand that someone who is an advocate is not only going to be great for you, but will potentially support and create change for many others. Their communication on your behalf is what can ultimately create that access to others for you and your career.

I regularly check in with my advocates and work with them to drive systemic change for my diverse community. I like to think of this like entrusting someone, sort of like you would in a mentoring relationship. You need to mentor someone to help them fulfill their ability to be an advocate and ally, but also understand that, just like any other mentoring relationship, this can go both ways. Oftentimes when people are presented with seemingly insurmountable issues that are affecting a community or an organization, the thought of creating change can be

252

overwhelming. You need to be prepared to share action steps that advocates can take and use immediately. When people know what they can do to create change, they are more likely to be an advocate. Even small actions that a person can do, whether that is cosigning on a letter demanding action, urging executive leadership to incorporate more educational training, or to hire more diverse candidates. Once people have actions they can take, and an understanding of what changes need to be made, they will be an advocate for you and those that follow.

Being Comfortable Being Uncomfortable

In many cases, trying to educate someone will make either you, or your audience uncomfortable. Oftentimes, they are uncomfortable with the societal systems that discriminate against certain groups of people, or they are uncomfortable because of actions that they themselves have made in the past. Reflecting and coming to terms with certain things can be uncomfortable. In these cases, you have to make sure that you have the confidence in what you are saying. The people around you will only be as comfortable as you make them. This is why it's crucial that you come into conversations knowing what you want to communicate and how you are going to say it.

You also need to make sure that they are comfortable being uncomfortable. Have the confidence in what you are saying and stand firm in the case that someone tries to refute it. Sometimes it's hard to push back on someone and educate them, especially when it's a topic they should know. Something that affects the both of you in the same way, but they aren't able to see where you are coming from initially. It takes time and it may wear on you and the other person. Be sure to take time for yourself, this is a marathon, not a sprint. No one said fighting for equality and justice would be easy, but it is crucial in empowering those around you.

Uplifting Other People's Stories

Every person has the chance to empower others. Everybody also has the chance to help control the narrative for communication of diverse communities. By speaking out against injustices that you see, this helps to stop systemic issues in society. Another thing that I recommend that anyone can do is to amplify someone's voice. An example would be conducting a simple retweet for someone on a constant basis. Saying it a little louder for someone in the back to hear. These are small actions that everyone should be doing, and actions that allies can take after hearing your story.

I'm often quoted at events when I state that all of our diverse communities are stronger together. This goes back to why empowering others is so important. You may have developed the relationship with the senior leader in the organization, so now you have earned that access. That's not the time to stop influencing change for other people. Reaching a milestone, or making a great connection, is always something to be excited about, but there is always more work that needs to be done. Whether that is on a larger scale within an organization, or even with individuals.

I typically mentor someone from the trans community a couple of times a week. I use these discussions to highlight my story and teach them how they can do exactly the same thing that I did. I check in with them to be sure that they aren't hiding their identity and empowering themselves. We have to communicate what we've been through so others don't make the same mistakes. Our stories need to be told and heard; it's how we learn from each other and grow together as a community. The more we tell our stories, listen, and learn from those around us the more we work towards a more inclusive society.

Appearance Awareness

Your Dress and Authenticity

What you wear and your style are a part of your individuality and brand. It is your way to be different and showcase yourself. This is a fine line in the sand, so please use caution here. I think we all have a general want and need to impress others; to put our best foot forward. Being your whole self, in how you dress and appear each day, is the heart of my overall message in this story of empowering differences. When you feel good about the way you look, you become more confident in yourself. That confidence in yourself will lead to you being able to focus on your inspirational message and so much more.

Sadly, what others think of your style matters way more than it should. It can be the difference between getting the job offer or not. It can also be a factor in getting passed over for a promotion. How you dress, and how you present yourself to people, will influence how they interact with you. Much like how there is workplace attire, you need to consider how you are dressing and how people perceive you.

For me, this was a huge process as I really needed to find my own sense of style and fashion. I was incredibly lucky to have my sponsors support me in this process. They encouraged me, and the organization hired an image consultant. I was actually pretty scared to do this, I was worried that I was not going to fit in, or fail my appearance check. Through the process we talked about jewelry, clothes, sizing, makeup, and hair. I decided to go into these sessions with an open mind and I ended up learning that I was not that far off from finding my own comfort and sense of style. Most of the changes I decided to make were actually very minor, but the overall impact was very major.

The biggest leap I made was cutting about 6 inches in length from my hair. For me, I had developed my hair as my signature, personal branding concept. Though my issue was that it didn't have a style that suited the look I was aiming for. The foundation of my hair being a branding concept was built on my hair color, but I didn't really have a style, other than it being long. The other issue with my hair was that it was so long and thick, it became difficult to manage. I needed a third, forth, and even fifth opinion, alongside encouragement, to make my decision to finally cut my hair. I also decided to make an investment in good hair days. I began budgeting for bi-weekly hair blowouts. This was key for me to keep my confidence. My hair was still my focal point of my style and fashion, so taking care of it well helped keep me at ease. This freed me up to focus on the other items in my wardrobe and appearance.

While these changes were minor, the people around me started to take notice. I was treated with more respect by my colleagues, and the results that I was producing carried more weight in the eyes of my managers. It was hard to believe at first that making such seemingly minor changes affected the way that people interacted with me. It was almost like night and day. That isn't to say that I was treated poorly prior, but the amount of respect and how others held me in a much higher regard was easy to tell. Having a style allowed me to physically embody my own brand, and gave me access to people that I wouldn't have been able to reach. This ultimately influenced more people around me and amplified my own voice.

Take Notice of the Attitude and Attire of Those Around You

Think about all the decisions you make each day that relate to what you are going to wear. This is more important than you think. People tend to assume the best dressed person is the manager or leader of the business. Use this tactic with caution. Don't wear a tuxedo or ball gown to work. Also, be aware of what the normal attire is. If everyone wears t-shirts and jeans, then a full suit might be oversell for yourself. What I am saying is that you should highlight yourself in a confident manner within the structure of the organization.

Take notice of how everyone around is dressing. How do people in a similar position dress? What are they wearing, and how are they interacting with other people? Compare what you noticed to those who are in a higher position than you. What are your supervisors doing differently, and how are they presenting themselves to others? Take what you've noticed, and if you are able to, adapt your sense of style in a professional setting to those who have higher positions than you. This will not only put you in the mindset of being a higher level executive, but also gives others the same impression.

Initially in my career, my personal goal was to always dress three levels above my current job level. For me, this was a way to garner more respect, especially working in the retail bank. Often, there were times

258

customers would assume I was a manager or someone important, at the very least, the leader of my job function. This led to inclusion and respect, which were crucial for me in building confidence in myself. I needed access to every single advantage that I could reach in order to allow the control of communication I was talked about in the prior chapter. Your attitude and your attire make up a portion of nonverbal communication. The moment that people see you, they immediately begin to create an opinion of who you are and what you're doing. All this will factor in before you've even said one word. That is why I was thankful to have Patty Soltis as my personal image consultant. What follows from here are her thoughts around attitude, attire, and appearance, and how those contribute to your overall communication strategy and goals for advancing your career.

Guest Contributor Patty Soltis, STYLEdge Fashion LLC CEO/Principal Consultant

A first impression is made in 1/10 of a second[30] or in seven seconds.[31] In that literal blink of an eye, a first impression is made. A judgment has been made about your competence, abilities, dominance and trust, and it takes seven more times of seeing that person to change the first impression. Who has that kind of time in today's fast-paced world? You want to achieve pinnacles of success, now.

Have you defined your image and your brand? Your image is what you project and how it is being perceived by others, that first impression you make. While your mind is brilliant, your look needs to match that. Too often people think that being great at what they do will get them to the final steps. This is not about feminism, romanticism, sexism or any other ism. This is about POWER, SUCCESS and RESULTS.

There are three things that an image consultant must understand and have a high level of experience. The first one is understanding strategic objectives, short and long-term goals and the image that a business wants to reflect. What message is the professional sending to the clients, colleagues and the community about your business, who you are and what you stand for? A cohesive message of brand marketing comes into play here. The reason that clients do business is not because of the amazing marketing materials, they do business because they trust you, your image needs to reflect this.

The second level of expertise comes from thorough knowledge about fashion and style. These are two very different things that intertwine. An image consultant understands fashion from the standpoint of keeping their client updated and modern. Style is about realizing what the client is comfortable in while upping the ante with the fashion component, creating self-confidence.

Lastly, an image consultant needs to understand the lifestyle of a busy executive. This includes their professional life with high impact meetings, casual Friday and all other places that business is done, including on the weekend, at events, dinners, cocktail/black tie events. An image consultant knows the time constraints both professionally and personally of the executive. The focus of the image consultant is on the functions of their client's lifestyle to pull together the looks for the executive and all components of their life.

When you work so hard to pull together business plans, strategies, presentations, products, and marketing, remember how equally important your appearance is in determining your abilities. Your confidence radiates outward and others respond to this, you can make a first impression last with one that says power, success and results.

Be Open to Criticism

What worked for me may not work best for you, that is why I truly recommend relying on a few key others to provide guidance and feedback for you. Think about how a company chooses to market a new product. They compile a focus group. The company does this for many reasons: to gauge the product, packaging, branding, appearance, and many other things. Why shouldn't you do the same thing? You should prepare yourself to go to market. Assemble your own focus group to find out how people are perceiving you. An image that you are trying to project may not be seen by other people for any number of reasons. Be sure to enlist a diverse selection of people for your internal focus group, this will help maximize exposure. We can only see the world through our own eyes. How other people see us can be very different from how we see ourselves.

Please keep an open mind. Not everyone will agree with you or your sense of fashion and style. Criticism is a necessary thing, as long as it's constructive. I encountered many people who would never understand me, but I can still listen to their opinion. It was my chance to hear what others think, and that in its own right not a bad thing. Think about this as a mentoring relationship, where it's access to an open dialogue between both of you. You need to make sure that you are building this strategic relationship like that with your adviser. An adviser is there to offer suggestions about areas that could use changes or improvements. Whether or not you take that criticism and change is up to you, but it's good to be aware of what people are thinking and saying.

It can be disheartening to hear criticism about your personal style, what you are wearing, or what you are doing. Keep in mind, if the criticism is constructive it can be helpful. For example, if someone approaches you and says, "Hey, I noticed this about what you were wearing and I think you might be better suited with this instead.", they have enough trust with you to voice their opinion and let you know what they think. This is a teaching moment where you may want to follow their advice and change a part of your style. Especially when you are trying to adjust your style, it can be easy to just throw your hands up and say, "well this didn't work", and go back to what you were doing before. Making any change in your life is hard, even changing your style. It may take time to fully develop your own sense of self, so don't give up upon receiving criticism, but focus on the fact that you are growing, and it will take time.

With that in mind, I also want to say, choose your guidance people carefully. I recommend someone who knows you very well, and someone who may not know you as well. This will give you someone who truly understands what is important to you, your goals, and most importantly your style history. Then, the other person could be someone whose style you like or aspire to have. They could also be an expert in a style field. This person would be someone who knows, for example, the work that you've done, but may not necessarily know your entire background and history. I recommend at least two people to guide you here, but you are welcome to ask more people.

People's Perception of Your Attitude and Diversity

Keep in mind that your attitude is also always on display, especially for diverse minorities. The more marginalized, intersectional identities you have, the higher the intensity is for you. We are under a microscope. People are always watching and waiting for us to slip up and make a mistake. The last thing that I want to be known as is the angry, militant trans woman. There are stereotypes for virtually every diverse person having strong emotions. The angry black man stereotype, women being considered "hormonal" the minute they have any reaction to anything, or Hispanic people being considered too loud. These stereotypes are hurtful and wrong on so many levels.

Perception comes into play here exponentially. It may not be reality, but others will perceive and assume many things about you just by looking at you, your style, your attitude, and your appearance. You are who you are. I would never change who I am for someone else, but as it relates to the other components, they each depend on the situation. Yes, I may change what I wear and how I act around certain people, but I make sure to stay true to myself and who I am. I don't become a completely different person when I enter a conference room vs when I'm at an event with executive leaders of an organization. I may code-switch and focus on different aspects of either myself or my community when talking and educating people, I may change some parts of how I dress depending on where I'm going, but at the core of it, I'm still presenting myself authentically. It may be different shades of me, but it's still me.

It's a fine line to walk on here. Being authentic and true to yourself, while trying to adapt to the situations that you are in each moment. What I've learned is to be as authentic as possible and try to have allies close by. They are the people who can, and will, back you up when you need it. If someone feels that you are being too authentic, if they have an unconscious or conscious bias about you, allies are there to help support you and reaffirm what you are saying and who you are. Allies are also the people who you can turn to ask how they perceive your attitude. This mentoring is very crucial. This is why I ultimately recommend the focus group style. They can give you honest feedback when you are ready to meet that interviewer for the first time, or are talking with a high level executive trying to pitch an idea.

In many cases, I've let my results speak for themselves. People may have had a bias against me, but they couldn't deny that the work that I was doing, both on the clock and off, was bringing more business to the organization. That coupled with the mentors I had access to who could vouch for me. What I brought to the table made the difference in me getting noticed and people having a positive impression of me before I even met them. Once we did meet, they already knew me to an extent, and I capitalized on that by making sure that before even speaking a word, they saw a confident leader looking to make a difference. All of these combined are actions that you should be taking that will help you fast track your career and get you to where you want to be in your journey. Don't be afraid to speak up and share your voice. You know who you are and nobody can take that away from you. This is why your attitude is so important. It connects your resume, attire, and style to what you are seeking to communicate. Use all of these tools to increase your influence towards others.

Changing Perspectives

Perspective is in the Eye of the Beholder

While you may look up people's information and background before meeting them, there are very few times others will look up your bio or background. Outside of someone who's potentially hiring you, the first impression that you make is how they will remember you going forward. Once you've made that first impression, you have to decide whether it will be worth the investment to educate them on your perspective. People only know what you tell them, which goes to the core of why communication is so important. They don't know your background, your history, what you've done, or what you've gone through. They see you through their own perspective and from that, they form their first impression of you.

The perspective that people have of you is based on many things that you cannot control in the moment, the majority of those things are processed unconsciously. You can't control how someone's perspective has been shaped throughout their life before meeting you. The biases a person may have when entering a conversation is something you can't control. You are, however, able to control the first impression you make based on your appearance, this is why appearance awareness is so important.

We all walk through the world with our own perspectives on how we see different situations, people, organizations, movements, and even our careers. The way we interact with these things are dependent on the perspectives that we have. Thankfully, perspectives can and do change. The way we view the world can change in a moment's notice. We grow and learn by understanding the perspectives of others, their lived experiences, their stories, and the lessons that people have to share. All it takes is one person's advice, or one person's story, to shift the trajectory of our career and lives onto a completely different path.

Think about the way you currently view your career; the people that you've met, and the experiences you have had. These have led you to the current point you are at, and how you view your career trajectory. I'm here to tell you that you need to keep expanding your perspective. Force yourself to go outside your comfort zone. This needs to happen for you to see things through a different lens. It is by no means easy to put yourself into something you aren't familiar with, but if you want to make waves in your career, to empower others and yourself, you need to get comfortable with being uncomfortable.

You only know what you know, your lived experiences are exactly that. This is at the central core of why being able to seek out other experiences and perspectives is so important. For example, in order to structure an inclusive virtual meeting that didn't exclude anyone based on ability, I had to research technology communication platforms and how they interact with people who have differing abilities. I had to do my own research and talk to people I knew with differing abilities to get their perspectives; learning about what they need and what I can do to make things more accessible for everyone.

This goes to why I stressed about getting to know other people earlier in this book. Research what you don't know, and have an open mind about another person's point of view. Change your own perspective of what you witness, see, and surround yourself with, and it will have a lasting impact on how you are able to create a more inclusive environment and empower the people around you. Keep in mind that the eye of the beholder is all based on someone who sees and considers, it is their personal opinion.

Diversity of Thought

At the heart of this chapter is a concept referred to as diversity of thought. Diversity of thought means expanding your knowledge about other people by intentionally putting yourself in different communities, listening to other people's stories, and/or doing your own research into different cultures. Through this, you are able to gain some understanding of how a diverse person might see things from their perspective. That doesn't mean that you become an expert on someone else's experiences and can speak for them, rather you are better able to understand the needs and concerns that diverse people have in a given society.

You also have to be ready to meet people that you have never met. Each time this happens to you, it will increase your diversity of thought and your cultural agility. You have to aim for that to happen every day. You can learn a lot from an affinity group that doesn't represent your community, diversity, or even your inner circle of friends. For example, I joined the Asian employee network because it was one of the employee networks that I knew the least about. I started attending their events and learning about their culture.

I was there as an ally, wanting to learn more. I made sure not to bog down the network with constant questions, but rather focused more on listening. I know what it's like to have numerous people ask a barrage of questions about my personal experiences, and it does get exhausting. I soaked up as much knowledge as I could and educated myself on the basics that I was unfamiliar with. When I did ask a question, I kept it focused on how I could help be an ally. I focused on where I could leverage my influence and power to help the people in the network and beyond. From my time spent getting to know the network and the people there, I learned what I could and needed to be doing better, not just for the employee group, but also for the people I was working with. It helped me build relationships with multiple people and taught me more about how to be an inclusive leader.

I encourage each of you to do this process of engaging diversity of thought. Invest in getting to know another community as an ally because that will help increase your diversity of thought. Educating yourself around other people's lived experiences gives you the knowledge of their perspective. This also helps you adapt because you have more cultural agility. Through this, you will be a better advocate with more access and influence. When you help others, they in turn will help you.

Changing Other People's Perspectives

There will be times when you will have to win others over at all cost. That is usually reserved for people who are closest to you, like your family or very close friends. When you are trying to drive meaningful change, this also applies to managers and business leaders. For people in those categories, it's a worthwhile investment. You have to put in the time and help them see a different perspective. One of the things that helped me with this space is all the resources that we have for educating another person. Many of these things did not exist 10 years ago. Think about all of the documentaries, training sessions, educational workshops, and many more tools and resources that exist now. All of those things help drive perspective changes in others. Utilize these tools and resources and it will be a worthwhile strategic investment.

Diversity of thought is an equalizer that exists for many people out there that don't value inclusion work. Often I see white male executives who are threatened by this movement of belonging. I think that together, everyone who is empowering differences should be empowering more privileged people to think about how diversity of thought plays into their day-to-day actions. Many people are averse to change, especially when they aren't able to see that there are problems and areas that need to be improved upon. This is where you need to bring the knowledge that you've learned, and the allies that you've gained, to change their perspective. Again, diversity of thought is not meant to be a way to bypass diversifying a workforce, but to get people, especially those that have more power, to see things from a diverse person's perspective, what the needs and wants are for multiple communities, and what can be done to support them.

Change Your Surroundings

Go where nobody would ever expect to see you. Trust me, this can be very hard. People will give you looks or stares but you need to focus on your goal of why you are there and what you hope to gain. Whether that is putting yourself in a networking event for a specific group of people, a club that several co-workers are a part of, even sporting events. Consider who is going there and what you hope to gain by putting yourself out there. I would look for the most off the wall place for a transgender female banker to go network with other business professionals.

 It was terrifying at first, putting myself in those situations, trying to be a fly on the wall. Not drawing too much attention by being there, but also trying to engage with people where I could. Think about it from my perspective; before I shared openly that I was trans, what was life like for me. I was living a double life, lying to myself and sometimes the people I loved. The perspective that I had was just to try to survive each day.

When I started to live more authentically, it did take a while to build the confidence that I needed in order to feel comfortable in those seemingly awkward situations, but I came to each of them with a goal and a mission. To gain access to the meaningful connections that I needed to move forward in my career. From Mad Men groups to health festivals, you name it, I would check them all out. The more that I

271

went, the more that I realized that I had nothing to lose. We are all people, and in the end I was actually making lasting connections. Once I started to build relationships, I started to feel more confident in myself. As I continued to grow, I realized that I wasn't just surviving anymore, my perspective now is all built around thriving.

Do What's Strategic for Your Career, Put Yourself in the Shoes of People Above You

While you are working to change your perspective externally, you also need to do this internally in an organization. Think where all the white male executives are each day. You need to network with them on their turf. That will require you to hop out of that comfort zone a bit. It may mean going to the private members only club, or the clubhouse of the golf course, for example. However secure an exclusive a club or place may seem, there shouldn't be any place that would be off limits. When it comes to getting into 'invite only' places, they all do events to recruit new members and that is your way in, just be confident. They are not going to ask you to prove income or credit score or anything. Even if you aren't able to break through once, don't give up. Keep putting yourself in those situations and continue to try.

There have been plenty of times that I've tried to put myself in the areas that the executives would be, only to be met with disappointment. There were times that I wasn't able to meet any of them, or if I did, I wasn't able to build a connection. One of those times was when I decided that I needed to put myself on the golf course. I was winning the annual sales awards and I would go on the fun reward trip. We got to choose our fun activity each year. The first year, I chose to do a fun thing, so I went shopping. That was all well and good, and I made sure that this was a moment where I treated myself. The second year I was able to go on another trip, but this time I decided to change my strategy and went to play golf.

Trust me, I felt extremely out of place and way out of my comfort zone. I had not picked up a club on a real good course in years. I tried to prepare in advance so that I could at least pull off the impression that I knew what I was doing. If you are looking to take the same route, you do need to understand some etiquette on the course, so please do some research on this. You don't need to be the best player, there are plenty of people that go out there and have no clue what they are doing, but you do need some base knowledge. My recommendation is to be good at one facet of the game; that can be putting, driving, or chipping. You're going to be paired with three other people, and oftentimes in tournaments, they will be playing the best ball type of match, which means that you play off the person who had the best shot. That will help make golf much easier if you aren't proficient. Just go out and have fun with it, and remember the focus of why you're putting yourself out there.

While on the course you have four hours of direct relationship building with someone, think of these opportunities as an investment. This is your chance to get to know people as you're going to be with them for at least half a day. I was hoping I would get paired with an executive, but when I showed up to the course, I was paired with other bankers and a regional manager. It turns out my plan was a lofty goal. I hadn't realized that the executive leaders typically play with other executives. They work together regularly so it makes sense that they'd be playing together as well. I was disappointed at first, and now I was committed to playing instead of doing what I did last year. Instead of being upset, I decided that I needed to own my decision and have fun playing golf.

This actually led to a great day of talking and networking. I learned a bunch about a co-worker who was a business banker, and I found out that he was inducted into the employee hall of fame the prior year. I was amazed at his accomplishment, and began to think how great it would be if I was inducted into the hall of fame one day. I was grateful for getting to meet the people there, and hadn't even considered that I had planted a seed of opportunity. Three months later, I got a random phone call from the CEO of the company telling me that I was being inducted into the hall of fame that year. I was amazed, shocked, and excited about what this meant for me. It was a dream come true seeing all of my hard work paying off in a big way. It may not have been how I had originally envisioned, but I eventually got to meet all the executives at my induction. There was a reception with the CEO, then lunch in the boardroom with the entire team of chief level officers.

I networked with these contacts and then built a relationship with them. I was able to share my story about how I arrived at that moment, and educate them about what we could be doing better. I came into those conversations fully prepared to make the absolute most out the opportunity that was dropped in my lap. I told them about the importance of having a more diverse workforce, to reach out to more of the LGBTQ+ community, how this would help the organization, and how I was the person who could tie all of this together.

They took in everything that I was saying, and I was tasked with figuring out how this could be put together. About six months later, I put together a business plan for a new role where I would focus on what I do best for the company. This role was then created for me as a pilot program. That role is the Vice President of Diversity and Inclusion. Now I'm one of the executives that is driving change in the financial services organization, and throughout several communities.

The largest "aha" moment happened a few months later when I got a calendar invite to be a part of the organization's hall of fame selection committee. I was very curious about it and I emailed the organizer of the meeting. I found out that the prior years winners make the selections for the current year. The opportunity and realization hit me like a ton of bricks. I started to think about all the people I had networked with. I remembered my business banker friend who was one of the few on the selection committee that was advocating for me. In a roundabout way, that golf outing was absolutely worth it in a way I never could have expected. The strategic access that I received by changing my perspective about a golf outing, made a huge difference.

My takeaway for you is that even if you aren't able to obtain your exact goal in networking, don't discount the opportunities you are able to access. Sometimes the best opportunities in our careers, and even in life, are the ones that we don't expect or plan for. You never know what a new person has to share with you, or what opportunities can come with getting to know someone new. You'll never know unless you change your thinking, put yourself in places you wouldn't think of going, and keep seeking what you don't know.

Step 4

Empowering Actions

Chapter 16

Leadership Adaptation

How Leaders are Made

It's the time to start putting your differences into action to empower others. Lead by example and work to help those around you. All of the lessons that I've learned and have been imparting onto you have been leading up the importance of being a leader. One key element that all 10 empowering actions add up to is leadership. It's one trait that binds all of these actions together. Leaders empower their differences, they don't hide or run away from them. Leaders empower their differences and encourage those around them to do the same. Leaders provide power and authority to amplify other people's voices.

I will say that I didn't wake up one day and all of a sudden become a leader. Leaders aren't born that way. Leaders are sculpted, and crafted through time, experience, and culture, among other things. Becoming a leader is something that will take time and constant work. People often ask me what my keys to leadership are, and the first thing that comes to mind is having to overcome obstacles. The struggles that certain leaders have gone through are what have shaped the person they are today. Of course, not all leaders are going to be put in a fire drill situation. That also doesn't mean that all leaders have had to overcome insurmountable odds to get to where they are, or that that is a

279

prerequisite for being a leader. The way someone handles a pressure-packed situation is going to depend on how well they prepared themselves and the experiences they have had in a leadership role. The best leaders are the ones that are able to guide others and lift them up in their own strife.

My experience as a leader has been crafted over all 40 years of my life. Experiences as a youth watching teachers and community volunteers lead team sports activities, or school fundraisers, has helped shape who I am. Every single experience that I've encountered throughout my time on this earth has been something that I personally thought through. I've either studied or mimicked the actions of the leaders around me. Taking in as much information as I could, and emulating what I had believed was the right thing to do. Basically, I lived through my own experiences and made the choice to take away the best parts of what I witnessed. Taking each item, discussion, and action from others, all led to a form of being mentored.

I saw that work ethic made a huge impact from a leadership point of view. I saw how coaches of team sports encouraged others, and were teaching fundamental principles. As I grew up, I entered the workforce as a young adult and learned from leaders in restaurant management. They taught me principles around customer service, training, and education. I learned from some of my early leaders the importance of punctuality. Being forced to grow up early on as a teen, I started to craft my own leadership style based on all I had experienced in my first seventeen years of my life. Having my first management role when I turned 18, this is when I started to develop my own leadership style.

Adapting to Your Situation

I define my early leadership style as friendly leadership. I say that because the people I was leading were all my friends. When this proved to be incredibly difficult long-term, I had to adapt as a leader. I couldn't be friends with everyone, so I shifted to trying to make myself as available as possible for the people that I couldn't create long-term connections with. This is when I learned that an amazing leader is adaptable. They aren't stuck in their own ivory tower and are always open to trying something new or changing something that isn't working. Not all leadership styles are going to work for every organization, team, or specific individual. That was the biggest thing that I wish I knew more about when I was starting to manage and lead people.

If I was going to keep improving myself, as my position and role changed, I needed to learn what was best for the current situation. Know what the end goal is that you are striving for as a team, and understand that there are always going to be multiple pathways to get you there. In many cases, you're going to have to adapt on the fly depending on the role that you serve, and you may not have all the answers in those moments. That is why I mentioned early on that you should take mentorship from other diverse leaders, but also anyone else that you have access to so that you can increase your education.

Leadership lessons can come from the most unexpected places. So being adaptable can give you an edge to find that unexpected lesson from an unexpected person. When you find these opportunities, jump on them. An example would be having the opportunity to work on a

281

project with a marginalized individual. Use this opportunity to soak up all of their experiences, and their leadership point of view. Understand that it requires huge amounts of leadership skills as a marginalized person to make it in this world. Think about all of the obstacles that are in their way, and the systemic issues that their community faces on a daily basis. They've had to combat these obstacles and adapt to make it in this world. They have a unique perspective on navigating society, and their experiences can enlighten you about what you can be doing better as a leader.

I've learned from people of color about the struggles that they have gone through and how they have risen to certain positions. I've listened to the stories of immigrants and people with differing abilities about what their experiences have been like, and what I can be doing to help improve their quality of life. I've been mentored by people of multiple generations, each teaching me how they've become their own leaders and what they wished they knew when starting out. Each person has taught me lessons that I carry with me, and they have helped to shape me into a better leader.

I also want to highlight that leadership learnings can come from people who are not titled as a leader in an organization. For example, I've spent the better part of 10 years not managing others directly. Just because I'm not a manager of people doesn't mean that I can't be a great resource for others. Be sure to surround yourself with senior leaders, but also individuals that make an impact in your organization or community. Individual contributors display leadership skills that can make you a much better leader. Be adaptable, learn, and have a conversation with these key members of your organization. There is always something to learn from people you've never met, and especially those that are driving change, whether it is a senior manager or someone who is an active member in their community. This was why networking is such a huge part of your goal in empowering differences, giving you the increased access to more leaders with differing opinions and experiences.

Building Up Your Bold Leadership Traits

A common thread between just about any leader is that they carry similar traits. I call these bold leadership traits. These are traits that shine when they are speaking to a crowd, an audience, or even a group of friends. These can include being outspoken in front of people, and being knowledgeable about what they are speaking about. Bold leaders take in feedback or criticism that is given to them, and they are grounded in themselves.

If you've watched anyone who's spoken in front of a crowd, or even led a group of people, they give a commanding presence in a room. They don't hesitate with their words, and their body language is relaxed and confident. Bold leaders like this are unapologetic. They are passionate and confident about what they are saying. They know who they are, who they are talking to, and they want their voices to be heard. Bold leaders have told their stories time and time again. They know how to convey who they are, what they've learned, and what they want to impart onto others through inspirational storytelling and educating. Those are the traits that you can see in big speeches given to hundreds of people, and the traits that I hope to begin to instill in you. These traits are in people in smaller settings as well. Working with a team of people, a leader is someone who usually directs everyone on what they need to be doing, but they are also open to any ideas that their team members have, and they motivate those around them to do their best.

Like I said, I don't think that anyone is born a leader. We all take in our surroundings and our past experiences. The people we meet and what we take in determines how we see the world and ourselves. All of this goes back to building your confidence and knowing who you are. Be unapologetic in who you are, your story, what you have done and what you can do. Also share what you can't do, lean on to others to deliver in ways you are not able. No one knows you better than yourself. Be sure that your authenticity shines in all of your actions. Take inspiration from leaders around you, and take things one step at a time. Wherever you are in terms of being a leader and seeing yourself as one, know that it takes small steps to get to the point that you want to be at. Changes won't happen overnight, but if you work on it every day changes will happen over time.

Other than taking and mimicking the traits of leaders around you and learning from them, the other piece of advice that I can give you in building yourself as a leader is fake it until you make it. I know that may sound silly, but many parts of being a leader come down to mentality. When you feel confident in yourself, you're unafraid to voice your opinion, to call out something, and to lead people. Even if you feel like the least confident person in a room, you have to tell yourself that you are confident, that you are a leader. Telling others what you have to say is more than valuable, it is necessary for them to hear what you have to say. Over time, you start to feel that you aren't faking it; you are it. Making the decision to live authentically, to stop just surviving and start thriving, is by no means an easy choice. Truthfully speaking, it takes courage and strength, and it is terrifying. It was a scary time in my life putting myself forward the way that I did, but I knew that it was necessary and the benefits led me down the career path I'm at now, to the point of sharing this with you. Even if you make a mistake, speak at the wrong point, or come off offhandedly, keep going harder. Learn from where you may have made a mistake and keep pushing yourself to be a better leader.

I do want to make a note that it's okay to feel uncomfortable or not confident. Give yourself permission to feel however you might be feeling. If you have a day when you aren't able to fully show up, that's okay. I want you to be as authentic and true to yourself as you can be, whatever that may look like. You don't have to be speaking to a huge amphitheater filled with people in it to be a bold leader, you can take smaller actions, inspire a team of people, or try to do your part in a community. Whatever being authentic looks like for you, I want you to keep doing it. Building up your bold leadership traits will take time. Take things in stride, or dive right into the deep end, whatever is best for you to push your boundaries and get out of your comfort zone.

Leadership Actions

The foundation of Empowering Differences is built on the 10 empowering actions. The same can be said when it comes to leaders. Many of the leaders that I've met have utilized all 10 of these actions throughout their daily lives. When building up your bold leadership traits, I also want you to incorporate these actions into your style of leadership.

Empower

Empowerment is such a huge factor when determining whether someone is a leader or not. Through the last 10 years I've had leaders who have gone out of their way to empower me. Something as simple as scheduling a meeting and having a conversation to learn more about me was extremely impactful. Conversations like this have led to deeper understanding and future opportunities. When I was still anxious about sharing myself with others, leaders that I knew would encourage me to speak my story. They shared that my voice and my story were something that people needed to hear and that it was worth the time to share with others. Those early encouraging words meant all the difference for me in being confident in myself and in who I was presenting to the world. Those leaders were also the ones who were sharing my name when I wasn't in the room. Once a leader has the opportunity to share your name with others when you're not there, it's a great way of empowering you and showcases them as a true leader. Do the same for those around you. Support and uplift the marginalized people. Even small actions can make the biggest difference in someone's life.

Inspire

Inspiration is one of my most favorite leadership traits. I think about inspirational leaders from my diverse community and how they continue to inspire me to do more every day. Their stories, and their daily commitment to making a difference, are what drive me to take action. For many leaders, including myself, knowing that my story has inspired someone and made a difference in their life is part of what keeps me going; to continue improving and keep sharing more of my journey with more people. I've learned that actions of leadership should always drive inspiration for their team and others. Oftentimes, those who have overcome difficult obstacles are most equipped to teach others how to do the same. Don't forget that inspiration can come in numerous forms. Inspiration can be drawn from current actions you are taking, or from a time you were able to overcome overwhelming obstacles. Inspiring leadership gets people to create change either in their life, another person's life, a community, or on a large scale with laws and policies.

Educate

This goes back to bold leadership traits. I love when a leader takes the time to learn more about my community. Education is such an important leadership trait. A true leader learns about privileges and equity each and every day, whether it is their own or another person's point of view and experience. Anytime I'm faced with something that I don't know a lot about, I take the time to research the topic to learn more. I encourage you to do the same. You can't educate someone about something that you're unfamiliar with. Sometimes a leader also has to fight for others to be educated. You could host training sessions for your team to make sure that everyone understands their privileges. Leaders work to educate others on their own perspective, as well as be there to teach others about topics that they don't understand. Leaders are knowledgeable about a number of things, and they understand the value of educating those around them.

Inclusion

Inclusive leaders are all about creating a welcome environment for others. Cultivating a sense of belonging for everyone on their team, as well as visitors or guests. These leaders also create a safe space for everyone they come in contact with on a daily basis. The concept of a safe space is built by the inclusive environment a leader has cultivated. For me, I want to be around leaders that display inclusion on a daily basis because they are just fun to be around. Inclusive leaders foster an environment that feels welcoming for everyone, and every time I'm around them I learn a lot and have a good time. I can feel the engagement that surrounds an inclusive leader and their team; everyone's voice and opinion matters, and no one is ever left out of a conversation. If someone is feeling left out, a leader will be the one to uplift their voice to be sure that they are heard.

Motivate

Motivation is something that moves us forward, and leaders that highlight this skill make a huge difference in empowering others. Whether someone is feeling down, or has been struggling with something, a leader will motivate them to keep going stronger. They listen to a person's struggles and offer advice to help that person keep moving forward. Seeing leaders that share motivational stories also makes a huge impact. Personally, I get motivated from a leader who leads by example. Motivating others has to be a key tool in every single leader's repertoire. When you see a motivational leader, do your best to soak up what they say. Use their words and experiences to fuel you in moving forward. Have their motivational words and actions stand out for you on a daily basis. Seek out and find these leaders that motivate others, you want to be a part of their circle.

Invest

Investing in diverse communities is a great way to highlight your leadership. Leaders have the direct opportunity to financially, personally, and professionally invest in others. They make sure that they are doing business with others who support diverse communities, small businesses, and organizations that work to create change. Even the seemingly smallest investments into a person, such as listening to their story, may make all the difference. You don't need to have a high standing position or a lot of money in order to invest and make a positive impact in someone's life. Thinking back to when I mentioned time, treasure, and talent, keep that as an investment model for leaders that create environments that uplift diverse people. The time that you invest is invaluable. What you have to share through your investment helps cultivate change. That could be through lessons you learned to share with others or donating resources to drive impact.

Mentor

When you get a chance to witness a leader who constantly mentors others, it will be a huge treat. Learning directly from a leader, and having them impart what they have learned onto you, is an excellent learning opportunity. Make the most of the moment, whether it is a single meeting or a reoccurring mentorship. Remember from previous chapters that mentoring can be a large time commitment for both parties. Be mindful of that commitment when asking someone to be your mentor. This is why you need to come prepared to maximize their chance of agreeing. Keep in mind that this applies to you being a mentor as well. Leaders make sure they take the opportunities to mentor people of multiple communities. Mentoring is one of the ways that we are able to pass on what we know, and what we wish we knew, to people who are in a similar position to where we once were. Much like a generation of people passing the torch to the next, you can be both the person passing on the torch, as well as the one receiving it. Mentoring needs to be key to the leadership style you are crafting if your intention is to impact others.

Influence

Leaders have a degree of influence they are able to use to create change for others. That influence can come from their position at work, status in the community, or with the people that are around them. Regardless of what or who they lead, they make sure that they use their influence to create a more inclusive environment. I think about some of the leaders that I've encountered through my life that utilize their influence, and a majority of them worked to advocate for others. These are the leaders that have power in an organization or a community. It's how they use that influence that defines them as a leader. The way they are able to use their own influence helps set the stage for others to follow in their footsteps. Everyone, regardless of their position, has a degree of influence that they can leverage. The key is understanding how you are able to use your influence, and recognizing when you have more of it.

This all connects to the overarching concept of influential leadership. Influential leaders achieve exceptional results through powerful partnerships with others.

Access

Have you ever heard of an open door policy? Who actually keeps their door open? Not everyone has the policy, but leaders that believe in an open door policy are able to make a much greater impact than those that do not. Open door policy is not a myth. I've had the pleasure of working with leaders who actually practice this policy on a regular basis. I could literally step in their office and be able to ask them anything. It was a huge relief to know that I could physically walk into their office and not have to worry about if I'm overstepping my boundaries with them. I've adopted this into my own practices and I've made sure that people have access to me. If people need me, I make time for them. Whether an open door policy works for you and how you operate, the important thing is to be available to others when you can be. It can be invaluable for other people to know that they have access to you, or that you have a dedicated block of time available for them to ask you anything. Think about who you would love to have more access to and what it would mean for you. Allow people to have access to you, whether that's as a co-worker, a mentor, a manager, and especially a leader. Leaders go out of their way to create an accessible space for all.

Enlighten

Enlightenment is one of the hardest types of traits that a leader can demonstrate. This type of leader gets to the heart and mind of the matter. They work with many of these other empowering actions to turn on a light bulb for someone who does not believe in empowering themselves and others. Educating and storytelling are the two biggest factors when a leader is enlightening someone. They are able to teach people about their diverse background and get people to see things from a different perspective. This is largely done through sharing their story. As I said earlier, storytelling is a way of cultivating allies and getting people to understand a different point of view. It teaches people about what they can do to help empower others and create change. Be sure to enlighten those around as you work to empower them.

Your Own Uniqueness and Being Memorable

What Would You Do? (WWYD)

When you are developing yourself as a leader and showcasing your leadership, people will start to take more notice of you. Being in a leadership role means standing in the spotlight. People that you talk to and meet will be more likely to remember you. Your authenticity should shine as a leader, and you need to be inspiring others to do the same. Empower others so they can also be their authentic selves. Once you've made that first impression, you want to deliver on the follow up with what you say and how you act. This is especially true when you are in the middle of critical conversation with someone. For instance, when you talk with a board member of an organization you are trying to partner with, you need to make sure they walk away from that conversation having had a positive experience.

When it comes to being memorable and making a splash, have a signature move, or like in wrestling, a finishing move; one that's going to really rile up the crowd. You need to have things that people will immediately take away and remember you for. It is always nice to be remembered for your accomplishments, but that's not how the world works sometimes. We live in a, "what have you done for me lately?", society. You want to have something that people see as exclusively you, and yours. Jokingly, I sometimes refer to these as Ashleyisms. Some of the things that I do or say that are unique to me, and part of my identity and my brand. I count these as my family, style, fashion, hair, experiences, voice, and everything else that makes me who I am. Think about what makes you unique. Ask the people close to you what it is about you that stands out and makes the biggest impression when meeting you for the first time? Their answers will give a general sense of what other people are thinking. From there you can fine tune your brand to the image that you want to leave in peoples minds.

As you are putting yourself out there, expanding past your comfort zone, and shining as a leader, I want you to get to the point where others may ask what you would do in a situation. That's when you know that people look to you as a change maker. I also jokingly call this a WWAD (What Would Ashley Do) moment. In all seriousness, it should be something that is fun to highlight. It's your individuality shining every moment of every day and people are taking notice. Getting to a point like this, the people around you view you as an expert who knows exactly what to do in certain situations. They value not only you, but also your unique viewpoint and your take on a problem or question. I think of these moments as a, "I live for this moment" situation. These are the moments where you shine personally but where others see it, or they sense it, which is honestly even way cooler. Keep demonstrating your authenticity and what makes you unique because that uniqueness just might be the thing that drives people to ask, "WWYD?".

Being Remembered vs. Being Memorable

Having these moments happen are a good benchmark in knowing your effort to empower your differences is having a positive impact on the people around you. It's good to have mentors that you can also turn to judge the impact that you are having, much like consulting with someone on how they view you based on your appearance or your delivery. As with many things that can be considered "in your face", or flashy, you have to balance your uniqueness in everything that you do each and every day. The important thing when you are making an impact and building your brand, is to know if you are being memorable, or being remembered. There is a fine line that exists between the two. The difference determines how much of an impact you are leaving on people's minds, and the value of the information you continue to provide.

The dictionary definition of the word remember is: "have in or be able to bring to one's mind an awareness of".[32]

I'm not sure about you, but I certainly don't want someone to just be aware of me, that only got me so far in my career. People were aware of me and the work that I was doing, but they didn't know the person that I was and the value that I brought to the team apart from my assigned job duties. Of course it feels good to have people remember who you are, that's always a nice, warm feeling, but warmth isn't going to quickly land you a promotion. Having people be "aware" of you implies they only know the bare minimum about you. They aren't aware of all that you provide, and unfortunately, you're not going to stand out in an impactful way. You have to start to bring your special sauce to the daily briefing and change the way people think about you. Creating this change, and cultivating a more inclusive environment where people feel empowered to be themselves is your mission here. You need to live outside the world of just being remembered.

The dictionary definition of being memorable: "worth remembering or easily remembered, especially because of being special or unusual".[33]

When you are memorable, you easily come to someone's mind because of that special something that you bring to the table. That can be any number of things that you have, whether it's an important piece of work that you've done, being an educator, or a part of your identity. As I mentioned before, you want to have that special move; something that will move you into the memorable category. This is something that will help you stand out so that when a position opens up, you are the first person who comes to mind for the job. Being memorable will impact the number of eyes that are on you. Take these opportunities and capitalize on them.

I want to make a quick note to say that it's okay to be special or unusual. That's all part of the messaging I've been talking about in this book. Don't be afraid to stand out and let a part of yourself shine. Overall, what I'm suggesting you do in your career is stand out. Make that strong impression on someone's mind. In order to do this you have to be memorable, special, visible, and active. Use your distinct qualities and experiences, alongside all of the 10 empowering actions. Manage your uniqueness in an appropriate way, then be sure to make sure it's memorable.

Authenticity in Action

Being unique and memorable is built into how you need to display your authenticity. I've mentioned quite a lot about how I exhibit my authenticity. This includes being unapologetically trans, out in everything that I do, and very vocal about my identity. My authenticity is linked into how I demonstrate inspiration, and how I motivate myself and others on a constant basis. In a way, being authentic and being yourself unapologetically, is like giving a person permission to do the same; to inspire them to be their own authentic self. Bold leaders I have learned from taught me that I could follow in the same footsteps. I needed to see someone who was authentic and confident in who they are, and who is also successful in the workplace. It opened my eyes and made me realize that I could do the same. That was one of those shifting moments in my life where I went from surviving to thriving.

The other thing that I find important to highlight surrounding my authenticity is how much it leads to enlightening others. I can think about tons of times that I've had conversations with people who tell me that they've never met anyone from the transgender community, and by meeting me, it has led them to open up their eyes and be able to see that we exist in society. It's situations like this that drive change for my community. Knowing just one person from a diverse community can change their perspective about how they see a whole cross-section of people. By being visible and open to educate, there's a level of trust that people have with me where they feel comfortable asking me questions. Your authenticity can create change where you are through enlightenment of others. All it takes is getting to know one person to shift the way they see, not only a group of people, but also their own relations to that community and what they can do to help empower and uplift others.

Creating a Sense of Belonging

As you're building out your branding, and highlighting your authenticity to become more memorable, I also want you to fundamentally understand how belonging is linked to these concepts. The foundation of you empowering others needs to happen in an environment where you feel like you actually belong. Imagine it as like you're part of a family, and this family loves and cares for everyone regardless of their differences. You will have to make sure that the people you surround yourself also understand belonging as a foundational concept. That the people around you value you for who you are and uplift you as much as you uplift them. They see your authentic self and welcome all of you. Though you're going to have to build and work towards the environment that you want to be in, and one that others want to be in as well. This feeling will then begin to lead to the path of belonging.

Everyone that I've ever met has wanted to feel like they belong to something, whether it is a community, a group of friends, or people who share similar interests. Whatever the case may be, they want to feel accepted for who they are. Inclusion is a key ingredient for creating an environment where people feel that they belong. When thinking about helping people feel comfortable in being themselves, and highlighting their authenticity and uniqueness, they need to feel that they are in an inclusive environment.

I sought out to find and surround myself with other inclusive individuals. These individuals made me feel more comfortable, and allowed me to shine. I would never have been able to fully bring my whole self to work without constant access to an inclusive environment, which includes leaders who cultivated a sense of belonging. It may seem silly, but me wanting to wear a really bold necklace, bright color jacket, or high heels, are all things that I would want to do to increase my visibility, and be more memorable. These leaders were also the ones who encouraged me to keep being myself and motivating me to push myself further. If I ever doubted myself in any way, they were there to help give me that extra boost that made all the difference. Surround yourself with inclusive people to drive that feeling of belonging because it is going to be the major support that drives you to be more memorable and unique.

Workplace Culture

All of the items that I've been talking about in this chapter lead to one major item that you want to look for in an organization that you partner with on a daily basis. This major item is culture. You can read a job requisition posting, or you can look on the internet about an organization, but those items aren't going to teach you about the workplace culture and the overall culture of the organization. Individuals in an organization can contribute to a negative culture just by the things that they say or do. Think about the comments on a provocative social media thread. You can quickly shift the culture of a discussion without much work. Cultivating a sense of belonging and an inclusive environment, not just for yourself but also those around you, and being authentic and memorable, culminates in shifting the culture that an organization has.

Know that your individuality is helping to drive that change. You need to be making sure that people feel included and welcome. Educate others where you can, and when you are able to. You can be the catalyst to make sure that others are highlighting their authenticity, as well as working to change the culture of an organization for the better. This is not something that you do by yourself. Having allies and advocates will help you accomplish the larger shifts. Remember that the biggest changes you can see are never done alone. Start small with shifting culture, but think big and strategic. Work to empower one person at a time, and cultivate the environment you want to be in, thus making your own dream job.

Driving culture changes will take time, which means you will need to be in this for the long game. It is something that you are going to need to invest time and energy into, but the end results will be well worth it. The biggest question you need to ask yourself is, how big of an investment are you willing to put into creating that more inclusive culture? Think about your long-term career prospects, and if the organization that you are working for will value and recognize you for the leadership work that you're doing. You want to work for an organization that values the work you are doing now, and the work you will be doing in the future. This work will require you to leverage all of the pieces from this chapter, combined with the 10 empowering actions, to ultimately drive change.

Organizations Empowering Others

Plant the Seeds of Diversity

As an individual, you should be doing all that you can to empower, lead, and create change around you. The many things that you do, can contribute to the culture that surrounds you each and every day. I want you to think about who you are directing your empowering efforts towards. Think on a larger scale about the changes that can happen when you connect with the right person or group of people. I also want you to consider the work that an organization can have in this process. Please understand that I don't want you to ever stop empowering individuals after reading this chapter, but know that organizations can make an impact more quickly and affect more people in a shorter time. An organization is the one that can fund programs, sponsor events, develop leaders, and even influence other organizations to create change. The organizations that you are affiliated with may already be doing some of these actions, but wherever your organization is on their journey, if you want to empower people, you have to empower them so they know what is needed.

For those that might be wondering how you empower an organization, it starts with the people who make up that organization. Keep focusing on individuals, but be smart in who you choose to empower. You will

301

want to make sure that you're empowering and inspiring strategic decision makers in an organization. This will lead to a larger cultural shift, thus impacting people more quickly than you can do alone. I often refer to this as seed planting. You will want to plant seeds with many leaders who have the greater access to make change, or people who have access to those change makers. Individuals who have access to make the change are the ones that ultimately need to be educated, inspired, mentored, and empowered.

Once you know who you should plant seeds in, stay connected with them, your access needs to be constant. Check in with them on a regular basis to make sure that they understand what your diverse community is going through. Make sure they understand the systematic issues that you're facing. For me, this is where I would present the health care challenges that the trans community face, the systematic problems with changing names, and changing gender markers, just to name a few items. Now that you've enlightened them about your community, you have to keep them engaged. Be sure to give positive reinforcement for the impact that they're making. Together, their work with your guidance, mentorship and impact can truly make a difference in how an organization begins to empower those around you and other diverse communities.

Three Goals for Your Organization

Organizational diversity is no longer a taboo topic. It needs to be discussed frequently. Diversity should be on the fore-front continually within Human Resources, especially when considering new candidates. Same for executives when planning the future of the company, and for everyone involved in the hiring process, including department leads as well. Diversity does not just pertain to hiring. Retention and inclusion are just as important. You have to be sure your diverse employees are not being tokenized, and that they have a sense of inclusion and belonging. A corporation's commitment to corporate social responsibility is just the first step in the direction they need to move. This intentional focus on inclusion of individuals who are inherently different needs to be a major focus. This can be done in numerous ways including talent management and how corporations intentionally recruit, retain, and develop talent. These are three things that an organization can do to empower people, and are goals that you should be moving towards in your organization.

Recruiting

Today, many organizations are creating different strategies to attract diverse candidates. For some, it is a goal based on compliance or to keep up with changing times, but for many, it is an understood effort that will increase top talent and create an advantage over competitors. A diverse team gives a distinct advantage in remaining up to date with customers changing needs. Companies who want to be competitive thrive when they attract the best talent. A company wide diversity and inclusion initiative lays the foundation for diverse talent to feel more connected to the organization. Job seekers are being purposeful to make sure a potential employer values diversity and inclusion before accepting a position. Having a solid base will attract more diverse talent, but there also must be intention to diversify the workforce, making sure no one is overlooked in the hiring process.

The first step to a complete internal change, or amping up your diverse hiring and recruiting efforts, is to have clear policies and procedures set in place, as well as a long-term vision for the organization. To change your recruiting efforts, you must first understand the culture and what diverse communities think about your organization. The organization needs to be aware of unconscious biases, with a plan to assess candidates appropriately for the current and future goals of the organization. Take a look at the statistics of other companies that are in the same line of business. What are they doing, and what could be implemented in your organization that would have a lasting impact? It's easier for change to be implemented when there is a reference to how it was done before, with results to show afterwards. This will mean seeking information, either from online sources, or meeting other people in your field. Be mentored and educated by those who have done this work. Have them show you what you can do, or how you can influence those above you to create the lasting change that will benefit the organization.

With a plan of action in place, an organization will need to make sure that the people who are hiring have been trained. They aren't excluding people based on any biases that they have or looking over people who have the work experience and potential but are overshadowed because of their background. One very common requirement to consider is an advanced degree. There are positions in many fields that require extra school or training. However, there are many more positions that do not, and requiring higher education can be stifling your diverse recruiting efforts. Especially since numerous minority communities have less access to higher education. This same logic can be applied to having a certain number of years in the field; you will be excluding some candidates that may have great potential who are newly out of school, switching careers, or returning to work. This is why I emphasize the importance of your organization having training, or even having a diversity consultant come in and conduct an assessment. They will look at the policies in place, the culture and environment that people are working in, and give their recommendations on areas to improve. It's always good to have multiple diverse people to look into the policies and practices to make sure that they are inclusive.

Another piece to this is intentionally partnering with diverse organizations to grow your company's recruiting platform. Realistically though, not every company is going to have a limitless budget to recruit from every single diverse organization in your area, but at least be intentional in rotating through numerous diverse recruiting events. This should allow the opportunity to continuously recruit from multiple diverse pools. Also, partner with these organizations in a high-level way. That should include people from your organization volunteering, and serving on their board, or on committees. These are great ways for your organization to get exposure in these diverse communities. An organization should be empowering their employees to be involved, and should make it part of their job deliverables. Recruiting should be owned by all people within the organization, not just the lead recruiter or the human resources professional. An organization has to have the buy-in of all employees to make a full scale impact.

Retention

Once your organization has more diverse talent on board, now it's important to make sure they don't leave. There are many other organizations who are constantly trying to recruit the good people, who may already have jobs. Your company isn't going to be the only one that recognizes the value and importance of having some of these people on their team. They may get offers with another organization, or be talking with another person to learn how differently they treat their employees. You want to also consider what your company is doing for its employees to make sure that they retain them. What the organization as a whole stands for, and how much it is giving back to local, diverse communities, are huge incentives to retaining the diverse talent that your organization has been working so hard to recruit.

Think about what kind of programs you have in place to excite your diverse employees. Not every organization will have a budget to have a Diversity and Inclusion Officer, but your executive leaders should all serve in a capacity partnering with the diversity and inclusion program. If one is already established, then that's great, look into what they are already doing and what more that they could be doing by researching into other organizations. If there isn't an inclusion program established, you can be the one to lay the foundation and present it to your organization. You don't have to go through it alone, talk to your allies and advocates about coming together, and address the importance of having a diversity and inclusion program. Any size company can have a diversity and inclusion program, it's not just for big companies. Smaller organizations can still make big changes through having purposeful engagement. Open up a dialog with diverse groups of people in your organization to find out what they need. Leverage the connections that you make and stress the importance of having this program with the change makers of your organization.

Employee affinity groups are a major benefit in how you empower your employees to celebrate who they are and to feel included at work. These groups can cultivate a sense of belonging in your organization. The budget that is put forth for these programs matters. Understand that each dollar that is being put forth should be returning an investment due to the natural retention happening within those groups. Smaller organizations can benefit by teaming diverse people together. Creating culturally diverse groups, where different cultures are working together to highlight inclusion in your organization, is a great way to empower people. Having affinity groups represented in the talent recruitment process is a great way to coordinate and provide current employees more engagement. Employees typically join an affinity group to get more resources for their time in an organization. By engaging these employees across your organization's efforts for inclusion, the byproduct is then increasing the time they spend in your organization. Retention should be an amazing key benefit of creating affinity groups.

Another key element of an employee affinity group is to make sure that they are rewarding the employees who help run these programs. This doesn't mean that they need to pay them to run the program, it means that they need to be getting some benefit to support their increased engagement in your organization. Benefits can range from getting to attend one of those talent focused conferences, attending other diverse conferences within their intersectionality to give your organization more exposure, or visibility and recognition on the organizational social media channels. These are just a few examples, but there needs to be something to show that the employees who are volunteering are valued and that they aren't doing this for just a pat on the back and a gold star, but rather for an enhanced employee experience.

Development

Developing diverse talent should be a key component of your organization. Specific development programs to empower diverse individuals need to exist in your organization to really make a difference. Mentoring programs can be a huge key to how you accomplish your development goals for diverse employees. Pass on key information and be sure that the diverse people who are working for your organization have the tools that they need to be successful in their roles and as leaders in their fields. Mentoring programs need to be linked within all of your other diversity and inclusion efforts. These programs can also help diverse people with getting sponsored and recognized by the higher executives within your organization, leading to more visibility and helping them further their career.

It's also important that everyone has equal access to all of the programs that an organization is offering, and that they are aware that these programs exist. Having access also means making sure that the meeting days aren't on a religious holiday or that there aren't physical obstacles that bar people with disabilities from participating. The program needs to have the input of those that it is designed for so that no one is excluded from the program because of a part of their identity.

Developing talent can also extend beyond programs that your organization is hosting. Part of my development as a leader was through key initiatives including having an image consultant, media training, being on the corporate advisory council for the National LGBT Chamber of Commerce, even speaking and sharing my story at multiple events which all helped to develop the person that I am today.

There are opportunities that will exist outside of your organization that can bolster your skills as a leader. They can come from a nonprofit that you're volunteering in, a civic organization, or a chamber of commerce. I want you to be a part of and join as many as you are able to because each of these are opportunities to grow.

A large part of being aware of opportunities is up to you, and you have to seize them anyway you can. Organizations can also do their own part in making these aware to their employees, especially if your organization doesn't have the financial capacity to host their own training and programs. They can make employees aware of opportunities they never would have known about. Whether that is checking in with specific employees about opportunities or letting the people in your organization know in a blanket way via emails. At the core of being aware of these opportunities is being engaged with a community and their organizations. Know what's happening and then relay the information. Influence the change makers in your organization about the importance of making sure that more people are aware that these opportunities exist and motivate diverse people to seize them.

Supplier Diversity

Outside of your organization focusing on empowering its employees, it also has the opportunity to diversify who they are doing business with including marginalized and underrepresented businesses. This is what's called, supplier diversity; it is a proactive approach to support these diverse owned businesses. Supplier diversity is one of my most favorite discussion topics. I may be a "homer" on this one, since I used to run a regional supplier diversity advocacy organization. My close to five years running the local LGBTQ+ Chamber of Commerce in my city was immensely rewarding, but even more rewarding for the members was the fact that our chamber, just like the other LGBTQ+ chambers, operates with a supplier diversity focus. Businesses that are 51% owned, operated, and controlled by a diverse person can potentially qualify for a supplier diversity certification. Each certifying body may require slightly different criteria. In the case of my local chamber, membership covers the cost for certification through the NGLCC-National LGBT Chamber of Commerce. The cool thing here is that by purchasing this book you are contributing to economically empower a trans owned business, since my business is a certified LGBTBE (LGBT Business Enterprise, a certification from the NGLCC).

The foundation of supplier diversity is deeply connected to every single one of the 10 empowering actions. Organizations have an opportunity to showcase supplier diversity in all of their efforts, which can lead to economic equality which could include creating mandates on making sure there is a diverse supplier who has access to bid on every contracting opportunity, or creating an inclusive registration process where everyone is welcome to apply. Creating goals on diverse spending for your organization should also be in their foundation. There are many opportunities to empower diverse owned businesses, these examples are just a few. The organizations that make investments in a supplier diversity program are ones that are truly working to empower others.

Organizations also have an opportunity to work closely with a diverse supplier network. Investments in these types of community partnerships can have numerous positive impacts on the diverse supplier businesses. This can include educational sessions on the various topics that an organization is knowledgeable about. Giving a diverse owned business an opportunity to learn from a major organization can be extremely impactful. This also ties directly to mentoring as well. Having some representatives from an organization host training sessions for smaller businesses and business leaders about what they can be doing to grow their businesses. Hopefully, an organization that you are tied to can participate in mentoring diverse owned businesses.

Organizations have constant opportunities to invest in their community driven actions. Partnering with supplier diversity advocacy organizations is a great opportunity to invest in diverse owned businesses, which will grow a community. These can be national level organizations like the National Minority Supplier Development Council[34], the Women's Business Enterprise National Council[35], or National LGBT Chamber of Commerce.

It can be exciting when a company creates an educational program to impact diverse communities without having to recreate the wheel. It can just be as simple as sponsoring their regional supplier diversity advocacy organization. These organizations are constantly making investments to economically empower their diverse owned constituent businesses. Many of these advocacy organizations have access to programming that includes empowerment, education, and mentoring programs. I've personally taken part in inspirational programming through one of these advocacy organizations. I have also benefited from a leader of one of the advocacy organizations who went out of their way to influence an organization to hire my company for a speaking engagement. Constant investments in economically empowering diverse owned businesses can be incredibly impactful for your community.

Another opportunity around investing in diverse communities is through general community driven partnerships. Supplier diversity is part of that, but there are many other community organizations that exist in all areas where people live. As part of my diverse community, I immediately think about LGBTQ+ Community Centers as a great way to connect and develop my diverse community. Personally, that's where I went for resources when I was struggling and those resources were key in helping me get my feet on the ground to move forward. The list of non-profit organizations that support a geographical community is usually pretty big, depending on where you live. Think about earlier in the book when I asked you to research your community, you should get to know all of the organizations that are key in supporting diverse communities where you live. Follow the steps that I'm outlining here to build the relationship with the leaders in your organization who have the ability to make investments which will create change for your community. You will need to continue to influence them to maximize their efforts to truly make an impact.

Two Pronged Sponsorship

This should be a two-way focus for organizations. Make financial investments in community organizations that you're partnering with constantly. For example, if I'm on the board of the local homeless shelter, my organization could be investing in the homeless shelter to support my efforts. Sponsorship should be a process that exists through a request system, and all of your teams should know the process for this. The system could be where either a person, or a group of people, put forth a request or a proposal about who they want to sponsor, for how much, how long, and outline the lasting benefits of sponsorship. Your organization's teams should know how to structure their sponsorship request, including important information about the organization, and the impact and the effect it is going to have on the organization and the community. The key information here is the return on investment. Be sure to include that information as it will lead to more empowerment faster.

Other ways sponsorship needs to show in your organization is through your development programs. If none of your senior leaders are promoting the names of diverse individuals when they're not present, then you won't have truly diverse succession plans in place. Succession planning and diversity should be owned by your senior leaders and executives to intentionally include, mention, and openly discuss career trajectory for your employees, but especially your diverse employees. Many organizations I have interacted with create a mandate on these senior leaders to empower others, and this leads to more access for those diverse groups. Within some organizations this might be senior leaders influencing an affinity group, employees, or mentoring. I want you to think about taking this a step further because forced mentoring, or sponsoring is not going to end well. These senior leaders need to want to empower others who are diverse which will make the biggest impact. Remember the importance of educating the influential leader that you have access to, which is going to drive the engagement for these senior leaders.

You want your organization to reach the point where it's truly walking the walk by building engagement in the community, and investing internally with diverse talent development. Whatever you do from that moment, don't stop there! Use your individuality, and your authenticity, to continue to influence the strategic leaders that you have access to because there is much more work to be done. If your organization gets a perfect 100 score on the human rights campaign corporate equality index, that doesn't mean there aren't ways to improve. To use an example, even if your organization has a perfect score, there is likely much more work to do in the area of corporate LGBTQ+ equality. Your organization can work to advocate for them to sponsor the equality act, or advocate for more organizations to follow the same path and drive them to also make a more inclusive environment. There is always more work that needs to be done and your organization can be the one who sets the trend for others to follow suit. Empowering those around you starts on a small scale, but continuing to do so can change the culture and direction of an organization to move towards empowering others and creating social change.

Continuous Innovation

<u>Change Requires Innovation</u>

The last point that I mentioned in the ground rules is that you want to repeat the process that I outlined. Keep learning and empowering yourself and those around you. Each day we continue to grow as people, both in our fields, and as leaders. We need to be adaptable to whatever the situation calls for and how the times change. You have to keep innovating and reinventing yourself over and over again. Remember how I mentioned the importance of being memorable? Innovation is a key way that you can continue to do this, but take it even further. Don't be afraid to bring up your ideas, even if they seem off the wall to other people. The way things are done may be working, but there may be a target that either you, someone else, or even an organization is missing. Change and innovation don't have to mean reinventing the wheel. They can also mean building on what is already there and making it better.

Think about how a millennial, who's just getting into the industry, might offer fresh, new ideas to how an organization could be marketing. They could come into the organization with new ideas of expanding their marketing efforts to include more types of social media to attract the millennial market that the organization has been missing.

315

Sometimes it takes a fresh perspective, self reflection, making a mistake, or research to drive ourselves to innovate. It's important to take in these sources and soak up what we can. This is not just for people, but also important for organizations. Keeping up with changing times means continuing to recognize where you are, and what you can be doing better, or what you need/want to learn more about. One of the key takeaways that has been at the heart of this book is to be adaptable and open to change, the way you think, act, and see the world, which will then change how others view you.

Brand Leadership

I want you to have the most amazing career possible. Knowing that sometimes workplaces can be very hard to break through as a diverse individual, I want you to see the value you bring value to any business that you come in contact with. Part of breaking through, to get people to view the value that you bring, is by having your own brand and continuing to innovate and evolve that brand. Your brand is defined by who you are, what you do, how you present yourself, and what you stand for and believe. Defining your brand is critical. Your brand allows people quick and easy access to get to know you. As a leader in your field, your brand is something you're already showing off each and every day. How people perceive you and how you present yourself to the world, through your actions and appearance is all a part of your branding identity.

Your brand is essentially an extension and representation of who you are, what you bring to the table, and what makes you unique. How far you choose to showcase your brand is dependent upon you. Whether you want to stick to social media branding, or connecting with others directly, it will make those connections more memorable because of your brand. You also can take things a step further and use the skills that you have to start your own business. An important factor is for you to differentiate yourself from the rest, that is how to rise up quickly in an organization. Think about the unique perspective you have to offer that no one else has, and how your perspective can enlighten others. Whichever direction you decide to take your brand, I want you to have a clear mindset of what your brand is, and what you want it to be in the future. Keep in mind that both of these might change with time and that's okay. Start with a solid baseline for now, but be open to the possibility that things can change. Take measure of what your end goal is in this mission of empowering differences, as it will impact your strategic decisions you make along the way.

I'll use my business as an example. I branded myself as a public speaker, motivational speaker, and an inclusion and leadership training expert. Upon doing competitive landscape analysis, all of those things separately exist within many speaker and training companies. Then I researched and saw that there are also plenty of transgender people who are speakers or trainers. What I didn't see were people from my diverse community that were motivational speakers who are able to encapsulate my unique career experience and journey. No one had a story like mine, or shared the exact same experiences that I have gone through. That was the line that I knew I needed to build on; the piece that would separate me from others.

From the point that I had a baseline about what my brand and business were, then through the years they have continued to evolve. I wanted to focus on empowering others to follow in similar footsteps to my own, but it has grown to include speaking on various issues surrounding multiple diverse communities including what people can do to help drive change and support the people around them. What started as a motivational story also grew to address systemic issues and hurdles that needed to be addressed to create a more inclusive and accessible environment for everyone.

This was made possible by the relationships that I had built through networking, the advice that was given to me by mentors and sponsors, as well as what I had taken away from listening to other motivational speakers from multiple backgrounds. I took in all of this information and added it like a building block to my own brand and business. All of their enlightenment has helped me become a better leader, speaker, and businesswoman. Utilize the relationships that you have, take in all of the knowledge that other people have to offer; listen to their perspectives and be open to changing how you operate. It can lead you down a path of great opportunities that you never would have seen or realized beforehand. I also want you to do this for those around you as well. Help cultivate someone's brand by offering them advice, teaching them something that they could use, or offer constructive criticism. For the amount of advice and guidance that you receive, you should be doing what you can to do the same for someone else who needs it. Be a mentor for someone else and then pass down what you know. You never know when that investment will come back to help you in the long run.

Business Certifications

Another lesson that I've learned while innovating is diverse business certifications. These are intended if you are running your own diverse business, or a part of an organization that is largely made up of diverse people. While the focus for this is on business, and you may or may not be a part of a diversely operated business, keep these in mind for future consideration. Your career path may lead to you starting a sole proprietorship, single member LLC, or an S-Corporation on the side where you take your skills outside the organization you're working. You may also meet business leaders that had no idea that there was such a thing as a diverse business certification and would be immensely grateful for the information. You might be partnering with a diverse business, or working for a diversely run organization that could grow and reach new audiences with these certifications. Even if you feel this may not apply to you at the current moment please keep these in mind as it can be great information to leverage empowerment of others.

As I mentioned in the last chapter on supplier diversity, this would be the diverse owned and/or run business lens side of this program. An example of this is, before I got my business certified as a diverse supplier, I would talk to organizations and ask if they would ever think about bringing me in to talk to their employees. Every once in a while I would gain their attention. I would get an introduction to their women's, or LGBTQ+ affinity groups, and then go from there about what I talk about and what I bring to the table. After gaining my diverse business certification, in those similar conversations I would say that I count towards their diverse spending goals if they make an introduction and bring me in for a training or speaking engagement. The change that

319

I've experienced has been night and day. Roughly 90% of the companies that I talk to now are more than eager to introduce me to someone who I can talk to discuss the details of having me speak. Once that initial connection has been made, I'm much more likely to be brought in to speak about my experiences and/or educate people on the importance of highlighting their diversity.

When I think about diverse business certification, and why someone would want to get their business certified, I sum this up in two main reasons for the certification. Reason one is you want to sell more goods, services, or products to more people. This reason usually suffices for most business entity types out there in society. Some businesses are going to be more sourceable than others. By sourceable, I mean the level at which a business can sell and mass produce more items, products, or have higher in demand services from larger organizations. Some examples of extremely sourceable businesses might be construction and related industries, or products that are needed by mass amounts of people in society. For me, I'm just one person, but a consulting agency that has five or more consultants is able to reach more of a wider audience and sell themselves to more entities.

The other reason that someone would get their business certified as a diverse supplier goes a little more to the empowerment side of the equation. Being counted economically as a diverse business is incredibly important, as strength is typically found in numbers. This can never be understated. Having the ability to have your business count economically is the key to economic parity for your diverse community. A couple of years ago I found out that there were only 26 businesses in the entire United States that were transgender or non-binary owned businesses. I knew the number was going to be low, but being that low scared me, and it made me wonder why my own community wasn't being counted. I knew in that moment, personally, I could count more than a hundred people from my community that owned a business. I talked to a mentor of mine who I mentioned earlier in the book, Justin Nelson, and together we worked with the team at NGLCC to create the Trans and Gender Non-Conforming Inclusion Task Force. This task force served as a focal point to getting the word out around diverse business certification for my community. I've been proud to co-chair this task force alongside a great friend, Sabrina Kent. In less than a year and a half, we were able to increase the number of certified businesses, including pending certification, by more than 400%. The effect of this was our way to make sure that the community was being counted economically. Empowering your business can't be done without being counted economically. Everyone wants to sell more good services and products, but true change happens when we empower others and show them there's a key to their economic future.

There are lots of options to certifying your diverse owned business. Many municipalities certify women, and minority businesses, and those certifications usually are not too expensive. My recommendation would be to engage with the regional affiliate of one of those national certifying organizations for diverse suppliers. These national organizations are NGLCC, Women's Business Enterprise National Council, United States Hispanic Chamber of Commerce[36], Disability:IN[37], and the National Veteran Owned Business Association[38], to name a few. These organizations provide valuable resources that you need to leverage for your business or organization.

There are national organizations for almost every diverse community that you can research and then gain certification.

Maximize Connections with Regional and National Organizations

Regardless of where you are in your career and what position you have, utilize the opportunities and access to programs, training, and lessons that these national level organizations have, as well as those on a more local level. These are opportunities for you to continue to learn and develop yourself further on your career journey, so take advantage when you come across them. Mentoring programs exist within these organizations, and the mentors that participate are usually the exact people that you would hope to meet in the procurement teams of the major organizations that support those national non-profits. The mentoring programs run by these organizations are top-notch, and supply you with information and resources to help you grow in your field. Also consider serving as a mentor to a diverse owned business as you can provide great resources, and in return you're also building your network.

Another benefit that comes from partnering with these organizations is from a diverse owned business perspective. As a diverse supplier, the advocacy work that they're doing on your behalf is immensely helpful and can get some businesses started. I got a chance to volunteer closely during some of those advocacy outreach efforts, and I can tell you that the collective power when diverse organizations are supporting one another is limitless. Matchmaking is unbelievably good for your business. The first time I was able to attend a matchmaking session I was super nervous. Here I was, an extreme minority, getting the opportunity to talk about my business with a buyer from a major organization. The matchmaking helped to change my outlook on my diverse business and it helped to empower me to do more and to highlight what I actually bring to the conversation. In a little more than a year of having my business registered as a diverse supplier with NGLCC, I have been able to have conversations with more than fifty organizations that I may never have had a chance to speak with in that setting. When organizations provide an opportunity to support businesses, that's all a person needs. That opportunity can give someone who is ready to take the next step and grow as a leader in their field, career, and business, a chance to compete, an opportunity to empower, and to innovate their business.

Business to business opportunities are plentiful within diverse organizations like the ones I've mentioned. I've had the opportunity to collaborate with five other LGBT certified businesses that I have met through NGLCC. They have each provided me with business opportunities that I would've never had, and they've also helped me establish myself as a business owner within the community. Through partnership, I've been able to gain credibility from long-established organizations and businesses, as well as getting my name out there within different social circles. Partnership and advocacy work is something that I continue to do for other businesses. Other certified diverse supplier businesses have huge incentives from the national organization to partner with other diverse suppliers. We all work collectively together to help one another establish ourselves and grow. However, partnership is only as strong as what you put into it, you have to be purposeful to go out of your way and make sure that you're partnering with organizations that have diverse business owners and that share your value system, motivation, and your personal belief structure.

What Have You Done for Me Lately?

What have you done for me lately? When was the last time you asked yourself that question? Has a supervisor ever asked you that question? They could be thinking that question currently about you. The point of that question is in the eyes of many people: managers, executives, and community partners, you are only as good as your latest, greatest, and best idea that you provided. Your manager has you on the team because of all the things that you bring to the table. Bringing a great idea that helps the organization is going to get you recognition for the work that you've done, but you have to continue to capitalize on this. The same can be said for work you do outside of your organization. The influence that you have is based on what you've done in the past, but it is due in large part to what you've accomplished more recently. If you got your organization to sponsor a local community event, that's great, but it loses some of the impact that it had when that event was five years ago. Part of innovating yourself is making sure that you are continually pursuing new ideas and goals in your work.

Continuing to capitalize on the work that you have done is thinking about your sales strategy. Whether you work in a sales capacity or not, you should be continually trying to market either yourself or your organization to other people. Continue to build connections that you will use professionally. This goes back to engaging strategically and leveraging your communication. These are two crucial pieces that you need in order to put together your pitch when you are networking with other people about why they should partner, invest, or do business with yourself or your organization.

When I was sharing my journey through the financial services organization, I spoke at great length about how I was able to highlight my results, think outside the box, and build relationships with my own diverse community. Highlighting the numbers behind it, that was my innovation. I continued to drive more people and business to the organization, and because I continued to bring more business, it was seen as more than a one-time thing. It became something that was soon expected of me. It was always recognized, but once it was established as a part of my brand and what I bring to the table, I had to think about who else I could bring and what more I could do to continue to innovate myself. That's what led me to creating the business plan for the organization. It was the next step in my own personal innovation that no one expected, but it allowed me to move forward in my career. Teaching others to do what I was doing on a localized level across the organization was the kind of innovation that was going to drive real change and results.

It was an ambitious goal that I created for myself, and I still wanted to go further in my field and as a business leader. My mentality and goals were once just to scrape by; the only goal I had was being sure my rent was paid and having the lights stay on. That has now evolved into doing everything I can to make sure that I am thriving and that I am doing everything I can to give back to my community and those who have helped me through my journey. This is part of what I want you to take away: don't ever settle or be comfortable with where you are in an organization. Continue to strive for more, set those ambitious career goals and go for it! Always take a moment to think about what you can be doing and how you are able to meet the goals you have in mind. If you are a member of a diverse community, then you have to have that chip on your shoulder to keep fighting for more. If you're an ally, then you have to work twice as hard to empower others, lifting up their voices. Wherever you are on the diversity spectrum, keep being a champion for others, motivating them to strive for more, and serving as an inspirational model for what they can accomplish. Set an example and keep empowering those around you to create a continuous model of engagement.

Takeaways & Actions

Keep Growing and Let the Numbers Amplify Your Voice

Work to empower your differences each and every day. Utilize the strategies that you come up with on how you want to highlight yourself and work with what is best for you. Take the lessons that I've shared with you and adapt them to your own unique self. Only you know what will work best for you, but you need to try different things. Even if you fail, if you make a mistake, or realize that something isn't right, then take a step back and process what happened. Realize where you can make a change or improve, and then make it happen. Experiment with all the ways that you present yourself to the world, and remember that it's okay to mess up or try something new, the important thing is that you are making a conscious effort to push yourself to where you want to be.

Take ownership of your career, within each and every moment. This is how I want you to move forward to take action. Keep talking about what makes you who you are and especially, use data to highlight and drive your successes. Keep track of your wins, anything relating to your successes. Leaders need access to this data. Anything that has a number attached to it, should be something you keep track of to empower yourself and others. This can be many including the number of sales that you've made, the number of leaders that you've connected with, and the number of engagements on a social media post that you made. Keep track of all of these numbers, including results from others on your team.

Remember that keeping metrics does not only apply to sales people. Sales personnel may have an easier path to tracking data, but don't get discouraged from this advantage. Having worked several years in human resources, I can tell you anytime I bought a metric to a meeting or discussion I immediately got people's attention. Once I was able to quantify some of what I was talking about, people could put it in terms they understood. A universal language in corporate America is numbers. Human Resources has tons of data, from humans, to the cost to replace them, train them, recruit them, and many more. If the organization sells something and you don't work in sales, this doesn't mean that you still shouldn't be making introductions for sales teams. Follow the motto of, "all for one, one for all". The organization name is the same on each of your paychecks. You can also team up with your co-workers on tracking results, and if working together actually saves time on a project, then time is money and that saved time should be tracked as well.

Tracking metrics should be fun and easy, a way to give yourself a pat on the back for the good work that you're doing. Call it your personal brags, whatever you want, just keep a log of what you're doing to make an impact constantly. This can't be taken as a once in a while thing though, you will have to be very purposeful to track everything. Use your calendar as that might be easier. Assuming you put each thing you do daily on your calendar, this will give you a historical reference guide as well. Then in the calendar appointment record put what you did, who you met, and what came from your time there. If you treat your own time as an investment this will be a great way to show the fruits of your labor.

Remember that data and metrics are your friend, they are the access keys to your future. Empowering your differences only works when you take record of how you showcased your differences, and how they helped to create positive change for your organization. When you walk in with data showing your impact, it is going to increase your confidence in everything you are about to do, and it will enlighten the leadership about the work that you have been doing. Numbers can sometimes speak for themselves and you want to have them on your side when you come into different meetings like:

- Annual Performance Review
- Mid-year review
- Job interview
- Evaluating your team
- Sales meeting
- Meeting with senior leadership
- Team meetings
- Non-profit board
- Other uses (Conversations with community leaders, educating and enlightening someone, etc.)

Combine the data that you've gathered with everything that makes you who you are. Walk into that sales meeting with the confidence of the world, knowing that you have data to back up everything that you say.

When you have your annual performance review, let your authenticity shine, and then allow the numbers to exemplify the work that you've put in over the past year. Coming into a conversation with someone who doesn't understand your diverse background, you're able to educate them with your personal story as well as point to larger systemic issues around your diverse community with data. Enlightening them about how pervasive an issue is, and what they can do to help be an ally and advocate. Come prepared with all of this knowledge, wherever you go, let the data and metrics back up every single part of your authenticity.

Allyship

I want to have my life-saving ally, my wife, and mother of our children, Whitney Brundage, share her perspective on what it means to be an ally. It was having her support in one of my darkest hours that helped me keep going. Honestly, if it wasn't for her being supportive and being there as an ally, I don't think I would even be alive today. Having her support meant a literal world of difference for me. It allowed me to keep living, and subsequently, allowed me to thrive.

Whitney Brundage, VP Digital Transformation Programming and Strategy at Computer Measurement Group, Inc.

I think the most important attribute of being an ally is not that you understand what it feels like to identify as a minority or to live within an oppressed community, but that you use your voice to amplify their fight and their struggles. Being an ally means you stand up for people who do not have the same platform. That you are there for them in what they need. Being there for them as someone who listens, supports them, and raises them up.

An ally is someone who utilizes all of these actions but listens to what each individual person and each community needs. Sometimes people want you to be there to help amplify their message, sometimes they just need to know that someone cares and understands what they are going through, other times they need an advocate and sponsor who can vouch and help them get to where they want to be. The important thing is to ask for what a person or community needs and act accordingly.

Being an ally at the beginning for Ashley meant showing my support and acceptance for who she is. It was hard at first to come to terms with what her identity would mean for me and the kids. Over time, I listened and learned more about what it means to be trans, what her personal struggles have been, and we got to know each other again. I kept showing my support throughout the years but I was now advocating for her and the trans community. Educating those close to me about what it meant and being at different events as an ally, showing my support for the community. It's been a journey for us both and we've both learned and have grown together as friends, as partners, and me as an ally.

The impact that you can make on a diverse person's life by being an ally cannot be stated enough. For some people, it can save their lives to know that they have someone in their corner and make a world of difference in them building their confidence in themselves. I encourage you to do your part and do what you can to show your support for diverse people. All the above elements of allyship are cultivated through implementing the 10 Empowering Actions by:

- Empowering others because you are paving the way for them by showing others you are invested in their equality. Showing them that they matter, that they can tell their stories and raise their voice and when they do, they'll have someone in their corner cheering them on all the way.

- Inspiring others by showcasing your commitment to being self-aware to injustices and inequalities. Setting the example for others that they do have allies who may not specifically experience the same struggles but understand them and are working to help alleviate them.

- Educating yourself continuously on systemic oppression, on how to create change, and on any way you may have contributed in the past. Being an ally means being knowledgeable about these topics and committing yourself to using that knowledge to help each and every day.

- Including others in your journey to be a better ally. Listen to feedback, listen to community struggles. What concerns people have and transforming your environment into one that doesn't discriminate against anyone and is open to everyone.

- Motivating others through support. You are working as an ally but the people you are championing for are living this life. Make sure you cheer them on and support them. The seemingly smallest supportive actions can make all the difference in someone's life.

- Mentoring others who want to be better allies. You may not have all the answers but you are further along than someone who is just starting their journey and you can help guide them to be a better ally.

- Investing in learning the specific hardships of a community and how to also be a better ally. Get to know the people who you are striving to be a better ally for and be there for them when they need it.

- Influencing others through appropriate actions as an ally, which means not taking credit for advances made within the community, finding out what people need and how to support them- do not make assumptions.
- Accessing avenues you have because of your privilege. That means speaking up when you notice someone's being put down or amplifying someone's voice to make their words carry further. Utilize the access that you have to critical people and be the bridge that someone needs to voice their concerns, promote their ideas, or advance their career.
- Enlightening others about a community's struggles or why you chose to advocate for certain minorities. This is key to creating a more inclusive environment where everyone is on the same page and knows the struggles that minorities communities and people go through.

Empowering Actions

I created this book with the intention of highlighting all the key actions that were taken to make a difference in my career journey. I wanted to simplify the process of sharing by picking the top 10 empowering actions used throughout this book. I'm sure you've noticed that there were a whole lot more than 10 actions. What follows are my ten best takeaways for each of the top 10 empowering actions that you should implement to empower others whenever and wherever you can. Please take action with others, as it will empower people and have a lasting change that can be measured in the amount of lives that you impact.

Empower

Raise your voice for others! Scream to the top of your lungs, especially when you see injustice. We are fighting for our lives for intersectional, diverse communities, all out injustices that you see, and raise the voices of those around you. Be an amplifier for their voices, and help to create the space where they are able and comfortable to share themselves. Encourage others to be their authentic selves, and to bring their authentic selves to every part of their lives. Lead by example, be confident in who you are and what you do, and work to teach others to do the same. Share the lessons that you've learned throughout this book, and throughout your personal story, to help empower those around you to follow in the same footsteps. Above all, build a platform for others to stand on, and not a wall to block them out. Raise their voices so that everyone can hear and listen to them.

Inspire

Tell the inspirational parts of your story over and over. Remember how I was able to leverage sharing my story to create change, and how I made sure to highlight the inspirational parts of it to make the biggest impact. In many cases, that is what led me to develop deeper relationships with people, to get others to listen to me, and make myself known in different communities. Everyone has a story to share. People need to hear your story. Keep sharing it with others, both those who want to listen, and those who are just getting to know you. It's through storytelling that we are able to forge more meaningful relationships with people. Oftentimes, we make ourselves vulnerable, open ourselves up to someone, and they will do the same in return. Embracing all of yourself and being confident in the way you're able to tell your story will inspire people to want to do the same. Shine bright and people will take notice of your demeanor, knowing that if someone else can be that way, then they can too.

Educate

Aim to educate one person per day about your fight for visibility and equality. Whether that person is a colleague, acquaintance, or someone you've connected with online. When I say to educate one person, remember that you need to educate them enough to arm them to educate another person per day. Your education of others should include many of the other empowering actions. This is the foundation to creating any change. Keep in mind, you can't change something that you are unfamiliar with. You must first take time to learn about another person's struggles. Education means constantly learning more about yourself and others. Learn something new every day; be it something that you've been meaning to research, or something someone teaches you. Education is a constant. We all continue to learn more and teach others each and every day. Tying education to inspiration and motivation is going to make a bigger impact daily.

Inclusion

Follow up with someone to ensure that you know they feel welcomed. Do your best to cultivate a sense of belonging. I know how important it is to have that feeling that you're in a place where you know you belong. It makes a world of a difference to know that you are in an environment where you are accepted, and where no one is going to judge you or talk behind your back. It's an incredibly welcoming feeling knowing that where you are is an inclusive environment and that you don't have to constantly worry if who you are is "too much" for others. People who feel comfortable in their environment perform better, and help to cultivate a workplace culture that is welcome to all. Check in with the people closest to you to make sure that they feel they're in an inclusive environment. Then, work outside of that comfort zone to get to know the people you don't know as well. Find out what their needs are, and if there is anything that you can do to make it so that they feel more included. Wherever you go, do what you can to help cultivate a sense of belonging for everyone.

Motivate

Light a fire under a new ally for your diverse community, motivate them to create change. Bring in the facts, the reasons why change is needed, how it affects them, and what they can do to help your communities. You may have to constantly keep in contact with this person, getting someone motivated to help create change might not be a one and done situation. This goes back to the planting of seeds and how you get people on your side to help with the heavy lifting of creating an inclusive culture. The need for change, and how something can affect them or someone they care about, is a good way to motivate someone to be an advocate and help put in the work that's needed for that change to happen. Motivating is also being there to support others in their time of need. Trying to make a difference and change anything that exists beyond our immediate control is going to be a marathon, not a sprint. Even achieving your goals and rising in your career is something that will take time. You may not see the end goal quickly, and you may be facing obstacles on your way, but keep yourself motivated. Keep the end goal in mind, you may not get there today or tomorrow, but keep working towards it and you will achieve the goals you have in your mind.

Invest

If you or if your organization is able, make a financial investment in a non-profit organization fighting for equality and justice. Large or small, the investment will make a major impact. Large dollar investments make a large impact, that is not a secret, but small dollar investments can actually lead to larger investments, depending on how you amplify the message. If you plan to make a small dollar investment, utilize the social component of that donation, along with the other empowering actions to drive more people to make a similar investment. This can be posting about it on your social media or talking with your friends and family. Also, keep in mind that investments made to an organization don't have to be financial. You can make investments by volunteering for events and donating your time to the organization, helping out where you can. Share the work that you are doing and motivate others to make similar investments. Outside of making investments in organizations, make sure that you are also investing in diverse people that you are working with. Get to know them, their stories, and their struggles, and do what you can to help as an ally and as an advocate.

Mentor

Part of that investment into people is mentoring someone from your diverse community. This is one of my most favorite takeaways in this chapter. Even if you do not have the time for occurring mentoring meetings, at least have a one-time connection for someone from your diverse background. The measured impact from these kinds of meetings is tremendous. Making that thirty minutes or an hour happen for someone, is something that both of you will cherish long term. Being able to pass on what I've learned onto youth in my communities has been immensely rewarding for me. It felt like I was passing the torch, making sure that the person I was mentoring had the tools that they needed to succeed. A lot of what I pass on is what I wish I knew when I was starting out. Think about everything that you wished you knew when you started your career, that insider knowledge you can pass onto the next generation. You may also be surprised what wisdom and insight they are able to pass onto you. Like I said before, mentoring is a two-way street, and as much knowledge as you give to someone they can return the same amount. Be purposeful in seeking out mentees, but also mentors throughout your career journey.

Influence

Influence an organization to invest in a community organization that will create change. This could take time, so you may need to follow my steps that I laid out earlier in the book around seed planting. This takeaway is built around how you manage your influence on a constant basis. Managing those seeds and continually watering them is a way to maintain future influence. Plant those seeds in your organization to create larger structural changes, but also in the change makers of an organization. Change starts on a small level, like a wave in the ocean. It slowly gains more and more momentum, and eventually builds on itself until it becomes a massive wave of change. Use the power that you have and access to the change makers of an organization, and influence them to create the lasting differences that you want to see in your organization, your community, and in your own career.

Access

Leverage your contacts to create access for someone from a diverse community other than your own. Remember the walk of privilege, and how this is tied to equity. It's hard to have access to get ahead when you're starting the race thirty steps behind everyone else. Utilize the opportunities and privileges that you have to uplift those around you. Everyone, at some point, needs access either to a specific person, an organization, or a community partner to get their footing and receive what they need to empower themselves. Utilize the access that you have and make a connection for someone. If you are in a position of power, make sure that people have access to you. Make it known that people are able to approach you and ask you for something that they need. Doing this has helped to make sure that the people I was managing knew that they were in an inclusive environment, where their concerns were being heard and met, and they felt part of a team working together. Utilize the access you have, whether it is to other people or other people to you, and help to create a more inclusive culture in your organization.

Enlighten

Give someone the insight of what you actually go through in the world. This is tied to sharing your story, but the awakening that comes with someone truly seeing what you go through will make a bigger impact.

This will then lead to the other empowering actions, the lessons, and takeaways that you want to impart on someone after enlightening them. The person can be an advocate for change for you and your communities. I think about some of the people that I've enlightened versus educated through the years, and those that I've enlightened are my biggest allies and champions for equality. The people that I've enlightened got to hear the raw and real parts of my story, how certain policies and decisions affect me in my everyday life, and what they can do to help make sure that no one has to endure the same struggles. Enlighten the people that you meet throughout your journey, and guide them in the direction they need to go to be your allies and champions for equality.

Empowering Differences

Now that you have the takeaways for all of the empowering actions, let's cover the differences and discuss what we can do to create change. These were the ones that I had mentioned around these 10 intersectional differences. Remember the immediate takeaway action to empower others in these communities because change happens from your purposeful engagement.

Ability

Create accessible spaces for those that have differing abilities. Accessibility will always be a key takeaway for everyone. This will require you to do multiple things including advocating for the right technology, influencing others for the right kind of investments to be made in a building, and getting people to understand the struggles that people with disabilities go through on a daily basis. Help the organization understand that the investments made are worth it in the short and long term. In the more than 30 years since the ADA passed, there has not been enough focus in advocacy done for those who have differing abilities. Now is the time for you to step up and create that accessible space. Get to know the struggles, what needs to change, what you can do to help, and make it happen!

Age

Regardless of your age, you should be proud of how old you are and share it. I know this seems like a simple action, but honestly, there's so much shame involved on both ends of the spectrum for age, which has led to a lot of ageism from all sides. Ageism is discriminatory actions based on a person's age. As I was writing this book, I had always set a goal that I wanted to be published by the time I turned 40. As it turns out, I was so nervous about that number and meeting my self-imposed goal that it put extra, unneeded stress on me. If you're young, use that as your advantage and empower it. You bring a fresh perspective to how an organization operates and can shine a light on where an organization might miss the mark when it is marketing itself. If you're older, all of your lived experiences and lessons are important for all people involved in an organization and you should empower that as well. Don't get caught up in what other people think in society about what it means to be a certain age. You need to just be you, regardless of how old you are, and continue to impact your diverse community.

Class

Speak your truth! Regardless of what class you're from, you need to speak up so others can be empowered. Talking about how I was homeless is tough, but it's inspirational to know how much I've overcome. It's taken a while for me to even feel remotely comfortable sharing that part of my life with one person, let alone to write it and include it in this book. It was when I realized the impact that it had, and how it affected other people in such a positive way that I realized I needed to be telling this part of my story. It's hard to remember that time in my life where I didn't know what was coming in the next day, where me and my family would end up, or what was going to happen. Knowing the impact that it has had by telling it though, for as hard as it has been to recall that time, I'm glad that I continue to share it because it truly enlightens others. I encourage you to share your story, share your truth especially the hard parts, more people will relate to your experiences than you might think. If you're from the upper class, then share how you've gotten there and use that class privilege to uplift others. Build a platform and an environment where they can share their experiences and utilize the empowering actions to help impact other people.

Education

Uplift the voices of those that don't have as high an education as others, and if you don't have a higher education don't be afraid to speak up and have yourself be heard. Your voice and your value should not be measured by your education level. Much like with sharing my experiences being homeless, I was terrified to even draw attention to

342

the fact that I only have a high school diploma. I felt that I could never surmount to a higher position in a company, or that my voice would even be valued when I got there. What I learned is that added to the motivational and inspirational parts of my story. It showed perseverance to get to where I was and where I wanted to go. That I was dedicated to the job and getting work done. That's a part of what stood out in the minds of the executives when they saw my resume and background. College isn't for everyone, and not everyone has the opportunity to go to college. Don't let it discourage you or make it feel like you aren't worth it. Oftentimes, what employers are really looking for is that you can do the job and do it well, which translates to work experience and past positions. Work to change the culture in your organization; call out the lie that people need to have a higher education to perform in a role. Act as a platform for those who don't have a higher education so their story can be heard.

Ethnicity

Immersing yourself in a community's culture is the immediate takeaway action. This goes way deeper than just education being your empowering action. You need to connect all the empowering actions to immerse yourself in a community's culture. From listening to inspirational stories on cultural differences, to researching historical access issues. Be cognizant that you will need to do something to actually drive a cultural shift in yourself and others. As you are immersing yourself in the culture of different ethnicities, take notes and come up with your own empowering actions to create change. Taking action with what you've learned is how you are going to be able to shift the culture in your organization to be inclusive of all people. Start by listening to the concerns that people of different ethnicities have, don't just go off and do something that you think will help. Be an active listener and truly get to know the challenges that people face. Let them take the lead on the actions that need to be taken, and do what you can to drive that cultural shift.

Gender

Expand your horizon on the gender continuum. Understand that there is more to gender than just being male or female, and the way that people are treated in your organization can depend on their gender expression. Call out inequalities when you see them, and make sure that someone isn't overlooked or undervalued because of their gender expression. Be the ally that other people need in situations where they aren't being treated in the same way as a male colleague, or a cisgender co-worker. This is especially important for our non-binary and gender non-conforming friends. They need our support in the mission of gender equality now more than ever. Looping them in with just the trans communities fight is not enough to create change quickly. We have to make sure that when we're having a gender parity, equity, or equality discussion, that these have to include our non-binary friends. Lastly, be aware of your use of pronouns and gender inclusive language, as this will show a huge amount of inclusion.

Language

Learn five words or phrases in a language you don't currently know, especially one that people around you speak fluently. The amount of respect that this will show to someone who speaks the other language will be remembered. In addition to this, look into how important organizational documents and websites are being translated for those that need it. If they aren't being translated, then bring this up with the change makers in your organization. It is important having these be accessible for people that speak different languages. I've noticed that too often this investment is only reserved for vital documents, but there needs to be access to translations for those who need it. Much like with ability, language has everything to do with access and being able to read, understand, and communicate effectively. Listen and work with people who speak another language about their struggles, and use your influence and power to make sure that they have what they need.

Race

Be an advocate for racial justice and raise your voice. The takeaway here is very simple; Black Lives Matter! In the face of multiple systems that constantly treat and value non-white lives as if they don't matter, or that they matter less because of the color of their skin, we need to come together and address the history and the power structures at their core. That means having hard conversations with one another about the privileges that white people have in this country, and what specific changes need to be made to address the ongoing systemic injustices that continue. It's not enough to just be "not racist", white people have to also be anti-racist. Hundreds of years of systemic racism in our society can't be broken down by keeping the status quo. Speak up for injustices that you witness and enlighten those that don't understand systemic racial issues that continually affect non-white people.

Religion

Advocate for your religious organization to display their inclusion for others. This can be as simple as creating a marketing flyer, or sponsoring a diverse community event. It could be something more like marching in a pride parade, or creating a policy of inclusion. Whichever path you take, know that if you're advocating for change, it should lead to success eventually. Encourage your religious organization to invest in the communities it serves and help them achieve opportunities that people wouldn't otherwise have. This can be housing for those who are homeless, opening its door to host classes, events, and support groups, and making people aware of opportunities for jobs. The key is advocating for your religious organization to empower it's community members. Also, stand up and call out discriminatory behaviors and practices that you see in your organization. Be it a manager denying someone a religious request, or slurs being tossed around about a person's religious background. Be an ally and don't let that moment slip by without being addressed.

Sexuality

Educate yourself and others about a person's sexuality. Work to create an inclusive environment where people feel comfortable and confident in themselves, and expressing who they are. Something as seemingly small as a male co-worker saying, "my husband or boyfriend", can be one of the most terrifying things, especially if they don't know how their co-workers are going to react. Be an advocate and ally for LGBTQ+ people, the person that they know they can go to who is not going to judge them and who will listen openly and honestly about their concerns. Being an advocate also means making sure that your organization has inclusive policies that don't tolerate discrimination, either from the organization or it's employees. Ensure that LGBTQ+ people can't be fired for being LGBTQ+, or that they aren't held back from a promotion or are treated differently because of their sexuality. Having inclusive policies in place ensures that LGBTQ+ people are protected from discriminatory practices, and helps create an inclusive environment.

Now that you have the last keys to empowering differences, I would like to hear from you. I want to know the bold, strategic thing you did today to empower yourself and others. We can hold each other accountable for our future. We can see other people's best practices on how they made a difference, and how they are empowering others constantly. Share the connections that you're making in community. Together we will always be stronger and together we can empower our differences! #EmpoweringDifferences #EmpoweringActions

Afterword

Thank you for reading this book. I look forward to connecting with you and learning how you have been using the 10 empowering actions to leverage change. I want to give the last word to my biggest advocate and ally, my wife, and mother of our children Whitney Brundage. Her strength and resiliency are qualities that I can only dream to possess in the future. Ultimately, none of this would have been possible without her guidance and support. For everything you have done to save my life countless times and all you do to constantly empower differences, I offer a final thank you.

Whitney Brundage, VP Digital Transformation Programming and Strategy at Computer Measurement Group, Inc.

We all find ourselves at a crossroads some point in our life. Whether it is realizing we are on a new path, wanting to change or grow, needing to change or grow, or working on our impact on others and our community. There are a few key parts to how you handle this: an accurate and in depth self-assessment, introspection on what you discovered and what to do with that, then putting it into action. Also, contributing greatly to where your path in life takes you, are those who you surround yourself with. Remember that life is a journey and obstacles are part of the process.

Discovering who you are and uncovering your differences on your self-assessment will guide you through life, personally and professionally. For me, it was a change in my personal life that led to professional growth. My assessment originated from needing to change. I was diagnosed with celiac, which is an autoimmune disease and the only cure is to live a gluten free lifestyle. My life changed as I took care of my body and gained more knowledge. I have spent years educating myself, researching autoimmune responses and the way the body responds to foods, and how to make lifestyle changes in an area that is affected every day. People saw the change and began to ask what I was doing, they asked how they too could feel better. The outside effect of my difference is what people began to notice, but the visible change was caused by an invisible difference that only became visible after embracing my diagnosis. I am now able to speak on a topic that so few people want to discuss: chronic illness and feeling unwell.

You may notice, as you begin to discover more about yourself and embrace what life has handed you, that people and social situations around you no longer look or feel the same. It could be a natural change because of growth, because you lost or gained shared interests, or the most difficult one: not everyone is able to accept change. It is important to remember that this is a normal part of progress and to be cognizant that the people surrounding you are appropriately supportive and inclusive. As my life transformed, it led to reframing my view of the things that make me different. I had to accept a major life change and a physical, but invisible, difference that can be a perceived weakness.

An autoimmune disease is rare, so is the knowledge of how to incorporate the change into your life and make it work. If you feel called to do so, I encourage you to share your knowledge with others. Your personal evolution may be the inspiration someone else needs to see to begin their journey.

While your story may look different than mine and be different from Ashley's, we will all have one thing in common. We are working to empower our differences.

About the Author

Ashley T Brundage is the Founder and President of Empowering Differences. While seeking employment at a major financial institution, she self-identified during the interview process as a male to female transgender woman and subsequently was hired. She was offered a position and started as a part time bank teller and worked in various lines of business before moving to VP of Diversity & Inclusion in less than 5 years. Ashley recently celebrated 18 years of marriage to Whitney and together they have two sons; Bryce, 15, and Blake, 13.

Since beginning transitioning in 2008, she has worked tirelessly to promote awareness and acceptance of gender identity and expression. She works to accomplish this goal by volunteering in the community, and holding education sessions for corporations. She serves on the Corporate Advisory Council for the NGLCC-National LGBT Chamber of Commerce. Also is the co-chair for NGLCC's new global Trans+ Gender Non-Conforming Inclusion Task Force. She chaired the successful bid to host the NGLCC convention in 2019, and Visit Tampa Bay named her their Tourism Champion for 2017. In 2018, she started serving on the board of the Florida Museum of Photographic Arts. In 2019, she was voted on the National Board of Directors for GLAAD. GLAAD works to accelerate acceptance for the LGBTQ+ Community through media advocacy.

Ms. Brundage speaks locally and nationally about her transition, workplace equality, leadership, and Empowering Differences. She has also been interviewed in several publications and media outlets, including Tampa Bay Times, Watermark Magazine, Creative Loafing, The Tampa Bay Business Journal, The Miami Herald, Fox 13 News Tampa, ABC News 7 Ft Myers, CBS 10 Tampa, Las Vegas Review Journal, Milwaukee Biz Times, the Daily Beast, Fairygodboss, Auto Finance News, and a feature story with Bloomberg Businessweek in 2019.

Ashley has been recognized in many areas and has received numerous awards including: The University of South Florida 2014 Community Pride Award, 2015 St Pete Pride Grand Marshal, 2015 Commendation-City of Tampa, 2016 Tampa Bay Business Journal Business Woman of the Year, 2016 Voice for Equality Award from Equality Florida, and LGBT Leadership Award from the Florida Diversity Council. In 2017, she was awarded a Leadership Award from Metro Inclusive Health. Also in 2017 she was a winner of the Inaugural People First Award by the Tampa Bay Business Journal, and the TBBJ Power 100 list, the most influential and powerful people in business. In 2018, she was given the Champion Award from international non-profit Out & Equal as well as named one of Florida's Most Powerful and Influential

Women from the National Diversity Council. In 2019, she was named one of the Top 40 under 40 in the LGBTQ community nationally by Business Equality Magazine, TBBJ Outstanding Voice for the LGBTQ community and the Inaugural Transgender Rising Star by Trans New York.

Acknowledgements

This book would not have been possible without many key contributing partners:

My content strategist, development editor, and confidant, Brandi Lai from Best Laid Pens. Your help in the book process was instrumental. The help you provided with writing, development, organization, research, and weekly strategy meetings helped get this project from the ideas I had in my head onto paper. Thank you for helping me complete this book, and accomplish more than I ever thought possible. Thank you for coming alongside this journey together with me. I enjoyed every minute of our meetings together and feel like our friendship has grown through this process. If you are reading this thinking about writing a book but not sure how or where to start, or are looking to have someone help you write your book, then I highly recommend contacting Brandi. She has a passion for diversity and inclusion, and is committed to helping people of diverse communities, especially in the trans and LGBTQ+ communities. She has been integral in bringing my book to life and she can help turn your ideas, your stories and experiences, into your own book.

You can contact her at Brandi@bestlaidpens.com or find her at her website bestlaidpens.com

My Marketing + Creative Agency, BKN Creative. CCO Brandon Tydlaska-Dziedzic helped to create an awesome design for the cover as well as all of the illustrations inside. CEO Kevin Tydlaska-Dziedzic, I loved our photoshoot together, and our creative strategy sessions. Your agency provided top-notch service and expertise, which made it such a pleasure working with you all.

www.bkncreative.com or contact them at info@bkncreative.com

My amazing copy editor, Alyssa Courtoy. Your attention to detail was second to none, and your turnaround time was impeccable. Thank you for your quick efforts and your awesome expertise. Also, thank you for being there for me throughout the years. You truly displayed constant allyship for as long as I have known you.

To my friend and mentor, Nicole Fielder. Thank you so much for giving me the opportunity to showcase what I could do by empowering my differences.

To my friend and style messiah, Patty Soltis, thank you so much for your contribution and even more for your continued friendship.

To the team at NGLCC, thanks for allowing me to always be me!

To the rest of my special book contributors, you all made such a huge contribution in showcasing how you bring empowering differences to life everyday in your actions:

Paul Ashley

Ambar Basu

Zora Carrier

Greg Pollock

Debra Quade

Todd Rice

For Sally Hogshead, Thank you for helping to inspire me to write a book in my own avant-garde way. Two of her books, How The World Sees You, and Fascinate, both were key in my professional development journey. Also thank you for being so approachable that fateful day we first met. I always feel inspired in your company and empowered to be my authentic self. Special shout out to your amazing son, Asher, he truly represents what is right with this world. Here is a Sally's official bio:

Growing up with the last name Hogshead would give anyone a quirky point of view.

After graduating from Duke University, Sally skyrocketed to the top of the advertising elite, creating TV commercials for brands like Nike and Coca-Cola. At age 24, she was the most award-winning copywriter in the U.S. By 27, she'd opened her first ad agency in Los Angeles. And at 30, her work was hung in the Smithsonian Museum of American History.

357

The press described her as "audacious" and "ultra-hip" ...a "superstar" and a "force of nature" who "changed the face of North American Advertising."

Today, Sally writes *New York Times* best sellers on the science of fascination… why we're impressed by certain people and brands. She has twice been named the #1 Global Brand Guru, and frequently appears on NBC's morning show, TODAY.

Sally is the creator of the Fascinate® test, the first personal brand measurement tool, which identifies your most fascinating and impressive qualities. More than one million professionals have taken her test, including leaders in companies such as Facebook, Porsche, NASA, and Twitter.

Oprah Magazine writes: "Sally helps you identify your unique talents so you can figure out what makes you different from others, then use that power to stand out—and shine."

Sally is one of only 189 professional living speakers to be inducted into the Speaker Hall of Fame® ...the industry's highest award for professional excellence.

- *New York Times* best-selling author of 4 books
- #1 *Wall Street Journal* bestseller
- Translated into 22 languages
- #1 award-winning copywriter at age 24
- Named #1 Global Brand Guru of 2016 and 2019

- Campaign leader of campaigns for Nike, Coca-Cola, MINI Cooper, Godiva, and BMW with over one billion in media dollars
- Showcased in Smithsonian Museum of American History
- Hall of Fame® speaker
- Word-of-Mouth Hall of Fame
- Huffington Post - Top Business Speakers
- LinkedIn Pulse - Top 10 Opening Speakers
- Evaluated over one million professionals
- Over 120 worldwide certified trainers in the Fascinate system
- Over a decade of proprietary market research
- Used by Porsche, Twitter, Facebook, Visa, Berkshire Hathaway, and NASA
- Inc.com columnist

Want to connect with Sally?

Instagram, Twitter: @sallyhogshead

Facebook: facebook.com/sallyhogshead

LinkedIn: linkedin.com/in/Hogshead

Email: hello@howtofascinate.com

Web: SallyHogshead.com

Web: HowToFascinate.com

There are key terms that have been used throughout this book. Use this guide if you would like to know more about a certain word or phrase. If you are unfamiliar with many of these terms, it would be good to take time to familiarize yourself with some of the terminology in this section.

Diverse Terminology

Privilege - An advantage that some people have based on certain aspects of their identity. These are unearned advantages that people have because they were born with certain identities. If you are a person who is born in the U.S., you have citizenship privilege. You are able to freely work in the country, able to travel throughout the states, have potential access to health care, potential access to schools, participate in elections by voting, have the ability to get a driver's license, and more. Privilege is not something that we usually think about unless we are the one's without it.

Class privileges - These are privileges that a person may or may not have depending on their socio-economic status. Depending on where a person is in terms of class (lower, middle, or upper class), grants them certain privileges that others may not have. For example, if a person is born in an upper class family, they may have the opportunity to go into a more prestigious school. In comparison, someone who was born into a low class family, may struggle to not only afford to attend a prestigious college, but even qualify for admission. The cost of application fees alone can feel astronomical to someone who is on a fixed income. There are many other financial barriers that can prevent low and middle class students from accessing Ivy League, or even a college education. These barriers could include, but certainly are not limited to; access to regular meals, access to reliable transportation, a supportive home environment, money for a tutor, money and transportation for extracurricular activities, access to reliable internet, and so much more. There is an inherent advantage in having more money compared to not. Oftentimes, the amount of opportunities one has is a direct correlation of their ability to access different resources. It is important to note, the root cause of poverty is not cut and dry, but it is often systemic and difficult to overcome, even with a tremendous work ethic.

Marginalized - This typically refers to communities or people groups who are pushed to the edge of society (i.e., outsiders). These are people that are disprivileged based on their identities; women, people of color, LGBTQ+, those experiencing poverty, those who lack higher education, non-English speakers, immigrants, and numerous other classifications of individuals.

Intersectionality - Each person has multiple social and political identities based on race, class, gender, sexuality, and religion to name a few. Intersectionality is looking at how those identities intersect with one another in social situations and how those intersecting identities affect the outcome of those situations. Think of it like a crossroads. One road could be race, while another is gender. They intersect with one another at a certain point. It is at the intersecting point that we can get a better understanding of how a social situation came to pass. Take the case of Anita Hill. When Anita testified to congress about the sexual harassment she endured from Clarence Thomas, a supreme court nominee at the time, she was not just testifying as a woman or a black person. Anita was testifying as a black woman. She was put through hell by the confirmation committee because she was being questioned and judged both as a woman and as a black person.

Intergenerational - This is similar to intersectionality. Intergenerational looks at the intersection of different generations and the common problems that these generations face. Student loans and student debt is something that multiple generations are struggling to deal with and have dealt with for years, meaning that this is an intergenerational issue.

Cultural References - These are references to a specific culture and cultural norms that a group of people share. These can be events, holidays, language or phrases that are used, clothing, and just about anything that relates specifically to a culture.

Cultural Dexterity - This refers to how a person is able to adapt to another culture. We all grow up in different cultures and speak our own languages. A group of kids may all speak English but the tones, emphasis, and meanings change depending on the people and group of people that you are with and with time.

Code-Switching - This means how we change the way we speak depending on who we are talking to and who we are around. Typically, you don't talk to your parents the same way that you talk to your friends or your partner. We change the way that we interact with different groups depending on who we are talking to and our relationship to the people we are talking to.

Unconscious Bias - These are deeply ingrained stereotypes that we have about certain groups of people that we are not consciously aware of and do not act upon in a conscious way. An example of this would be a hiring manager discriminating against applicants that have "black" or "Latino" sounding names. The hiring manager only considers names like "John" or "Krista" as potential hires. The manager may not be actively and intentionally doing this, but it does limit the applicants to "typical sounding" names.

Microaggressions - These are small off handed comments or phrases, directed at an individual or individuals of a marginalized group, that may seem insignificant, but overtime can cause harm. These can be directed consciously or unconsciously through comments, suggestions, physical acts, or body language. Comments like "you play like a girl", "you're Asian, you should be great at math", or "what are you, a sissy?" All of these may not be extremely harmful on their own, but hearing them and similar phrases repeatedly builds up and takes a toll on a person. Physical acts and body language, such as a woman clutching her purse when a black man steps on an elevator, or a person who moves to the other side of the street as they're walking home when they see a person of color wearing a hoodie. These actions may not be made consciously but they are noticeable for the people they are directed towards.

Macroaggressions - These are larger scale grievances and oppressions that target specific groups of people to keep them oppressed. Microaggressions use language and statements to target an entire population of people. An example would be stereotyping all poor people as being lazy and relying on the government for handouts.

Systemic Oppression - This is oppression and aggressions that target people on a systematic level. The policy of Stop and Frisk is specifically used to target people of color and treating them as criminals because of the color of their skin. On a systematic level of policing, people of color are unjustly targeted by police because of the color of their skin and because of the policy that was designed to make it that way. Systematic oppressions can be policies that specifically target a group of people, the way that industries view and put down certain groups of people, and the way that people are treated in the eyes of the law.

Ivory Tower - This is a metaphor referring to people who typically have a privileged point of view and don't take into consideration the lived reality of many people. This is typically used in academia and is a way of saying that a person who is in an ivory tower only looks at things from their point of view and doesn't take into account that people have different lived experiences. If someone has only learned about a disprivileged group of people's experiences and presumes to know the answer to this group's systemic problems, I.e. a person born into wealth telling a poor person that all they need to do is work harder to get ahead in life.

Prejudices - A perceived idea or notion about a person that isn't based on any fact or reason. Prejudices are often formed from harmful stereotypes about a group of people. If a stereotype is heard enough, people tend to believe them, even if they have no other facts or prior knowledge from anyone. There is the notion that it's been said and repeated enough times so it must be true.

Nationalism - Ideology that promotes the state or nation that a person resides in to retain sovereignty from any other nation, state, or people. This often means valuing one's own national ideas and sense of identity above all others and valuing people who fall within the same national background more favorably than others who come from a different nation or state.

Tokenism - To include only one or a few diverse people from the rest of the group in order to claim that the group is diverse. This is often seen by executives and boards of directors. There will be a boardroom led by ten white men and there will be one black woman in the room. Since there's some diversity in the boardroom, the organization is able to claim that they are diverse because of the one diverse person on the board.

Internalized Racism - Racism that is directed towards oneself or a person's racial group. This can be self hatred because of a person's skin color or dislike for people who share the same race because of stereotypes and negative connotations about their own racial group.

LGBTQ+ Terminology

A note about LGBTQ+ terminology: Ashley T Brundage has personally researched each of the terms and combined the research with her vast personal and business experience in the community. This is a representation of the most popular, common, and well known terms, it is by no means comprehensive. These terms are not meant to label an individual, but to understand how a person identifies themselves. Each person who uses one or more of these terms to represent themselves uses it in a way that is unique to them. It is appropriate to ask if you do not understand the way in which someone is using these terms, especially ones that typically have a negative connotation.

Lesbian - A woman who is primarily attracted to other women.

Gay - A person who is attracted primarily to members of the same sex.

Bisexual - A person who is attracted to both people of their own gender and another gender.

Transgender - A person whose sex is not aligned at birth, they feel they were born in the wrong body.

Transsexual - A person whose sex is not aligned at birth, this person takes the medical steps to confirm their correct gender.

Queer - All-encompassing term within the LGBTQ+ community for a person who does not feel they fit within a label. i.e. queer about their gender or their sexuality.

366

Questioning - A person in the process of exploring and discovering their sexual orientation, gender identity, or gender expression.

Intersex - A person who biologically does not fit within the gender markers of male or female. This person typically has XXY chromosomes.

Asexual - A person who does not have attraction to members of any group.

Agender - A term defined as without gender.

Ally - Non LGBTQ+ person who supports the rights of the LGBTQ+ community.

Pansexual - A person who is attracted to members of all gender identities/expressions.

Two Spirit - A Native American Term for an individual who has spirit of both genders in their body.

Gender Queer - A person who does not subscribe to conventional gender distinctions but identifies with neither, both, or a combination of male and female genders.

Cisgender - A person whose sense of personal identity and gender corresponds to their birth sex.

Trans+ - Inclusive term for someone in the trans spectrum.

M2F/MTF- Male to Female Transgender person.

F2M/FTM - Female to Male Transgender person.

Gender Identity - This is a person's, personal sense of gender.

Non-binary - Encompassing term for people whose gender identity doesn't fall into the traditional male or female binary.

Avoid using - transgendered, transgenders, transgenderism, transvestite, or tranny.

Individuals who identify as bi-gender, gender-questioning (queer), a-gender, or gender neutral may not choose to transition or never even consider it.

References

1. Mack, Lindsay. "12 Of the Biggest Challenges People with Disabilities Face When Pursuing an Office Job." Insider. Insider, August 20, 2019. https://www.insider.com/challenges-for-people-with-disabilities-who-have-office-jobs-2019-8.

2. Best Buddies - https://www.bestbuddies.org/

3. "Qualification Exams." Qualification Exams | FINRA.org. Accessed May 5, 2020. https://www.finra.org/registration-exams-e/qualification-exams.

4. "America's Women and the Wage Gap." National Partnership For Women & Families. March 2020. https://www.national partnership.org/our-work/resources/economic-justice/fair-pay/americas-women-and-the-wage-gap.pdf.

5. Chatterjee, Rhitu. "A New Survey Finds 81 Percent Of Women Have Experienced Sexual Harassment." NPR. NPR, February 22, 2018. https://www.npr.org/sections/thetwo-way/2018/02/21/587671849/a-new-survey-finds-eighty-percent-of-women-have-experienced-sexual-harassment.

6. Trotta, Daniel. "U.S. Transgender People Harassed in Public

Restrooms: Landmark Survey." Reuters. Thomson Reuters, December 8, 2016. https://www.reuters.com/article/us-usa-lgbt-survey/u-s-transgender-people-harassed-in-public-restrooms-landmark-survey-idUSKBN13X0BK.

7. Equality Florida - https://www.eqfl.org/

8. Gill Foundation - https://gillfoundation.org/

9. "Demand For Bilingual Workers More Than Doubled In 5 Years, New Report Shows". New American Economy. March 1, 2017. https://www.newamericaneconomy.org/press-release/demand-for-bilingual-workers-more-than-doubled-in-5-years-new-report-shows/.

10. Eswaran, Vijay. "The Business Case For Diversity Is Now Overwhelming. Here's Why". World Economic Forum. April 29, 2019. https://www.weforum.org/agenda/ 2019 /04/business-case-for-diversity-in-the-workplace/.

11. National LGBT Chamber of Commerce (NGLCC) – https://www.nglcc.org/

12. "LGBTQ Americans Aren't Fully Protected From Discrimination in 29 States." Freedom for All Americans. Accessed September 25, 2020. https://www.freedomforallamericans.org/states/.

13. The Editors of Encyclopedia Britannica. "Obergefell v. Hodges."

Encyclopedia Britannica. Encyclopedia Britannica, inc., June 19, 2020. https://www.britannica.com/event/Obergefell-v-Hodges.

14. Human Rights Campaign Corporate Equality Index https://www.hrc.org/resources/corporate-equality-index

15. Eswaran, Vijay. "The Business Case For Diversity Is Now Overwhelming. Here's Why". World Economic Forum. April 29, 2019. https://www.weforum.org/agenda/2019/04/business-case-for-diversity-in-the-workplace/.

16. Mirza, Shabab Ahmed, and Caitlin Rooney. "Discrimination Prevents LGBTQ People From Accessing Health Care." Center for American Progress, August 13, 2019. https://www.americanprogress.org/issues/lgbtq-rights/news/2018/01/18/445130/discrimination-prevents-lgbtq-people-accessing-health-care/.

17. National Association for the Advancement of Colored People (NAACP) - https://www.naacp.org/

18. Human Rights Campaign (HRC) - https://www.hrc.org/

19. National Organization for Women (NOW) - https://now.org/

20. GLAAD - https://www.glaad.org/

21. Wealthsimple. "Why It Costs More to Borrow If You're Black."

Wealthsimple, February 28, 2019.
https://www.wealthsimple.com/en-us/magazine/racial-
borrowing-gap.

22. Kralik, Joellen. "Bathroom Bill" Legislative Tracking, October 24,
2019. https://www.ncsl.org/research/education/-bathroom-bill-
legislative-tracking635951130.aspx.

23. Maza, Carlos, and Luke Brinker. "15 Experts Debunk Right-Wing
Transgender Bathroom Myth." Media Matters for America,
March 19, 2014. https://www.mediamatters.org/sexual-
harassment-sexual-assault/15-experts-debunk-right-wing-
transgender-bathroom-myth.

24. Auten, John Schneider and David. "The $1 Trillion Marketing
Executives Are Ignoring." Forbes. Forbes Magazine, August
14, 2018. https://www.forbes.com/sites/debtfreeguys/2018
/08/14/the-1-trillion-marketing-executives-are-ignoring/.

25. Farmer, David. "Trump Administration Announces Beginning of
Transgender Military Ban on April 12." National Center for
Transgender Equality, March 13, 2019.
https://transequality.org/press/releases/trump-administration-
announces-beginning-of-transgender-military-ban-on-april-12.

26. Kramer, Roderick M. "Rethinking Trust." Harvard Business
Review, August 1, 2014. https://hbr.org/2009/06/rethinking-
trust.

27. Watts, Sarah. "Our Brains Trick Us Into Trusting Rich People. Here's How." Forbes. Forbes Magazine, February 14, 2019. https://www.forbes.com/sites/sarahwatts/2019/02/14/our-brains-trick-us-into-trusting-rich-people-heres-how/.

28. Audre Lorde, "Age, Race, Class and Sex: Women Redefining Difference," in Sister Outsider: Essays and Speeches. (Berkeley, CA: Crossing Press, 1984), 281. © 1984, 2007 by Audre Lorde.

29. Tiger King. Directed by Eric Goode, and Rebecca Chaiklin. United States: Netflix, April 12, 2020.

30. Wargo, Eric. "How Many Seconds to a First Impression?" Association for Psychological Science- APS, July 1, 2006. https://www.psychologicalscience.org/observer/how-many-seconds-to a-first-impression.

31. Amber DeFabio, Marketing. "Making the Most of First Impressions." The Glatfelter Insurance Group Blog, June 30, 2017. https://blog.glatfelters.com/making-the-most-of-first-impressions.

32. "Remember: Definition of Remember by Oxford Dictionary on Lexico.com Also Meaning of Remember." Lexico Dictionaries | English. Lexico Dictionaries. Accessed September 4, 2020. https://www.lexico.com/en/definition/remember.

33. "Memorable." Dictionary.com. Dictionary.com. Accessed
    September 4, 2020.
    https://www.dictionary.com/browse/memorable.

34. National Minority Supplier Development Council (NMSDC)
    https://nmsdc.org/

35. Women's Business Enterprise National Council(WBENC)-
    https://www.wbenc.org/

36. United States Hispanic Chamber of Commerce - https://ushcc.com/

37. Diversity: Inc - https://www.diversityinc.com/

38. National Veteran Owned Business Association - https://navoba.org/

Printed in Great Britain
by Amazon

85577551R00224